JEWISH LITERATURE

AND OTHER ESSAYS

JEWISH LITERATURE

AND

OTHER ESSAYS

BY

GUSTAV KARPELES

PHILADELPHIA
THE JEWISH PUBLICATION SOCIETY OF AMERICA

Copyright 1895, by
THE JEWISH PUBLICATION SOCIETY OF AMERICA

PREFACE

The following essays were delivered during the last ten years, in the form of addresses, before the largest associations in the great cities of Germany. Each one is a dear and precious possession to me. As I once more pass them in review, reminiscences fill my mind of solemn occasions and impressive scenes, of excellent men and charming women. I feel as though I were sending the best beloved children of my fancy out into the world, and sadness seizes me when I realize that they no longer belong to me alone—that they have become the property of strangers. The living word falling upon the ear of the listener is one thing; quite another the word staring from the cold, printed page. Will my thoughts be accorded the same friendly welcome that greeted them when first they were uttered?

I venture to hope that they may be kindly received; for these addresses were born of devoted love to Judaism. The consciousness that Israel is charged with a great historical mission, not yet accomplished, ushered them into existence. Truth and sincerity stood sponsor to every word. Is it presumptuous, then, to hope that they may find favor in the New World? Brethren of my faith live there as here; our ancient watchword, "Sh'ma Yisrael," resounds in their synagogues as in ours; the old blood-stained flag, with its sublime inscription, "The Lord is my banner!" floats over them; and Jewish hearts in America are loyal like ours, and sustained by steadfast faith in the Messianic time when our hopes and ideals, our aims and dreams, will be realized. There is but one Judaism the world over, by the Jordan and the Tagus as by the Vistula and the Mississippi. God bless and protect it, and lead it to the goal of its glorious future!

To all Jewish hearts beyond the ocean, in free America, fraternal greetings!

GUSTAV KARPELES

BERLIN, Pesach $\frac{5652}{1892}$.

CONTENTS

	PAGE
A GLANCE AT JEWISH LITERATURE	9
THE TALMUD	52
THE JEW IN THE HISTORY OF CIVILIZATION	71
WOMEN IN JEWISH LITERATURE	106
MOSES MAIMONIDES	145
JEWISH TROUBADOURS AND MINNESINGERS	169
HUMOR AND LOVE IN JEWISH POETRY	191
THE JEWISH STAGE	229
THE JEW'S QUEST IN AFRICA	249
A JEWISH KING IN POLAND	272
JEWISH SOCIETY IN THE TIME OF MENDELSSOHN	293
LEOPOLD ZUNZ	318
HEINRICH HEINE AND JUDAISM	340
THE MUSIC OF THE SYNAGOGUE	369

A GLANCE AT JEWISH LITERATURE

In a well-known passage of the *Romanzero*, rebuking Jewish women for their ignorance of the magnificent golden age of their nation's poetry, Heine used unmeasured terms of condemnation. He was too severe, for the sources from which he drew his own information were of a purely scientific character, necessarily unintelligible to the ordinary reader. The first truly popular presentation of the whole of Jewish literature was made only a few years ago, and could not have existed in Heine's time, as the most valuable treasures of that literature, a veritable Hebrew Pompeii, have been unearthed from the mould and rubbish of the libraries within this century. Investigations of the history of Jewish literature have been possible, then, only during the last fifty years.

But in the course of this half-century, conscientious research has so actively been prosecuted that we can now gain at least a bird's-eye view of the whole course of our literature. Some stretches still lie in shadow, and it is not astonishing that eminent scholars continue to maintain that "there is no such thing as an organic history, a logical development, of the gigantic neo-Hebraic literature"; while such as are acquainted with the results of late research at best concede that Hebrew literature has been permitted to garner a "tender aftermath." Both verdicts are untrue and unfair. Jewish literature has developed organically, and in the course of its evolution it has had its spring-tide as well as its season of decay, this again followed by vigorous rejuvenescence.

Such opinions are part and parcel of the vicissitudes of our literature, in themselves sufficient matter for an interesting book. Strange it certainly is that a people without a home, without a land, living under repression and persecution, could produce so great a literature; stranger still, that it should at first have been preserved and disseminated, then forgotten, or treated with the disdain of prejudice, and finally roused from torpid slumber into robust life by the breath of the modern era. In the neighborhood of twenty-two thousand works are known to us now. Fifty years ago bibliographers were ignorant of the existence of half of these, and in the libraries of Italy, England, and Germany an untold number awaits resurrection.

In fact, our literature has not yet been given a name that recommends itself to universal acceptance. Some have called it "Rabbinical Literature," because during the middle ages every Jew of learning bore the title Rabbi; others, "Neo-Hebraic"; and a third party considers it purely theological. These names are all inadequate. Perhaps the only one sufficiently comprehensive is "Jewish Literature." That embraces, as it should, the aggregate of writings produced by Jews from the earliest days of their history up to the present time, regardless of form, of language, and, in the middle ages at least, of subject-matter.

With this definition in mind, we are able to sketch the whole course of our literature, though in the frame of an essay only in outline. We shall learn, as Leopold Zunz, the Humboldt of Jewish science, well says, that it is " intimately bound up with the culture of the ancient world, with the origin and development of Christianity, and with the scientific endeavors of the middle ages. Inasmuch as it shares the intellectual aspirations of the past and the present, their conflicts and their reverses, it is supplementary to general literature. Its peculiar features, themselves falling under universal laws, are in turn helpful in the interpretation of general characteristics. If the aggregate results of mankind's intellectual activity can be likened unto a sea, Jewish literature is one of the tributaries that feed it. Like other literatures and like literature in general, it reveals to the student what noble ideals the soul of man has cherished, and striven to realize, and discloses the varied achievements of man's intellectual powers. If we of to-day are the witnesses and the offspring of an eternal, creative principle, then, in turn, the present is but the beginning of a future, that is, the translation of knowledge into life. Spiritual ideals consciously held by any portion of mankind lend freedom to thought, grace to feeling, and by sailing up this one stream we may reach the fountain-head whence have emanated all spiritual forces, and about which, as a fixed pole, all spiritual currents eddy."[1]

The cornerstone of this Jewish literature is the Bible, or what we call Old Testament literature—the oldest and at the same time the most important of Jewish writings. It extends over the period ending with the second century before the common era; is written, for the most part, in Hebrew, and is the clearest and the most faithful reflection of the original characteristics of the Jewish people. This biblical literature has engaged the closest attention of all nations and every age. Until the seventeenth century, biblical science was purely dogmatic, and only since Herder pointed the way have its æsthetic elements been dwelt upon along with, often in defiance of, dogmatic considerations. Up to this time, Ernest Meier and Theodor Nöldeke have been the only ones to treat of the Old Testament with reference to its place in the history of literature.

Despite the dogmatic air clinging to the critical introductions to the study of the Old Testament, their authors have not shrunk from treating the book sacred to two religions with childish arbitrariness. Since the days of Spinoza's essay at rationalistic explanation, Bible criticism has been the wrestling-ground of the most extravagant exegesis, of bold hypotheses, and hazardous conjectures. No Latin or Greek classic has been so ruthlessly attacked and dissected; no mediæval poetry so arbi-

[1] Zunz, *Gesammelte Schriften*, I., 42.

trarily interpreted. As a natural consequence, the æsthetic elements were more and more pushed into the background. Only recently have we begun to ridicule this craze for hypotheses, and returned to more sober methods of inquiry. Bible criticism reached the climax of absurdity, and the scorn was just which greeted one of the most important works of the critical school, Hitzig's "Explanation of the Psalms." A reviewer said: "We may entertain the fond hope that, in a second edition of this clever writer's commentary, he will be in the enviable position to tell us the day and the hour when each psalm was composed."

The reaction began a few years ago with the recognition of the inadequacy of Astruc's document hypothesis, until then the creed of all Bible critics. Astruc, a celebrated French physician, in 1753 advanced the theory that the Pentateuch—the five books of Moses—consists of two parallel documents, called respectively Yahvistic and Elohistic, from the name applied to God in each. On this basis, German science after him raised a superstructure. No date was deemed too late to be assigned to the composition of the Pentateuch. If the historian Flavius Josephus had not existed, and if Jesus had not spoken of "the Law" and "the prophets," and of the things "which were written in the Law of Moses, and in the Prophets, and in the Psalms," critics would have been disposed to transfer the redaction of the Bible to some period of the Christian era. So wide is the divergence of opinions on the subject that two learned critics, Ewald and Hitzig, differ in the date assigned to a certain biblical passage by no less than a thousand years!

Bible archæology, Bible exegesis, and discussions of grammatical niceties, were confounded with the history of biblical literature, and naturally it was the latter that suffered by the lack of differentiation. Orthodoxy assumed a purely divine origin for the Bible, while sceptics treated the holy book with greater levity than they would dare display in criticising a modern novel. The one party raised a hue and cry when Moses was spoken of as the first author; the other discovered "obscene, rude, even cannibalistic traits"[1] in the sublime narratives of the Bible. It should be the task of coming generations, successors by one remove of credulous Bible lovers, and immediate heirs of thorough-going rationalists, to reconcile and fuse in a higher conception of the Bible the two divergent theories of its purely divine and its purely human origin. Unfortunately, it must be admitted that Ernest Meier is right, when he says, in his "History of the National Poetry of the Hebrews," that this task wholly belongs to the future; at present it is an unsolved problem.

The æsthetic is the only proper point of view for a full recognition of the value of biblical literature. It certainly does not rob the sacred Scriptures, the perennial source of spiritual comfort, of their exalted character and divine worth to assume that legend,

[1] G. Scherr, *Allgemeine Geschichte der Litteratur*, I., p. 62.

myth, and history have combined to produce the perfect harmony which is their imperishable distinction. The peasant dwelling on inaccessible mountain-heights, next to the record of Abraham's shepherd life, inscribes the main events of his own career, the anniversary dates sacred to his family. The young count among their first impressions that of "the brown folio," and more vividly than all else remember

> "The maidens fair and true,
>   The sages and the heroes bold,
> Whose tale by seers inspired
>   In our Book of books is told.
>
> The simple life and faith
>   Of patriarchs of ancient day
> Like angels hover near,
>   And guard, and lead them on the way."[1]

Above all, a whole nation has for centuries been living with, and only by virtue of, this book. Surely this is abundant testimony to the undying value of the great work, in which the simplest shepherd tales and the naïvest legends, profound moral saws and magnificent images, the ideals of a Messianic future and the purest, the most humane conception of life, alternate with sublime descriptions of nature and the sweet strains of love-poems, with national songs breathing hope, or trembling with anguish, and with the dull tones of despairing pessimism and the divinely inspired hymns of an exalted theodicy—

[1] F. Freiligrath, *Die Bilderbibel.*

all blending to form what the reverential love of men has named the Book of books.

It was natural that a book of this kind should become the basis of a great literature. Whatever was produced in later times had to submit to be judged by its exalted standard. It became the rule of conduct, the prophetic mirror reflecting the future work of a nation whose fate was inextricably bound up with its own. It is not known how and when the biblical scriptures were welded into one book, a holy canon, but it is probably correct to assume that it was done by the *Soferim*, the Scribes, between 200 and 150 B. C. E. At all events, it is certain that the three divisions of the Bible—the Pentateuch, the Prophets, and the miscellaneous writings—were contained in the Greek version, the Septuagint, so called from the seventy or seventy-two Alexandrians supposed to have done the work of translation under Ptolemy Philadelphus.

The Greek translation of the Bible marks the beginning of the second period of Jewish literature, the Judæo-Hellenic. Hebrew ceased to be the language of the people; it was thenceforth used only by scholars and in divine worship. Jewish for the first time met Greek intellect. Shem and Japheth embraced fraternally. "But even while the teachings of Hellas were pushing their way into subjugated Palestine, seducing Jewish philosophy to apostasy, and seeking, by main force, to introduce paganism, the Greek philosophers themselves stood awed by the majesty and power of the Jewish prophets. Swords and words entered the lists as champions of Judaism. The vernacular Aramæan, having suffered the Greek to put its impress upon many of its substantives, refused to yield to the influence of the Greek verb, and, in the end, Hebrew truth, in the guise of the teachings of Jesus, undermined the proud structure of the heathen." This is a most excellent characterization of that literary period, which lasted about three centuries, ending between 100 and 150 C. E. Its influence upon Jewish literature can scarcely be said to have been enduring. To it belong all the apocryphal writings which, originally composed in the Greek language, were for that reason not incorporated into the Holy Canon. The centre of intellectual life was no longer in Palestine, but at Alexandria in Egypt, where three hundred thousand Jews were then living, and thus this literature came to be called Judæo-Alexandrian. It includes among its writers the last of the Neoplatonists, particularly Philo, the originator of the allegorical interpretation of the Bible and of a Jewish philosophy of religion; Aristeas, and pseudo-Phokylides. There were also Jewish *littérateurs:* the dramatist Ezekielos; Jason; Philo the Elder; Aristobulus, the popularizer of the Aristotelian philosophy; Eupolemos, the historian; and probably the Jewish Sybil, who had to have recourse to the oracular manner of the pagans to proclaim the truths of Judaism, and to Greek figures of speech for her apocalyptic visions, which foretold, in biblical phrase and with prophetic ardor, the future of Israel and of the nations in contact with it.

Meanwhile the word of the Bible was steadily gaining importance in Palestine. To search into and expound the sacred text had become the inheritance of the congregation of Jacob, of those that had not lent ear to the siren notes of Hellenism. Midrash, as the investigations of the commentators were called, by and by divided into two streams—Halacha, which establishes and systematizes the statutes of the Law, and Haggada, which uses the sacred texts for homiletic, historical, ethical, and pedagogic discussions. The latter is the poetic, the former, the legislative, element in the Talmudic writings, whose composition, extending over a thousand years, constitutes the third, the most momentous, period of Jewish literature. Of course, none of these periods can be so sharply defined as a rapid survey might lead one to suppose. For instance, on the threshold of this third epoch stands the figure of Flavius Josephus, the famous Jewish historian, who, at once an enthusiastic Jew and a friend of the Romans, writes the story of his nation in the Greek language —a character as peculiar as his age, which, listening to the mocking laughter of a Lucian, saw Olympus overthrown and its gods dethroned, the Temple at Jerusalem pass away in flame and smoke, and the new doctrine of the son of the carpenter at Nazareth begin its victorious course.

By the side of this Janus-faced historian, the heroes of the Talmud stand enveloped in glory. We meet with men like Hillel and Shammaï, Jochanan ben Zakkaï, Gamaliel, Joshua ben Chananya, the famous Akiba, and later on Yehuda the Prince, friend of the imperial philosopher Marcus Aurelius, and compiler of the Mishna, the authoritative code of laws superseding all other collections. Then there are the fabulist Meïr; Simon ben Yochaï, falsely accused of the authorship of the mystical Kabbala; Chiya; Rab; Samuel, equally famous as a physician and a rabbi; Jochanan, the supposed compiler of the Jerusalem Talmud; and Ashi and Abina, the former probably the arranger of the Babylonian Talmud. This latter Talmud, the one invested with authority among Jews, by reason of its varying fortunes, is the most marvellous literary monument extant. Never has book been so hated and so persecuted, so misjudged and so despised, on the other hand, so prized and so honored, and, above all, so imperfectly understood, as this very Talmud.

For the Jews and their literature it has had untold significance. That the Talmud has been the conservator of Judaism is an irrefutable statement. It is true that the study of the Talmud unduly absorbed the great intellectual force of its adherents, and brought about a somewhat one-sided mental development in the Jews; but it also is true, as a writer says,[1] that "whenever in troublous times scientific inquiry was laid low; whenever, for any reason, the Jew was excluded from participation in public life, the study of the Talmud maintained the elasticity and the vigor of the Jewish mind, and

[1] D. Cassel, *Lehrbuch der jüdischen Geschichte und Literatur*, p. 198.

rescued the Jew from sterile mysticism and spiritual apathy. The Talmud, as a rule, has been inimical to mysticism, and the most brilliant Talmudists, in propitious days, have achieved distinguished success in secular science. The Jew survived ages of bitterness, all the while clinging loyally to his faith in the midst of hostility, and the first ray of light that penetrated the walls of the Ghetto found him ready to take part in the intellectual work of his time. This admirable elasticity of mind he owes, first and foremost, to the study of the Talmud."

From this much abused Talmud, as from its contemporary the Midrash in the restricted sense, sprouted forth the blossoms of the Haggada—that Haggada

"Where the beauteous, ancient sagas,
Angel legends fraught with meaning,
Martyrs' silent sacrifices,
Festal songs and wisdom's sayings,

Trope and allegoric fancies—
All, howe'er by faith's triumphant
Glow pervaded—where they gleaming,
Glist'ning, well in strength exhaustless.

And the boyish heart responsive
Drinks the wild, fantastic sweetness,
Greets the woful, wondrous anguish,
Yields to grewsome charm of myst'ry,

Hid in blessed worlds of fable.
Overawed it hearkens solemn
To that sacred revelation
Mortal man hath poetry called."[1]

[1] Heine, *Romanzero, Jehuda ben Halevy.*

A story from the Midrash charmingly characterizes the relation between Halacha and Haggada. Two rabbis, Chiya bar Abba, a Halachist, and Abbahu, a Haggadist, happened to be lecturing in the same town. Abbahu, the Haggadist, was always listened to by great crowds, while Chiya, with his Halacha, stood practically deserted. The Haggadist comforted the disappointed teacher with a parable. "Let us suppose two merchants," he said, "to come to town, and offer wares for sale. The one has pearls and precious gems to display, the other, cheap finery, gilt chains, rings, and gaudy ribbons. About whose booth, think you, does the crowd press?—Formerly, when the struggle for existence was not fierce and inevitable, men had leisure and desire for the profound teachings of the Law; now they need the cheering words of consolation and hope."

For more than a thousand years this nameless spirit of national poesy was abroad, and produced manifold works, which, in the course of time, were gathered together into comprehensive collections, variously named Midrash Rabba, Pesikta, Tanchuma, etc. Their compilation was begun in about 700 C. E., that is, soon after the close of the Talmud, in the transition period from the third epoch of Jewish literature to the fourth, the golden age, which lasted from the ninth to the fifteenth century, and, according to the law of human products, shows a season of growth, blossom, and decay.

The scene of action during this period was western Asia, northern Africa, sometimes Italy and France, but chiefly Spain, where Arabic culture, destined to influence Jewish thought to an incalculable degree, was at that time at its zenith. "A second time the Jews were drawn into the vortex of a foreign civilization, and two hundred years after Mohammed, Jews in Kairwan and Bagdad were speaking the same language, Arabic. A language once again became the mediatrix between Jewish and general literature, and the best minds of the two races, by means of the language, reciprocally influenced each other. Jews, as they once had written Greek for their brethren, now wrote Arabic; and, as in Hellenistic times, the civilization of the dominant race, both in its original features and in its adaptations from foreign sources, was reflected in that of the Jews." It would be interesting to analyze this important process of assimilation, but we can concern ourselves only with the works of the Jewish intellect. Again we meet, at the threshold of the period, a characteristic figure, the thinker Sa'adia, ranking high as author and religious philosopher, known also as a grammarian and a poet. He is followed by Sherira, to whom we owe the beginnings of a history of Talmudic literature, and his son Haï Gaon, a strictly orthodox teacher of the Law. In their wake come troops of physicians, theologians, lexicographers, Talmudists, and grammarians. Great is the circle of our national literature: it embraces theology, philosophy, exegesis, grammar, poetry, and jurisprudence, yea, even astronomy and chronology, mathematics and medicine. But these widely varying subjects constitute only one class, inasmuch as they all are infused with the spirit of Judaism, and subordinate themselves to its demands. A mention of the prominent actors would turn this whole essay into a dry list of names. Therefore it is better for us merely to sketch the period in outline, dwelling only on its greatest poets and philosophers, the moulders of its character.

The opinion is current that the Semitic race lacks the philosophic faculty. Yet it cannot be denied that Jews were the first to carry Greek philosophy to Europe, teaching and developing it there before its dissemination by celebrated Arabs. In their zeal to harmonize philosophy with their religion, and in the lesser endeavor to defend traditional Judaism against the polemic attacks of a new sect, the Karaites, they invested the Aristotelian system with peculiar features, making it, as it were, their national philosophy. At all events, it must be universally accepted that the Jews share with the Arabs the merit " of having cherished the study of philosophy during centuries of barbarism, and of having for a long time exerted a civilizing influence upon Europe."

The meagre achievements of the Jews in the departments of history and history of literature do not justify the conclusion that they are wanting in historic perception. The lack of writings on these subjects is traceable to the sufferings and persecutions that have marked their pathway. Before their chroniclers had time to record past afflictions, new sorrows and troubles broke in upon them. In the middle ages, the history of Jewish literature is the entire history of the Jewish people, its course outlined by blood and watered by rivers of tears, at whose source the genius of Jewish poetry sits lamenting. "The Orient dwells an exile in the Occident," Franz Delitzsch, the first alien to give loving study to this literature, poetically says, "and its tears of longing for home are the fountain-head of Jewish poetry."[1]

That poetry reached its perfection in the works of the celebrated trio, Solomon Gabirol, Yehuda Halevi, and Moses ben Ezra. Their dazzling triumphs had been heralded by the more modest achievements of Abitur, writing Hebrew, and Adia and the poetess Xemona (Kasmune) using Arabic, to sing the praise of God and lament the woes of Israel.

The predominant, but not exclusive, characteristic of Jewish poetry is its religious strain. Great thinkers, men equipped with philosophic training, and at the same time endowed with poetic gifts, have contributed to the huge volume of synagogue poetry, whose subjects are praise of the Lord and regret for Zion. The sorrow for our lost fatherland has never taken on more glowing colors, never been expressed in fuller tones than in this poetry. As ancient Hebrew poetry flowed in the two streams of prophecy and psalmody, so the Jewish poetry of the middle ages was divided into *Piut* and *Selicha*.

[1] F. Delitzsch, *Zur Geschichte der jüdischen Poesie*, p. 165.

Songs of hope and despair, cries of revenge, exhortations to peace among men, elegies on every single persecution, and laments for Zion, follow each other in kaleidoscopic succession. Unfortunately, there never was lack of historic matter for this poetry to elaborate. To furnish that was the well-accomplished task of rulers and priests in the middle ages, alike "in the realm of the Islamic king of kings and in that of the apostolic servant of servants." So fate made this poetry classical and eminently national. Those characteristics which, in general literature, earn for a work the description "Homeric," in Jewish literature make a liturgical poem "Kaliric," so called from the poet Eliezer Kalir, the subject of many mythical tales, and the first of a long line of poets, Spanish, French, and German, extending to the sixteenth or seventeenth century. The literary history of this epoch has been written by Leopold Zunz with warmth of feeling and stupendous learning. He closes his work with the hope that mankind, at some future day, will adopt Israel's religious poetry as its own, transforming the elegiac *Selicha* into a joyous psalm of universal peace and good-will.

Side by side with religious flourishes secular poetry, clothing itself in rhyme and metre, adopting every current form of poesy, and treating of every appropriate subject. Its first votary was Solomon Gabirol, that

> "Human nightingale that warbled
> Forth her songs of tender love,

> In the darkness of the sombre,
> Gothic mediæval night.
>
> She, that nightingale, sang only,
> Sobbing forth her adoration,
> To her Lord, her God, in heaven,
> Whom her songs of praise extolled."[1]

Solomon Gabirol may be said to have been the first poet thrilled by *Weltschmerz*. "He produced hymns and songs, penitential prayers, psalms, and threnodies, filled with hope and longing for a blessed future. They are marked throughout by austere earnestness, brushing away, in its rigor, the color and bloom of life; but side by side with it, surging forth from the deepest recesses of a human soul, is humble adoration of God."

Gabirol was a distinguished philosopher besides. In 1150, his chief work, "The Fount of Life," was translated into Latin by Archdeacon Dominicus Gundisalvi, with the help of Johannes Avendeath, an apostate Jew, the author's name being corrupted into Avencebrol, later becoming Avicebron. The work was made a text-book of scholastic philosophy, but neither Scotists nor Thomists, neither adherents nor detractors, suspected that a heretical Jew was slumbering under the name Avicebron. It remained for an inquirer of our own day, Solomon Munk, to reveal the face of Gabirol under the mask of a garbled name. Amazed, we behold that the pessimistic philosopher of to-day can as little as the

[1] Heine, *l. c.*

schoolmen of the middle ages shake himself free from the despised Jew. Schopenhauer may object as he will, it is certain that Gabirol was his predecessor by more than eight hundred years!

Charisi, whom we shall presently meet, has expressed the verdict on his poetry which still holds good: " Solomon Gabirol pleases to call himself the small—yet before him all the great must dwindle and fall.—Who can like him with mighty speech appall? —Compared with him the poets of his time are without power—he, the small, alone is a tower.—The highest round of poetry's ladder has he won.—Wisdom fondled him, eloquence hath called him son— and clothing him with purple, said: ' Lo!—my firstborn son, go forth, to conquest go!'—His predecessors' songs are naught with his compared—nor have his many followers better fared.—The later singers by him were taught—the heirs they are of his poetic thought.—But still he's king, to him all praise belongs—for Solomon's is the Song of Songs."

By Gabirol's side stands Yehuda Halevi, probably the only Jewish poet known to the reader of general literature, to whom his name, life, and fate have become familiar through Heinrich Heine's *Romanzero*. His magnificent descriptions of nature " reflect southern skies, verdant meadows, deep blue rivers, and the stormy sea," and his erotic lyrics are chaste and tender. He sounds the praise of wine, youth, and happiness, and extols the charms of his lady-love, but above and beyond all he devotes his song to Zion and his people. The pearl of his poems

> "Is the famous lamentation
> Sung in all the tents of Jacob,
> Scattered wide upon the earth . . .
>
> Yea, it is the song of Zion,
> Which Yehuda ben Halevy,
> Dying on the holy ruins,
> Sang of loved Jerusalem."[1]

"In the whole compass of religious poetry, Milton's and Klopstock's not excepted, nothing can be found to surpass the elegy of Zion," says a modern writer, a non-Jew.[2] This soul-stirring "Lay of Zion," better than any number of critical dissertations, will give the reader a clear insight into the character and spirit of Jewish poetry in general:

> O Zion! of thine exiles' peace take thought,
> The remnant of thy flock, who thine have sought!
> From west, from east, from north and south resounds,
> Afar and now anear, from all thy bounds,
>   And no surcease,
>   "With thee be peace!"
>
> In longing's fetters chained I greet thee, too,
> My tears fast welling forth like Hermon's dew—
> O bliss could they but drop on holy hills!
> A croaking bird I turn, when through me thrills
> Thy desolate state; but when I dream anon,
> The Lord brings back thy ev'ry captive son—
>   A harp straightway
>   To sing thy lay.

[1] Heine, *l. c.*
[2] M. J. Schleiden, *Die Bedeutung der Juden für die Erhaltung der Wissenschaften im Mittelalter*, p. 37.

In heart I dwell where once thy purest son
At Bethel and Peniel, triumphs won;
God's awesome presence there was close to thee,
Whose doors thy Maker, by divine decree,
        Opposed as mates
        To heaven's gates.

Nor sun, nor moon, nor stars had need to be;
God's countenance alone illumined thee
On whose elect He poured his spirit out.
In thee would I my soul pour forth devout!
Thou wert the kingdom's seat, of God the throne,
And now there dwells a slave race, not thine own,
        In royal state,
        Where reigned thy great.

O would that I could roam o'er ev'ry place
Where God to missioned prophets showed His grace!
And who will give me wings? An off'ring meet,
I'd haste to lay upon thy shattered seat,
        Thy counterpart—
        My bruisèd heart.

Upon thy precious ground I'd fall prostrate,
Thy stones caress, the dust within thy gate,
And happiness it were in awe to stand
At Hebron's graves, the treasures of thy land,
And greet thy woods, thy vine-clad slopes, thy vales,
Greet Abarim and Hor, whose light ne'er pales,
        A radiant crown,
        Thy priests' renown.

Thy air is balm for souls; like myrrh thy sand;
With honey run the rivers of thy land.
Though bare my feet, my heart's delight I'd count
To thread my way all o'er thy desert mount,
        Where once rose tall
        Thy holy hall,

Where stood thy treasure-ark, in recess dim,
Close-curtained, guarded o'er by cherubim.
My Naz'rite's crown would I pluck off, and cast
It gladly forth. With curses would I blast
The impious time thy people, diadem-crowned,
Thy Nazirites, did pass, by en'mies bound
      With hatred's bands,
      In unclean lands.

By dogs thy lusty lions are brutal torn
And dragged; thy strong, young eaglets, heav'nward
   borne,
By foul-mouthed ravens snatched, and all undone.
Can food still tempt my taste? Can light of sun
      Seem fair to shine
      To eyes like mine?

Soft, soft! Leave off a while, O cup of pain!
My loins are weighted down, my heart and brain,
With bitterness from thee. Whene'er I think
Of Oholah,[1] proud northern queen, I drink
Thy wrath, and when my Oholivah forlorn
Comes back to mind—'tis then I quaff thy scorn,
      Then, draught of pain,
      Thy lees I drain.

O Zion! Crown of grace! Thy comeliness
Hath ever favor won and fond caress.
Thy faithful lovers' lives are bound in thine;
They joy in thy security, but pine
      And weep in gloom
      O'er thy sad doom.

---

[1] Ezek. xxiii. 4. [Tr.]

From out the prisoner's cell they sigh for thee,
And each in prayer, wherever he may be,
Towards thy demolished portals turns. Exiled,
Dispersed from mount to hill, thy flock defiled
Hath not forgot thy sheltering fold. They grasp
Thy garment's hem, and trustful, eager, clasp,
      With outstretched arms,
      Thy branching palms.

Shinar, Pathros—can they in majesty
With thee compare? Or their idolatry
With thy Urim and thy Thummim august?
Who can surpass thy priests, thy saintly just,
      Thy prophets bold,
      And bards of old?

The heathen kingdoms change and wholly cease—
Thy might alone stands firm without decrease,
Thy Nazirites from age to age abide,
Thy God in thee desireth to reside.
Then happy he who maketh choice of thee
To dwell within thy courts, and waits to see,
      And toils to make,
      Thy light awake.

On him shall as the morning break thy light,
The bliss of thy elect shall glad his sight,
In thy felicities shall he rejoice,
In triumph sweet exult, with jubilant voice,
      O'er thee, adored,
      To youth restored.

We have loitered long with Yehuda Halevi, and still not long enough, for we have not yet spoken of his claims to the title philosopher, won for him by his book *Al-Chazari*. But now we must hurry on to Moses ben Ezra, the last and most worldly of the three great poets. He devotes his genius to his patrons, to wine, his faithless mistress, and to "bacchanalian feasts under leafy canopies, with merry minstrelsy of birds." He laments over separation from friends and kin, weeps over the shortness of life and the rapid approach of hoary age—all in polished language, sometimes, however, lacking euphony. Even when he strikes his lyre in praise and honor of his people Israel, he fails to rise to the lofty heights attained by his mates in song.

With Yehuda Charisi, at the beginning of the thirteenth century, the period of the epigones sets in for Spanish-Jewish literature. In Charisi's *Tachkemoni*, an imitation of the poetry of the Arab Hariri, jest and serious criticism, joy and grief, the sublime and the trivial, follow each other like tints in a parti-colored skein. His distinction is the ease with which he plays upon the Hebrew language, not the most pliable of instruments. In general, Jewish poets and philosophers have manipulated that language with surprising dexterity. Songs, hymns, elegies, penitential prayers, exhortations, and religious meditations, generation after generation, were couched in the idiom of the psalmist, yet the structure of the language underwent no change. "The development of the neo-Hebraic idiom from the ancient Hebrew," a distinguished modern ethnographer justly says, "confirms, by linguistic evidence, the plasticity, the logical acumen, the comprehensive and at the same time versatile intellectuality of the Jewish race. By the ingenious compounding of words, by investing old expressions with new meanings, and adapting the material offered by alien or related languages to its own purposes, it has increased and enriched a comparatively meagre treasury of words."[1]

Side by side with this cosmopolitanism, illustrated in the Haggada, whose pages prove that nothing human is strange to the Jewish race, it reveals, in its literary development, as notably in the Halacha, a sharply defined subjectivity. Jellinek says: "Not losing itself in the contemplation of the phenomena of life, not devoting itself to any subject unless it be with an ulterior purpose, but seeing all things in their relation to itself, and subordinating them to its own boldly asserted *ego*, the Jewish race is not inclined to apply its powers to the solution of intricate philosophic problems, or to abstruse metaphysical speculations. It is, therefore, not a philosophic race, and its participation in the philosophic work of the world dates only from its contact with the Greeks." The same author, on the other hand, emphasizes the liberality, the broad sympathies, of the Jewish race, in his statement that the Jewish mind, at its first meeting with Arabic philosophy, absorbed it as a leaven into its intellectual life. The product of the assimilation was—as early as the twelfth century, mark you—a philosophic conception of life, whose broad liberality culminates in the sentiment expressed by two most eminent thinkers:

[1] Ad. Jellinek, *Der jüdische Stamm*, p. 195.

Christianity and Islam are the precursors of a world-religion, the preliminary conditions for the great religious system satisfying all men. Yehuda Halevi and Moses Maimonides were the philosophers bold enough to utter this thought of far-reaching significance.

The second efflorescence of Jewish poetry brings forth exotic romances, satires, verbose hymns, and humorous narrative poems. Such productions certainly do not justify the application of the epithet "theological" to Jewish literature. Solomon ben Sakbel composes a satiric romance in the Makamat[1] form, describing the varied adventures of Asher ben Yehuda, another Don Quixote; Berachya Hanakdan puts into Hebrew the fables of Aesop and Lokman, furnishing La Fontaine with some of his material; Abraham ibn Sahl receives from the Arabs, certainly not noted for liberality, ten goldpieces for each of his love-songs; Santob de Carrion is a beloved Spanish bard, bold enough to tell unpleasant truths unto a king; Joseph ibn Sabara writes a humorous romance; Yehuda Sabbataï, epic satires, "The War of Wealth and Wisdom," and "A Gift from a Misogynist," and unnamed authors, "Truth's Campaign," and "Praise of Women."

---

[1] "Makama (plural, Makamat), the Arabic word for a place where people congregate to discuss public affairs, came to be used as the name of a form of poetry midway between the epic and the drama." (Karpeles, *Geschichte der jüdischen Literatur*, vol. II., p. 693.) The most famous Arabic poet of Makamat was Hariri of Bassora, and the most famous Jewish, Yehuda Charisi. See above, p. 32, and p. 211. [Tr.]

A satirist of more than ordinary gifts was the Italian Kalonymos, whose "Touchstone," like Ibn Chasdaï's Makamat, "The Prince and the Dervish," has been translated into German. Contemporaneous with them was Süsskind von Trimberg, the Suabian minnesinger, and Samson Pnie, of Strasburg, who helped the German poets continue *Parzival,* while later on, in Italy, Moses Rieti composed "The Paradise" in Hebrew *terza-rima.*

In the decadence of Jewish literature, the most prominent figure is Immanuel ben Solomon, or Manoello, as the Italians call him. Critics think him the precursor of Boccaccio, and history knows him as the friend of Dante, whose *Divina Commedia* he travestied in Hebrew. The author of the first Hebrew sonnet and of the first Hebrew novel, he was a talented writer, but as frivolous as talented.

This is the development of Jewish poetry during its great period. In other departments of literature, in philosophy, in theology, in ethics, in Bible exegesis, the race is equally prolific in minds of the first order. Glancing back for a moment, our eye is arrested by Moses Maimonides, the great systematizer of the Jewish Law, and the connecting link between scholasticism and the Greek-Arabic development of the Aristotelian system. Before his time Bechaï ibn Pakuda and Joseph ibn Zadik had entered upon theosophic speculations with the object of harmonizing Arabic and Greek philosophy, and in the age immediately preceding that of Maimonides, Abraham ibn Daud, a writer of surprisingly liberal views, had undertaken, in "The Highest Faith," the task of reconciling faith with philosophy. At the same time rationalistic Bible exegesis was begun by Abraham ibn Ezra, an acute but reckless controversialist. Orthodox interpretations of the Bible had, before him, been taught in France by Rashi (Solomon Yitschaki) and Samuel ben Meïr, and continued by German rabbis, who, at the same time, were preachers of morality—a noteworthy phenomenon in a persecuted tribe. "How pure and strong its ethical principles were is shown by its religious poetry as well as by its practical Law. What pervades the poetry as a high ideal, in the application of the Law becomes demonstrable reality. The wrapt enthusiasm in the hymns of Samuel the Pious and other poets is embodied, lives, in the rulings of Yehuda Hakohen, Solomon Yitschaki, and Jacob ben Meïr; in the legal opinions of Isaac ben Abraham, Eliezer ha-Levi, Isaac ben Moses, Meïr ben Baruch, and their successors, and in the codices of Eliezer of Metz and Moses de Coucy. A German professor[1] of a hundred years ago, after glancing through some few Jewish writings, exclaimed, in a tone of condescending approval: 'Christians of that time could scarcely have been expected to enjoin such high moral principles as this Jew wrote down and bequeathed to his brethren in faith!'"

Jewish literature in this and the next period consists largely of theological discussions and of commentaries on the Talmud produced by the hundred.

[1] Hirt, *Bibliothek*, V., p. 43.

It would be idle to name even the most prominent authors; their works belong to the history of theologic science, and rarely had a determining influence upon the development of genuine literature.

We must also pass over in silence the numerous Jewish physicians and medical writers; but it must be remembered that they, too, belong to Jewish literature. The most marvellous characteristic of this literature is that in it the Jewish race has registered each step of its development. " All things learned, gathered, obtained, on its journeyings hither and thither—Greek philosophy and Arabic, as well as Latin scholasticism—all deposited themselves in layers about the Bible, so stamping later Jewish literature with an individuality that gave it an unique place among the literatures of the world."

The travellers, however, must be mentioned by name. Their itineraries were wholly dedicated to the interests of their co-religionists. The first of the line is Eldad, the narrator of a sort of Hebrew Odyssey. Benjamin of Tudela and Petachya of Ratisbon are deserving of more confidence as veracious chroniclers, and their descriptions, together with Charisi's, complete the Jewish library of travels of those early days, unless, with Steinschneider, we consider, as we truly may, the majority of Jewish authors under this head. For Jewish writers a hard, necessitous lot has ever been a storm wind, tossing them hither and thither, and blowing the seeds of knowledge over all lands. Withal learning proved an enveloping, protecting cloak to these mendicant and pilgrim authors. The dispersion of the Jews, their international commerce, and the desire to maintain their academies, stimulated a love for travel, made frequent journeyings a necessity, indeed. In this way only can we account for the extraordinarily rapid spread of Jewish literature in the middle ages. The student of those times often chances across a rabbi, who this day teaches, lectures, writes in Candia, to-morrow in Rome, next year in Prague or Cracow, and so Jewish literature is the "wandering Jew" among the world's literatures.

The fourth period, the Augustan age of our literature, closes with a jarring discord—the expulsion of the Jews from Spain, their second home, in which they had seen ministers, princes, professors, and poets rise from their ranks. The scene of literary activity changes: France, Italy, but chiefly the Slavonic East, are pushed into the foreground. It is not a salutary change; it ushers in three centuries of decay and stagnation in literary endeavor. The sum of the efforts is indicated by the name of the period, the Rabbinical, for its chief work was the development and fixation of Rabbinism.

Decadence did not set in immediately. Certain beneficent forces, either continuing in action from the former period, or arising out of the new concatenation of circumstances, were in operation: Jewish exiles from Spain carried their culture to the asylums hospitably offered them in the Orient and a few of the European countries, notably Holland; the art of printing was spreading, the first presses in

Italy bringing out Jewish works; and the sun of humanism and of the Reformation was rising and shedding solitary rays of its effulgence on the Jewish minds then at work.

Among the noteworthy authors standing between the two periods and belonging to both, the most prominent is Nachmanides, a pious and learned Bible scholar. With logical force and critical candor he entered into the great conflict between science and faith, then dividing the Jewish world into two camps, with Maimonides' works as their shibboleth. The Aristotelian philosophy was no longer satisfying. Minds and hearts were yearning for a new revelation, and in default thereof steeping themselves in mystical speculations. A voluminous theosophic literature sprang up. The *Zohar*, the Bible of mysticism, was circulated, its authorship being fastened upon a rabbi of olden days. It is altogether probable that the real author was living at the time; many think that it was Moses de Leon. The liberal party counted in its ranks the two distinguished families of Tibbon and Kimchi, the former famed as successful translators, the latter as grammarians. Their best known representatives were Judah ibn Tibbon and David Kimchi. Curiously enough, the will of the former contains, in unmistakable terms, the opinion that "Property is theft," anticipating Proudhon, who, had he known it, would have seen in its early enunciation additional testimony to its truth. The liberal faction was also supported by Jacob ben Abba-Mari, the friend of Frederick II. and Michael Scotus. Abba-Mari lived at the German emperor's court at Naples, and quoted him in his commentary upon the Bible as an exegete. Besides there were among the Maimunists, or rationalists, Levi ben Abraham, an extraordinarily liberal man; Shemtob Palquera, one of the most learned Jews of his century, and Yedaya Penini, a philosopher and pessimistic poet, whose "Contemplation of the World" was translated by Mendelssohn, and praised by Lessing and Goethe. Despite this array of talent, the opponents were stronger, the most representative partisan being the Talmudist Solomon ben Aderet.

At the same time disputations about the Talmud, ending with its public burning at Paris, were carried on with the Christian clergy. The other literary current of the age is designated by the word Kabbala, which held many of the finest and noblest minds captive to its witchery. The Kabbala is unquestionably a continuation of earlier theosophic inquiries. Its chief doctrines have been stated by a thorough student of our literature: All that exists originates in God, the source of light eternal. He Himself can be known only through His manifestations. He is without beginning, and veiled in mystery, or, He is nothing, because the whole of creation has developed from nothing. This nothing is one, indivisible, and limitless—*En-Sof.* God fills space, He is space itself. In order to manifest Himself, in order to create, that is, disclose Himself by means of emanations, He contracts, thus producing vacant space. The *En-Sof* first manifested itself in the prototype of the whole of creation, in the macrocosm called the "son of God," the first man, as he appears upon the chariot of Ezekiel. From this primitive man the whole created world emanates in four stages: *Azila, Beria, Yezira, Asiya*. The *Azila* emanation represents the active qualities of primitive man. They are forces or intelligences flowing from him, at once his essential qualities and the faculties by which he acts. There are ten of these forces, forming the ten sacred *Sefiroth*, a word which first meaning number came to stand for sphere. The first three *Sefiroth* are intelligences, the seven others, attributes. They are supposed to follow each other in this order: 1. *Kether* (crown); 2. *Chochma* (wisdom); 3. *Beena* (understanding); 4. *Chesed* (grace), or *Ghedulla* (greatness); 5. *Ghevoora* (dignity); 6. *Tifereth* (splendor); 7. *Nezach* (victory); 8. *Hod* (majesty); 9. *Yesod* (principle); 10. *Malchuth* (kingdom). From this first world of the *Azila* emanate the three other worlds, *Asiya* being the lowest stage. Man has part in these three worlds; a microcosm, he realizes in his actual being what is foreshadowed by the ideal, primitive man. He holds to the *Asiya* by his vital part (*Nefesh*), to the *Yezira* by his intellect (*Ruach*), to the *Beria* by his soul (*Neshama*). The last is his immortal part, a spark of divinity.

Speculations like these, followed to their logical issue, are bound to lead the investigator out of Judaism into Trinitarianism or Pantheism. Kabbalists, of course only in rare cases, realized the danger.

The sad conditions prevailing in the era after the expulsion from Spain, a third exile, were in all respects calculated to promote the development of mysticism, and it did flourish luxuriantly.

Some few philosophers, the last of a long line, still await mention: Levi ben Gerson, Joseph Kaspi, Moses of Narbonne in southern France, long a seat of Jewish learning; then, Isaac ben Sheshet, Chasdaï Crescas, whose "Light of God" exercised deep influence upon Spinoza and his philosophy; the Duran family, particularly Profiat Duran, successful defender of Judaism against the attacks of apostates and Christians; and Joseph Albo, who in his principal philosophic work, *Ikkarim*, shows Judaism to be based upon three fundamental doctrines: the belief in the existence of God, Revelation, and the belief in future reward and punishment. These writers are the last to reflect the glories of the golden age.

At the entrance to the next period we again meet a man of extraordinary ability, Isaac Abrabanel, one of the most eminent and esteemed of Bible commentators, in early life minister to a Catholic king, later on a pilgrim scholar wandering about exiled with his sons, one of whom, Yehuda, has fame as the author of the *Dialoghi di Amore*. In the train of exiles passing from Portugal to the Orient are Abraham Zacuto, an eminent historian of Jewish literature and sometime professor of astronomy at the university of Salamanca; Joseph ibn Verga, the historian of his nation; Amatus Lusitanus, who came close upon the discovery of the circulation of the blood; Israel Nagara, the most gifted poet of the century, whose hymns brought him popular favor; later, Joseph Karo, "the most influential personage of the sixteenth century," his claims upon recognition resting on the *Shulchan Aruch*, an exhaustive codex of Jewish customs and laws; and many others. In Salonica, the exiles soon formed a prosperous community, where flourished Jacob ibn Chabib, the first compiler of the Haggadistic tales of the Talmud, and afterwards David Conforte, a reputable historian. In Jerusalem, Obadiah Bertinoro was engaged on his celebrated Mishna commentary, in the midst of a large circle of Kabbalists, of whom Solomon Alkabez is the best known on account of his famous Sabbath song, *Lecho Dodi*. Once again Jerusalem was the objective point of many pilgrims, lured thither by the prevalent Kabbalistic and Messianic vagaries. True literature gained little from such extremists. The only work produced by them that can be admitted to have literary qualities is Isaiah Hurwitz's "The Two Tables of the Testimony," even at this day enjoying celebrity. It is a sort of cyclopædia of Jewish learning, compiled and expounded from a mystic's point of view.

The condition of the Jews in Italy was favorable, and their literary products derive grace from their good fortune. The Renaissance had a benign effect upon them, and the revival of classical studies influenced their intellectual work. Greek thought met Jewish a third time. Learning was enjoying its resurrection, and whenever their wretched political and social condition was not a hindrance, the Jews joined in the general delight. Their misery, however, was an undiminishing burden, yea, even in the days in which, according to Erasmus, it was joy to live. In fact, it was growing heavier. All the more noteworthy is it that Hebrew studies engaged the research of scholars, albeit they showed care for the word of God, and not for His people. Pico della Mirandola studies the Kabbala; the Jewish grammarian Elias Levita is the teacher of Cardinal Egidio de Viterbo, and later of Paul Fagius and Sebastian Münster, the latter translating his teacher's works into Latin; popes and sultans prefer Jews as their physicians in ordinary, who, as a rule, are men of literary distinction; the Jews translate philosophic writings from Hebrew and Arabic into Latin; Elias del Medigo is summoned as arbiter in the scholastic conflict at the University of Padua;—all boots nothing, ruin is not averted. Reuchlin may protest as he will, the Jew is exiled, the Talmud burnt.

In such dreary days the Portuguese Samuel Usque writes his work, *Consolaçam as Tribulações de Ysrael*, and Joseph Cohen, his chronicle, "The Vale of Weeping," the most important history produced since the day of Flavius Josephus,—additional proofs that the race possesses native buoyancy, and undaunted heroism in enduring suffering. Women, too, in increasing number, participate in the spiritual work of their nation; among them, Deborah Ascarelli and Sara Copia Sullam, the most distinguished of a long array of names.

The keen critic and scholar, Azariah de Rossi, is one of the literary giants of his period. His researches in the history of Jewish literature are the basis upon which subsequent work in this department rests, and many of his conclusions still stand unassailable. About him are grouped Abraham de Portaleone, an excellent archæologist, who established that Jews had been the first to observe the medicinal uses of gold; David de Pomis, the author of a famous defense of Jewish physicians; and Leo de Modena, the rabbi of Venice, "unstable as water," wavering between faith and unbelief, and, Kabbalist and rabbi though he was, writing works against the Kabbala on the one hand, and against rabbinical tradition on the other. Similar to him in character is Joseph del Medigo, an itinerant author, who sometimes reviles, sometimes extols, the Kabbala.

There are men of higher calibre, as, for instance, Isaac Aboab, whose *Nomologia* undertakes to defend Jewish tradition against every sort of assailant; Samuel Aboab, a great Bible scholar; Azariah Figo, a famous preacher; and, above all, Moses Chayyim Luzzatto, the first Jewish dramatist, the dramas preceding his having interest only as attempts. He, too, is caught in the meshes of the Kabbala, and falls a victim to its powers of darkness. His dramas testify to poetic gifts and to extraordinay mastery of the Hebrew language, the faithful companion of the Jewish nation in all its journeyings. To complete this sketch of the Italian Jews of that period, it should be added that while in intellect and attainments they stand above their brethren in faith of other countries, in character and purity of morals they are their inferiors.

Thereafter literary interest centres in Poland, where rabbinical literature found its most zealous and most learned exponents. Throughout the land schools were established, in which the Talmud was taught by the *Pilpul*, an ingenious, quibbling method of Talmudic reasoning and discussion, said to have originated with Jacob Pollak. Again we have a long succession of distinguished names. There are Solomon Luria, Moses Isserles, Joel Sirkes, David ben Levi, Sabbataï Kohen, and Elias Wilna. Sabbataï Kohen, from whom, were pride of ancestry permissible in the republic of letters, the present writer would boast descent, was not only a Talmudic writer; he also left historical and poetical works. Elias Wilna, the last in the list, had a subtle, delicately poised mind, and deserves special mention for his determined opposition to the Kabbala and its offspring Chassidism, hostile and ruinous to Judaism and Jewish learning.

A gleam of true pleasure can be obtained from the history of the Dutch Jews. In Holland the Jews united secular culture with religious devotion, and the professors of other faiths met them with tolerance and friendliness. Sunshine falls upon the Jewish schools, and right into the heart of a youth, who straightway abandons the Talmud folios, and goes out into the world to proclaim to wondering mankind the evangel of a new philosophy. The youth is Baruch Spinoza!

There are many left to expound Judaism: Manasseh ben Israel, writing both Hebrew and Latin books to plead the cause of the emancipation of his people and of its literary pre-eminence; David Neto, a student of philosophy; Benjamin Mussafia, Orobio de Castro, David Abenator Melo, the Spanish translator of the Psalms, and Daniel de Barrios, poet and critic—all using their rapidly acquired fluency in the Dutch language to champion the cause of their people.

In Germany, a mixture of German and Hebrew had come into use among the Jews as the medium of daily intercourse. In this peculiar patois, called *Judendeutsch*, a large literature had developed. Before Luther's time, it possessed two fine translations of the Bible, besides numerous writings of an ethical, poetical, and historical character, among which particular mention should be made of those on the German legend-cycles of the middle ages. At the same time, the Talmud receives its due of time, effort, and talent. New life comes only with the era of emancipation and enlightenment.

Only a few names shall be mentioned, the rest would be bound soon to escape the memory of the casual reader: there is an historian, David Gans; a bibliographer, Sabbataï Bassista, and the Talmudists Abigedor Kara, Jacob Joshua, Jacob Emden, Jonathan Eibeschütz, and Ezekiel Landau. It is delight to be able once again to chronicle the interest taken in long neglected Jewish literature by such Christian scholars as the two Buxtorfs, Bartolocci, Wolff, Surrenhuys, and De Rossi. Unfortunately, the interest dies out with them, and it is significant that to this day most eminent theologians, decidedly to their own disadvantage, "content themselves with unreliable secondary sources," instead of drinking from the fountain itself.

We have arrived at the sixth and last period, our own, not yet completed, whose fruits will be judged by a future generation. It is the period of the rejuvenescence of Jewish literature. Changes in character, tenor, form, and language take place. Germany for the first time is in the van, and Mendelssohn, its most attractive figure, stands at the beginning of the period, surrounded by his disciples Wessely, Homberg, Euchel, Friedländer, and others, in conjunction with whom he gives Jews a new, pure German Bible translation. Poetry and philology are zealously pursued, and soon Jewish science, through its votaries Leopold Zunz and S. J. Rappaport, celebrates a brilliant renascence, such as the poet describes: "In the distant East the dawn is breaking,—The olden times are growing young again."

Die Gottesdienstlichen Vorträge der Juden, by Zunz, published in 1832, was the pioneer work of the new Jewish science, whose present development, despite its wide range, has not yet exhausted the suggestions made by the author. Other equally important works from the same pen followed, and then came the researches of Rappaport, Z. Frankel, I. M. Jost, M. Sachs, S. D. Luzzatto, S. Munk, A. Geiger, L. Herzfeld, H. Graetz, J. Fürst, L. Dukes, M. Steinschneider, D. Cassel, S. Holdheim, and a host of minor investigators and teachers. Their loving devotion roused Jewish science and literature from their secular sleep to vigorous, intellectual life, reacting beneficently on the spiritual development of Judaism itself. The moulders of the new literature are such men as the celebrated preachers Adolf Jellinek, Salomon, Kley, Mannheimer; the able thinkers Steinheim, Hirsch, Krochmal; the illustrious scholars M. Lazarus, H. Steinthal; and the versatile journalists G. Riesser and L. Philipson.

Poetry has not been neglected in the general revival. The first Jewish poet to write in German was M. E. Kuh, whose tragic fate has been pathetically told by Berthold Auerbach in his *Dichter und Kaufmann*. The burden of this modern Jewish poetry is, of course, the glorification of the loyalty and fortitude that preserved the race during a calamitous past. Such poets as Steinheim, Wihl, L. A. Frankl, M. Beer, K. Beck, Th. Creizenach, M. Hartmann, S. H. Mosenthal, Henriette Ottenheimer, Moritz Rappaport, and L. Stein, sing the songs of Zion in the tongue of the German. And can Heine be forgotten, he who in his *Romanzero* has so melodiously, yet so touchingly given word to the hoary sorrow of the Jew?

In an essay of this scope no more can be done than give the barest outline of the modern movement. A detailed description of the work of German-Jewish lyrists belongs to the history of German literature, and, in fact, on its pages can be found a due appreciation of their worth by unprejudiced critics, who give particularly high praise to the new species of tales, the Jewish village, or Ghetto, tales, with which Jewish and German literatures have latterly been enriched. Their object is to depict the religious customs in vogue among Jews of past generations, their home-life, and the conflicts that arose when the old Judaism came into contact with modern views of life. The master in the art of telling these Ghetto tales is Leopold Kompert. Of his disciples—for all coming after him may be considered such—A. Bernstein described the Jews of Posen; K. E. Franzos and L. Herzberg-Fränkel, those of Poland; E. Kulke, the Moravian Jews; M. Goldschmied, the Dutch; S. H. Mosenthal, the Hessian, and M. Lehmann, the South German. To Berthold Auerbach's pioneer work this whole class of literature owes its existence; and Heinrich Heine's fragment, *Rabbi von Bacharach*, a model of its kind, puts him into this category of writers, too.

And so Judaism and Jewish literature are stepping into a new arena, on which potent forces that may radically affect both are struggling with each other. Is Jewish poetry on the point of dying out, or is it destined to enjoy a resurrection? Who would be rash enough to prophesy aught of a race whose entire past is a riddle, whose literature is a question-mark? Of a race which for more than a thousand years has, like its progenitor, been wrestling victoriously with gods and men?

To recapitulate: We have followed out the course of a literary development, beginning in grey antiquity with biblical narratives, assimilating Persian doctrines, Greek wisdom, and Roman law; later, Arabic poetry and philosophy, and, finally, the whole of European science in all its ramifications. The literature we have described has contributed its share to every spiritual result achieved by humanity, and is a still unexplored treasury of poetry and philosophy, of experience and knowledge.

"All the rivers run into the sea; yet the sea is never full," saith the Preacher; so all spiritual currents flow together into the vast ocean of a world-literature, never full, never complete, rejoicing in every accession, reaching the climax of its might and majesty on that day when, according to the prophet, "the earth shall be full of the knowledge of the Lord, as the waters cover the sea."

THE TALMUD

In the whole range of the world's literatures there are few books with so checkered a career, so curious a fate, as the Talmud has had. The name is simple enough, it glides glibly from the tongue, yet how difficult to explain its import to the uninitiated! From the Dominican Henricus Seynensis, who took "Talmud" to be the name of a rabbi—he introduces a quotation with *Ut narrat rabbinus Talmud*, "As Rabbi Talmud relates"—down to the church historians and university professors of our day, the oddest misconceptions on the nature of the Talmud have prevailed even among learned men. It is not astonishing, then, that the general reader has no notion of what it is.

Only within recent years the Talmud has been made the subject of scientific study, and now it is consulted by philologists, cited by jurists, drawn upon by historians, the general public is beginning to be interested in it, and of late the old Talmud has repeatedly been summoned to appear in courts of law to give evidence. Under these circumstances it is natural to ask, What is the Talmud? Futile to seek an answer by comparing this gigantic monument of the human intellect with any other book; it is *sui generis*. In the form in which it issued from the Jewish academies of Babylonia and Palestine, it is a great national work, a scientific document of first importance, the archives of ten centuries, in which are preserved the thoughts and opinions, the views and verdicts, the errors, transgressions, hopes, disappointments, customs, ideals, convictions, and sorrows of Israel—a work produced by the zeal and patience of thirty generations, laboring with a self-denial unparalleled in the history of literature. A work of this character assuredly deserves to be known. Unfortunately, the path to its understanding is blocked by peculiar linguistic and historical difficulties. Above all, explanations by comparison must be avoided. It has been likened to a legal code, to a journal, to the transactions of learned bodies; but these comparisons are both inadequate and misleading. To make it approximately clear a lengthy explanation must be entered upon, for, in truth, the Talmud, like the Bible, is a world in miniature, embracing every possible phase of life.

The origin of the Talmud was simultaneous with Israel's return from the Babylonian exile, during which a wonderful change had taken place in the captive people. An idolatrous, rebellious nation had turned into a pious congregation of the Lord, possessed with zeal for the study of the Law. By degrees there grew up out of this study a science of wide scope, whose beginnings are hidden in the last book of the Bible, in the word *Midrash*, translated by "story" in the Authorized Version. Its true meaning is indicated by that of its root, *darash*, to study, to expound. Four different methods of explaining the sacred Scriptures were current: the first aimed to reach the simple understanding of words as they stood; the second availed itself of suggestions offered by apparently superfluous letters and signs in the text to arrive at its meaning; the third was "a homiletic application of that which had been to that which was and would be, of prophetical and historical dicta to the actual condition of things"; and the fourth devoted itself to theosophic mysteries—but all led to a common goal.

In the course of the centuries the development of the Midrash, or study of the Law, lay along the two strongly marked lines of Halacha, the explanation and formulating of laws, and Haggada, their poetical illustration and ethical application. These are the two spheres within which the intellectual life of Judaism revolved, and these the two elements, the legal and the æsthetic, making up the Talmud.

The two Midrashic systems emphasize respectively the rule of law and the sway of liberty: Halacha is law incarnate; Haggada, liberty regulated by law and bearing the impress of morality. Halacha stands for the rigid authority of the Law, for the absolute importance of theory—the law and theory which the Haggada illustrates by public opinion and the dicta of common-sense morality. The Halacha embraces the statutes enjoined by oral tradition, which was the unwritten commentary of the ages on the written Law, along with the discussions of the academies of Palestine and Babylonia, resulting in the final formulating of the Halachic ordinances. The Haggada, while also starting from the word of the Bible, only plays with it, explaining it by sagas and legends, by tales and poems, allegories, ethical reflections, and historical reminiscences. For it, the Bible was not only the supreme law, from whose behests there was no appeal, but also "a golden nail upon which" the Haggada "hung its gorgeous tapestries," so that the Bible word was the introduction, refrain, text, and subject of the poetical glosses of the Talmud. It was the province of the Halacha to build, upon the foundation of biblical law, a legal superstructure capable of resisting the ravages of time, and, unmindful of contemporaneous distress and hardship, to trace out, for future generations, the extreme logical consequences of the Law in its application. To the Haggada belonged the high, ethical mission of consoling, edifying, exhorting, and teaching a nation suffering the pangs, and threatened with the spiritual stagnation, of exile; of proclaiming that the glories of the past prefigured a future of equal brilliancy, and that the very wretchedness of the present was part of the divine plan outlined in the Bible. If the simile is accurate that likens the Halacha to the ramparts about Israel's sanctuary, which every Jew was ready to defend with his last drop of blood, then the Haggada must seem "flowery mazes, of exotic colors and bewildering fragrance," within the shelter of the Temple walls.

The complete work of expounding, developing, and finally establishing the Law represents the labor of many generations, the method of procedure varying from time to time. In the long interval between the close of the Holy Canon and the completion of the Talmud can be distinguished three historical strata deposited by three different classes of teachers. The first set, the Scribes—*Soferim*—flourished in the period beginning with the return from Babylonian captivity and ending with the Syrian persecutions (220 B. C. E.), and their work was the preservation of the text of the Holy Writings and the simple expounding of biblical ordinances. They were followed by the " Learners "—*Tanaïm*—whose activity extended until 220 C. E. Great historical events occurred in that period: the campaigns of the Maccabean heroes, the birth of Jesus, the destruction of the Temple by the Romans, the rebellion under Bar-Kochba, and the final complete dispersion of the Jews. Amid all these storms the *Tanaïm* did not for a moment relinquish their diligent research in the Law. The Talmud tells the story of a celebrated rabbi, than which nothing can better characterize the age and its scholars: Night was falling. A funeral cortege was moving through the streets of old Jerusalem. It was said that disciples were bearing a well-beloved teacher to the grave. Reverentially the way was cleared, not even the Roman guard at the gate hindered the procession. Beyond the city walls it halted, the bier was set down, the lid of the coffin opened, and out of it arose the venerable form of Rabbi Jochanan ben Zakkaï, who, to reach the Roman camp unmolested, had feigned death. He went before Vespasian, and, impressed by the noble figure of the hoary rabbi, the general promised him the fulfilment of any wish he might express. What was his petition? Not for his nation, not for the preservation of the Holy City, not even for the Temple. His request was simple: "Permit me to open a school at Jabneh." The proud Roman smilingly gave consent. He had no conception of the significance of this prayer and of the prophetic wisdom of the petitioner, who, standing on the ruins of his nation's independence, thought only of rescuing the Law. Rome, the empire of the "iron legs," was doomed to be crushed, nation after nation to be swallowed in the vortex of time, but Israel lives by the Law, the very law snatched from the smouldering ruins of Jerusalem, the beloved alike of crazy zealots and despairing peace advocates, and carried to the tiny seaport of Jabneh. There Jochanan ben Zakkai opened his academy, the gathering place of the dispersed of his disciples and his people, and thence, gifted with a prophet's keen vision, he proclaimed Israel's mission to be, not the offering of sacrifices, but the accomplishment of works of peace.[1]

The *Tanaïm* may be considered the most original expounders of the science of Judaism, which they fostered at their academies. In the course of centuries their intellectual labor amassed an abundant store of scientific material, together with so vast a number of injunctions, prohibitions, and laws that it

[1] *Midrash Echah*, I., 5; Mishna, *Rosh Hashana*, chap. II.

became almost impossible to master the subject. The task of scholars now was to arrange the accumulation of material and reduce it to a system. Rabbi after rabbi undertook the task, but only the fourth attempt at codification, that made by Yehuda the Prince, was successful. His compilation, classifying the subject-matter under six heads, subdivided into sixty-three tractates, containing five hundred and twenty-four chapters, was called Mishna, and came to be the authority appealed to on points of law.

Having assumed fixity as a code, the Mishna in turn became what the Bible had been for centuries— a text, the basis of all legal development and scientific discussion. So it was used by the epigones, the *Amoraïm*, or Speakers, the expounders of the third period. For generations commenting on the Mishna was the sum-total of literary endeavor. Traditions unheeded before sprang to light. New methods asserted themselves. To the older generation of Halachists succeeded a set of men headed by Akiba ben Joseph, who, ignoring practical issues, evolved laws from the Bible text or from traditions held to be divine. A spiritual, truly religious conception of Judaism was supplanted by legal quibbling and subtle methods of interpretation. Like the sophists of Rome and Alexandria at that time, the most celebrated teachers in the academies of Babylonia and Palestine for centuries gave themselves up to casuistry. This is the history of the development of the Talmud, or more correctly of the two Talmuds, the one, finished in 390 C. E., being the expression of what was taught at the Palestinian academies; the other, more important one, completed in 500 C. E., of what was taught in Babylonia.

The Babylonian, the one regarded as authoritative, is about four times as large as the Jerusalem Talmud. Its thirty-six treatises (*Massichtoth*), in our present edition, cover upwards of three thousand folio pages, bound in twelve huge volumes. To speak of a completed Talmud is as incorrect as to speak of a biblical canon. No religious body, no solemn resolution of a synod, ever declared either the Talmud or the Bible a completed whole. Canonizing of any kind is distinctly opposed to the spirit of Judaism. The fact is that the tide of traditional lore has never ceased to flow.

We now have before us a faint outline sketch of the growth of the Talmud. To portray the busy world fitting into this frame is another and more difficult matter. A catalogue of its contents may be made. It may be said that it is a book containing laws and discussions, philosophic, theologic, and juridic dicta, historical notes and national reminiscences, injunctions and prohibitions controlling all the positions and relations of life, curious, quaint tales, ideal maxims and proverbs, uplifting legends, charming lyrical outbursts, and attractive enigmas side by side with misanthropic utterances, bewildering medical prescriptions, superstitious practices, expressions of deep agony, peculiar astrological charms, and rambling digressions on law, zoology, and botany, and when all this has been said, not half its contents have been told. It is a luxuriant jungle, which must be explored by him who would gain an adequate idea of its features and products.

The Ghemara, that is, the whole body of discussions recorded in the two Talmuds, primarily forms a running commentary on the text of the Mishna. At the same time, it is the arena for the debating and investigating of subjects growing out of the Mishna, or suggested by a literature developed along with the Talmudic literature. These discussions, debates, and investigations are the opinions and arguments of the different schools, holding opposite views, developed with rare acumen and scholastic subtlety, and finally harmonized in the solution reached. The one firm and impregnable rock supporting the gigantic structure of the Talmud is the word of the Bible, held sacred and inviolable.

The best translations—single treatises have been put into modern languages—fail to convey an adequate idea of the discussions and method that evolved the Halacha. It is easier to give an approximately true presentation of the rabbinical system of practical morality as gleaned from the Haggada. It must, of course, be borne in mind that Halacha and Haggada are not separate works; they are two fibres of the same thread. "The whole of the Haggadistic literature—the hitherto unappreciated archives of language, history, archæology, religion, poetry, and science—with but slight reservations may be called a national literature, containing as it does the aggregate of the views and opinions of thousands of thinkers belonging to widely separated generations. Largely, of course, these views and opinions are peculiar to the individuals holding them or to their time"; still, every Haggadistic expression, in a general way, illustrates some fundamental, national law, based upon the national religion and the national history.[1] Through the Haggada we are vouchsafed a glance into a mysterious world, which mayhap has hitherto repelled us as strange and grewsome. Its poesy reveals vistas of gleaming beauty and light, luxuriant growth and exuberant life, while familiar melodies caress our ears.

The Haggada conveys its poetic message in the garb of allegory, song, and chiefly epigrammatic saying. Form is disregarded; the spirit is all-important, and suffices to cover up every fault of form. The Talmud, of course, does not yield a complete system of ethics, but its practical philosophy consists of doctrines that underlie a moral life. The injustice of the abuse heaped upon it would become apparent to its harshest critics from a few of its maxims and rules of conduct, such as the following: Be of them that are persecuted, not of the perse-

---

[1] Cmp. Wünsche, *Die Haggada des jerusalemischen Talmud*, and the same author's great work, *Die Haggada des babylonischen Talmud*, II.; also W. Bacher, *Die Agada der Tannaiten*, *Die Agada der babylonischen Amoräer*, and *Die Agada der palästinensischen Amoräer*, Vol. I.

cutors.—Be the cursed, not he that curses.—They that are persecuted, and do not persecute, that are vilified and do not retort, that act in love, and are cheerful even in suffering, they are the lovers of God.—Bless God for the good as well as the evil. When thou hearest of a death, say, " Blessed be the righteous Judge."—Life is like unto a fleeting shadow. Is it the shadow of a tower or of a bird? It is the shadow of a bird in its flight. Away flies the bird, and neither bird nor shadow remains behind.—Repentance and good works are the aim of all earthly wisdom.—Even the just will not have so high a place in heaven as the truly repentant.—He whose learning surpasses his good works is like a tree with many branches and few roots, which a wind-storm uproots and casts to the ground. But he whose good works surpass his learning is like a tree with few branches and many roots; all the winds of heaven cannot move it from its place.—There are three crowns: the crown of the Law, the crown of the priesthood, the crown of kingship. But greater than all is the crown of a good name.—Four there are that cannot enter Paradise: the scoffer, the liar, the hypocrite, and the backbiter.—Beat the gods, and the priests will tremble.—Contrition is better than many flagellations.—When the pitcher falls upon the stone, woe unto the pitcher; when the stone falls upon the pitcher, woe unto the pitcher; whatever betides, woe unto the pitcher.—The place does not honor the man, the man honors the place. —He who humbles himself will be exalted; he who exalts himself will be humbled.—Whosoever pursues greatness, from him will greatness flee; whosoever flees from greatness, him will greatness pursue. —Charity is as important as all other virtues combined.—Be tender and yielding like a reed, not hard and proud like a cedar.—The hypocrite will not see God.—It is not sufficient to be innocent before God; we must show our innocence to the world.—The works encouraged by a good man are better than those he executes.—Woe unto him that practices usury, he shall not live; whithersoever he goes, he carries injustice and death.

The same Talmud that fills chapter after chapter with minute legal details and hairsplitting debates outlines with a few strokes the most ideal conception of life, worth more than theories and systems of religious philosophy. A Haggada passage says: Six hundred and thirteen injunctions were given by Moses to the people of Israel. David reduced them to eleven; the prophet Isaiah classified these under six heads; Micah enumerated only three: "What doth the Lord require of thee, but to do justly, and to love mercy, and to walk humbly with thy God." Another prophet limited them to two: "Keep ye judgment, and do righteousness." Amos put all the commandments under one: "Seek ye me, and ye shall live"; and Habakkuk said: "The just shall live by his faith."—This is the ethics of the Talmud.

Another characteristic manifestation of the idealism of the Talmud is its delicate feeling for women and children. Almost extravagant affection is displayed for the little ones. All the verses of Scripture that speak of flowers and gardens are applied in the Talmud to children and schools. Their breath sustains the moral order of the universe: "Out of the mouth of babes and sucklings has God founded His might." They are called flowers, stars, the anointed of God. When God was about to give the Law, He demanded of the Israelites pledges to assure Him that they would keep His commandments holy. They offered the patriarchs, but each one of them had committed some sin. They named Moses as their surety; not even he was guiltless. Then they said: "Let our children be our hostages." The Lord accepted them.

Similarly, there are many expressions to show that woman was held in high esteem by the rabbis of the Talmud: Love thy wife as thyself; honor her more than thyself.—In choosing a wife, descend a step.—If thy wife is small, bend and whisper into her ear.—God's altar weeps for him that forsakes the love of his youth.—He who sees his wife die before him has, as it were, been present at the destruction of the sanctuary itself; around him the world grows dark. —It is woman alone through whom God's blessings are vouchsafed to a house.—The children of him that marries for money shall be a curse unto him,— a warning singularly applicable to the circumstances of our own times.

The peculiar charm of the Haggada is best revealed in its legends and tales, its fables and myths, its apologues and allegories, its riddles and songs.

The starting-point of the Haggada usually is some memory of the great past. It entwines and enmeshes in a magic network the lives of the patriarchs, prophets, and martyrs, and clothes with fresh, luxuriant green the old ideals and figures, giving them new life for a remote generation. The teachers of the Haggada allow no opportunity, sad or merry, to pass without utilizing it in the guise of an apologue or parable. Alike for wedding-feasts and funerals, for banquets and days of fasting, the garden of the Haggada is rifled of its fragrant blossoms and luscious fruits. Simplicity, grace, and childlike merriment pervade its fables, yet they are profound, even sublime, in their truth. "Their chief and enduring charm is their fathomless depth, their unassuming loveliness." Poems constructed with great artistic skill do not occur. Here and there a modest bud of lyric poesy shyly raises its head, like the following couplet, describing a celebrated but ill-favored rabbi:

"Without charm of form and face,
But a mind of rarest grace."

Over the grave of the same teacher the Talmud wails:

"The Holy Land did beautify what womb of Shinar gave;
And now Tiberias' tear-filled eye weeps o'er her treasure's grave."

On seeing the dead body of the Patriarch Yehuda, a rabbi laments:

"Angels strove to win the testimony's ark.
Men they overcame; lo! vanished is the ark!"

Another threnody over some prince in the realm of the intellect:

"The cedar hath by flames been seized;
Can hyssop then be saved?
Leviathan with hook was caught;
Alas! ye little fish!
The deep and mighty stream ran dry,
Ah woe! ye shallow brooks!"

Nor is humor lacking. "Ah, hamper great, with books well-filled, thou'rt gone!" is a bookworm's eulogy.

Poets naturally have not been slow to avail themselves of the material stored in the Haggada. Many of its treasures, tricked out in modern verse, have been given to the world. The following are samples:[1]

BIRTH AND DEATH

"His hands fast clenched, his fingers firmly clasped,
So man this life begins.
He claims earth's wealth, and constitutes himself
The heir of all her gifts.
He thinks his hand may snatch and hold
Whatever life doth yield.

But when at last the end has come,
His hands are open wide,
No longer closed. He knoweth now full well,
That vain were all his hopes.
He humbly says, 'I go, and nothing take
Of all my hands have wrought.'"

[1] M. Sachs, *Stimmen vom Jordan und Euphrat.*

The next, "Interest and Usury," may serve to give the pertinacious opponent of the Talmud a better opinion of its position on financial subjects:

"Behold! created things of every kind
    Lend each to each. The day from night doth take,
    And night from day; nor do they quarrel make
Like men, who doubting one another's mind,
E'en while they utter friendly words, think ill.
    The moon delighted helps the starry host,
    And each returns her gift without a boast.
'Tis only when the Lord supreme doth will
That earth in gloom shall be enwrapped,
    He tells the moon: 'Refrain, keep back thy light!'
    And quenches, too, the myriad lamps of night.
From wisdom's fount hath knowledge ofttimes lapped,
While wisdom humbly doth from knowledge learn.
    The skies drop blessings on the grateful earth,
    And she—of precious store there is no dearth—
Exhales and sends aloft a fair return.
Stern law with mercy tempers its decree,
    And mercy acts with strength by justice lent.
    Good deeds are based on creed from heaven sent,
In which, in turn, the sap of deeds must be.
    Each creature borrows, lends, and gives with love,
    Nor e'er disputes, to honor God above.

When man, howe'er, his fellowman hath fed,
    Then 'spite the law forbidding interest,
    He thinketh naught but cursèd gain to wrest.
Who taketh usury methinks hath said:
'O Lord, in beauty has Thy earth been wrought!
    But why should men for naught enjoy its plains?
    Ask usance, since 'tis Thou that sendest rains.
Have they the trees, their fruits, and blossoms bought?
For all they here enjoy, Thy int'rest claim:

>   For heaven's orbs that shine by day and night,
>   Th' immortal soul enkindled by Thy light,
>   And for the wondrous structure of their frame.'
>   But God replies: 'Now come, and see! I give
>   With open, bounteous hand, yet nothing take;
>   The earth yields wealth, nor must return ye make.
>   But know, O men, that only while ye live,
>   You may enjoy these gifts of my award.
>   The capital's mine, and surely I'll demand
>   The spirit in you planted by my hand,
>   And also earth will claim her due reward.'
>   Man's dust to dust is gathered in the grave,
>   His soul returns to God who gracious gave."

R. Yehuda ben Zakkaï answers his pupils who ask:

> "Why doth the Law with them more harshly deal
>   That filch a lamb from fold away,
> Than with the highwaymen who shameless steal
>   Thy purse by force in open day?"

> "Because in like esteem the brigands hold
>   The master and his serving man.
> Their wickedness is open, frank, and bold,
>   They fear not God, nor human ban.

> The thief feels more respect for earthly law
>   Than for his heav'nly Master's eye,
> Man's presence flees in fear and awe,
>   Forgets he's seen by God on high."

That is a glimpse of the world of the Haggada—a wonderful, fantastic world, a kaleidoscopic panorama of enchanting views. "Well can we understand the distress of mind in a mediæval divine, or even in a modern *savant*, who, bent upon following the most subtle windings of some scientific debate in the Talmudical pages—geometrical, botanical, financial, or otherwise—as it revolves round the Sabbath journey, the raising of seeds, the computation of tithes and taxes—feels, as it were, the ground suddenly give way. The loud voices grow thin, the doors and walls of the school-room vanish before his eyes, and in their place uprises Rome the Great, the *Urbs et Orbis* and her million-voiced life. Or the blooming vineyards round that other City of Hills, Jerusalem the Golden herself, are seen, and white-clad virgins move dreamily among them. Snatches of their songs are heard, the rhythm of their choric dances rises and falls: it is the most dread Day of Atonement itself, which, in poetical contrast, was chosen by the 'Rose of Sharon' as a day of rejoicing to walk among those waving lily-fields and vine-clad slopes. Or the clarion of rebellion rings high and shrill through the complicated debate, and Belshazzar, the story of whose ghastly banquet is told with all the additions of maddening horror, is doing service for Nero the bloody; or Nebuchadnezzar, the Babylonian tyrant, and all his hosts, are cursed with a yelling curse—*à propos* of some utterly inappropriate legal point, while to the initiated he stands for Titus the—at last exploded—'Delight of Humanity.' . . . Often—far too often for the interests of study and the glory of the human race—does the steady tramp of the Roman cohort, the password of the revolution, the shriek and clangor of the bloody field, interrupt these debates, and the arguing masters and disciples don their arms, and, with the cry, 'Jerusalem and Liberty,' rush to the fray."[1]

Such is the world of the Talmud.

[1] Emanuel Deutsch, "Literary Remains," p. 45.

THE JEW IN THE HISTORY OF CIVILIZATION[1]

In the childhood of civilization, the digging of wells was regarded as beneficent work. Guideposts, visible from afar, marked their position, and hymns were composed, and solemn feasts celebrated, in honor of the event. One of the choicest bits of early Hebrew poetry is a song of the well. The soul, in grateful joy, jubilantly calls to her mates: "Arise! sing a song unto the well! Well, which the princes have dug, which the nobles of the people have hollowed out."[2] This house, too, is a guidepost to a newly-found well of humanity and culture, a monument to our faithfulness and zeal in the recognition and the diffusion of truth. A scene like this brings to my mind the psalmist's beautiful words:[3] "Behold, how good and how pleasant it is for brethren to dwell together in unity. It is like the precious ointment upon the head, that ran down upon the beard, even Aaron's beard, that went down to the skirts of his garment; as the dew of Hermon, running down upon the mountains of Zion; for there hath the Lord commanded the blessing, even life for evermore."

[1] Address at the dedication of the new meeting-house of the Independent Order B'nai B'rith, at Berlin.
[2] Numbers, xxi. 17, 18.   [3] Psalm cxxxiii.

Wondrous thoughts veiled with wondrous imagery! The underlying meaning will lead us to our feast of the well, our celebration in honor of newly-discovered waters. Our order is based upon the conviction that all men should be banded together for purposes of humanity. But what is humanity? Not philanthropy, not benevolence, not charity: it is "human culture risen to the stage on which man is conscious of universal brotherhood, and strives for the realization of the general good." In early times, leaders of men were anointed with oil, symbol of wisdom and divine inspiration. Above all it was meet that it be used in the consecration of priests, the exponents of the divine spirit and the Law. The psalmist's idea is, that as the precious ointment in its abundance runs down Aaron's beard to the hem of his garment, even so shall wisdom and the divine spirit overflow the lips of priests, the guides, friends, and teachers of the people, the promoters of the law of peace and love.

"As the dew of Hermon, running down upon the mountains of Zion!" High above all mountains towers Hermon, its crest enveloped by clouds and covered with eternal snow. From that supernal peak grateful dew trickles down, fructifying the land once "flowing with milk and honey." From its clefts gushes forth Jordan, mightiest stream of the land, watering a broad plain in its course. In this guise the Lord has granted His blessing to the land, the blessing of civilization and material prosperity, from which spring as corollaries the duties of charity and universal humanity.

A picture of the olden time this, a lodge-address of the days of the psalm singers. Days flee, time abides; men pass away, mankind endures. Filled with time-honored thoughts, inspired by the hopes of by-gone generations, striving for the goal of noble men in all ages, like the psalm singers in the days of early culture, we celebrate a feast of the well by reviewing the past and looking forward down the avenues of time.

Less than fifty years ago a band of energetic, loyal Jews, on the other side of the Atlantic, founded our beloved Order. Now it has established itself in every part of the world, from the extreme western coast of America to the blessed meadows of the Jordan; yea, even the Holy Land, unfurling everywhere the banner of charity, brotherly love, and unity, and seeking to spread education and culture, the forerunners of humanity. Judaism, mark you, is the religion of humanity. By far too late for our good and that of mankind, we began to proclaim this truth with becoming energy and emphasis, and to demonstrate it with the joyousness of conviction. The question is, are we permeated with this conviction? Our knowledge of Judaism is slight; we have barely a suspicion of what in the course of centuries, nay, of thousands of years, it has done for the progress of civilization. In my estimation, our house-warming cannot more fittingly be celebrated than by taking a bird's-eye view of Jewish culture.

The Bible is the text-book of general literature. Out of the Bible, more particularly from the Ten

Commandments, flashed from Sinai, mankind learned its first ethical lesson in a system which still satisfies its needs. To convey even a faint idea of what the Bible has done for civilization, morality, and the literature of every people—of the innumerable texts it has furnished to poets, and subjects to painters—would in itself require a literature.

The conflicts with surrounding nations to which they were exposed made the Jews concentrate their forces, and so enabled them to wage successful war with nations mightier than themselves. Their heroism under the Maccabees and under Bar-Kochba, in the middle ages and in modern days, permits them to take rank among the most valiant in history. A historian of literature, a non-Jew, enumerates three factors constituting Jews important agents in the preservation and revival of learning:[1] First, their ability as traders. The Phœnicians are regarded as the oldest commercial nation, but the Jews contested the palm with them. Zebulon and Asher in very early times were seafaring tribes. Under Solomon, Israelitish vessels sailed as far as Ophir to bring Afric's gold to Jerusalem. Before the destruction of the Holy City, Jewish communities established themselves on the westernmost coast of Europe. "The whole of the known world was covered with their settlements, in constant communication with one another through itinerant merchants, who effected an exchange of learning as well as of wares;

---

[1] M. J. Schleiden: *Die Bedeutung der Juden für die Erhaltung der Wissenschaften im Mittelalter*, p. 7.

while the other nations grew more and more isolated, and shut themselves off from even the sparse opportunities of mental culture then available."

The second factor conducing to mental advancement was the schools which have flourished in Israel since the days of the prophet Samuel; and the third was the linguistic attainments of the Jews, which they owed to natural ability in this direction. Scarcely had Greek allied itself with Hebrew thought, when Jews in Alexandria wrote Greek comparable with Plato's, and not more than two hundred years after the settlement of Jews in Arabia we meet with a large number of Jewish poets among Mohammed's disciples, while in the middle ages they taught and wrote Arabic, Spanish, French, and German—versatility naturally favorable to intellectual progress.

Jewish influence may be said to have begun to exercise itself upon general culture when Judaism and Hellenism met for the first time. The result of the meeting was the new product, Judæo-Hellenic literature. Greek civilization was attractive to Jews. The new ideas were popularized for all strata of the people to imbibe. Shortly before the old pagan world crumbled, Hellenism enjoyed a beautiful, unexpected revival in Alexandria. There, strange to say, Judaism, in its home antagonistic to Hellenism, had filled and allied itself with the Greek spirit. Its literature gradually adopted Greek traditions, and the ripe fruit of the union was the Jewish-Alexandrian religious philosophy, the mediation between two sharply contradictory systems, for the first time brought into close juxtaposition, and requiring some such new element to harmonize them. When ancient civilization in Judæa and in Hellas fell into decay, human endeavor was charged with the task of reconciling these two great historical forces diametrically opposed to each other, and the first attempt looking to this end was inspired by a Jewish genius, Jesus of Nazareth.

The Jews of Alexandria were engaged in widespread trade and shipping, and they counted among them artists, poets, civil officers, and mechanics. They naturally acquired Greek customs, and along with them Hellenic vices. The bacchanalia of Athens were enthusiastically imitated in Jerusalem, and, as a matter of course, in Alexandria. This point reached, Roman civilization asserted itself, and the people sought to affiliate with their Roman victors, while the rabbis devoted themselves to the Law, not, however, to the exclusion of scientific work. In the ranks of physicians and astronomers we find Jewish masters and Jewish disciples. Medicine has always been held in high esteem by Jews, and Samuel could justly boast before his contemporaries that the intricate courses of the stars were as well known to him as the streets of Nehardea in Babylonia.[1]

The treasures of information on pedagogics, medicine, jurisprudence, astronomy, geography, zoology, botany, and last, though not least, on general

[1] *Moed Katan*, 26a.

history, buried in the Talmud, have hitherto not been valued at their true worth. The rabbis of the Talmud stood in the front ranks of culture. They compiled a calendar, in complete accord with the Metonic cycle, which modern science must declare faultless. Their classification of the bones of the human body varies but little from present results of the science of anatomy, and the Talmud demonstrates that certain Mishna ordinances are based upon geometrical propositions, which could have been known to but few mathematicians of that time. Rabbi Gamaliel, said to have made use of a telescope, was celebrated as a mathematician and astronomer, and in 289 C. E., Rabbi Joshua is reported to have calculated the orbit of Halley's comet.

The Roman conquest of Palestine effected a change in the condition of the Jews. Never before had Judah undergone such torture and suffering as under the sceptre of Rome. The misery became unendurable, and internal disorders being added to foreign oppression, the luckless insurrection broke out which gave the deathblow to Jewish nationality, and drove Judah into exile. On his thorny martyr's path he took naught with him but a book—his code, his law. Yet how prodigal his contributions to mankind's fund of culture!

About five hundred years later Judah saw springing up on his own soil a new religion which appropriated the best and the most beautiful of his spiritual possessions. Swiftly rose the vast political and intellectual structure of Mohammedan power, and as before with Greek, so Jewish thought now allied itself with Arabic endeavor, bringing forth in Spain the golden age of neo-Hebraic literature in the spheres of poetry, metaphysical speculation, and every department of scientific research. It is not an exaggerated estimate to say that the middle ages sustained themselves with the fruit of this intellectual labor, which, moreover, has come down as a legacy to our modern era. Two hundred years after Mohammed, the same language, Arabic, was spoken by the Jews of Kairwan and those of Bagdad. Thus equipped, they performed in a remarkable way the task allotted them by their talents and their circumstances, to which they had been devoting themselves with singular zeal for two centuries. The Jews are missioned mediators between the Orient and the Occident, and their activity as such, illustrated by their additions to general culture and science, is of peculiar interest. In the period under consideration, their linguistic accomplishments fitted them to assist the Syrians in making Greek literature accessible to the Arabic mind. In Arabic literature itself, they attained to a prominent place. Modern research has not yet succeeded in shedding light upon the development and spread of science among the Arabs under the tutelage of Syrian Christians. But out of the obscurity of Greek-Arabic culture beginnings gleam Jewish names, whose possessors were the teachers of eager Arabic disciples. Barely fifty years after the hosts of the Prophet had conquered the Holy Land, a Jew of Bassora translated from Syriac into Arabic the pandects by the presbyter Aaron, a famous medical work of the middle ages. In the annals of the next century, among the early contributors to Arabic literature, we meet with the names of Jews as translators of medical, mathematical, and astronomical works, and as grammarians, astronomers, scientists, and physicians. A Jew translated Ptolemy's "Almagest"; another assisted in the first translation of the Indian fox fables (*Kalila we-Dimna*); the first furnishing the middle ages with the basis of their astronomical science, the second supplying European poets with literary material. Through the instrumentality of Jews, Arabs became acquainted as early as the eighth century, some time before the learning of the Greeks was brought within their reach, with Indian medicine, astronomy, and poetry. Greek science itself they owed to Jewish mediation. Not only among Jews, but also among Greeks, Syrians, and Arabs, Jewish versatility gave currency to the belief that "all wisdom is of the Jews," a view often repeated by Hellenists, by the "Righteous Brethren" among the Arabs, and later by the Christian monks of Europe.

The academies of the Jews have always been pervaded by a scientific spirit. As they influenced others, so they permitted the science and culture of their neighbors to act upon their life and work. There is no doubt, for instance, that, despite the marked difference between the subjects treated by

Arabs and Jews, the peculiar qualities of the old Arabic lyrics shaped neo-Hebraic poetry. Again, as the Hebrew acrostic psalms demonstrably served as models to the older Syrian Church poets, so, in turn, Syriac psalmody probably became the pattern synagogue poetry followed. Thus Hebrew poetry completed a circuit, which, to be sure, cannot accurately be followed up through its historical stages, but which critical investigations and the comparative study of literatures have established almost as a certainty.

In the ninth century a bold, venturesome traveller, Eldad ha-Dani,[1] a sort of Jewish Ulysses, appeared among Jews, and at the same time Judaism produced Sa'adia, its first great religious philosopher and Bible translator. The Church Fathers had always looked up to the rabbis as authorities; henceforth Jews were accepted by all scholars as the teachers of Bible exegesis. Sa'adia was the first of the rabbis to translate the Hebrew Scriptures into Arabic. Justly his work is said to "recognize the current of thought dominant in his time, and to express the newly-awakened desire for the reconciliation of religious practice, as developed in the course of generations, with the source of religious inspiration." Besides, he was the first to elaborate a system of religious philosophy according to a rigid plan, and in a strictly scientific spirit.[2] Knowing Greek speculations, he controverts them as vigor-

[1] Cmp. "Israel's Quest in Africa," pp. 257-258
[2] Cmp. Gutmann, *Die Religionsphilosophie des Saâdja.*

ously as the *Kalâm* of Islam philosophy. His teachings form a system of practical ethics, luminous reflections, and sound maxims. Among his contemporaries was Isaac Israeli, a physician at Kairwan, whose works, in their Latin translation by the monk Constantine, attained great reputation, and were later plagiarized by medical writers. His treatise on fever was esteemed of high worth, a translation of it being studied as a text-book for centuries, and his dietetic writings remained authoritative for five hundred years. In general, the medical science of the Arabs is under great obligations to him. Reverence for Jewish medical ability was so exaggerated in those days that Galen was identified with the Jewish sage Gamaliel. The error was fostered in the *Sefer Asaf*, a curious medical fragment of uncertain authorship and origin, by its rehearsal of an old Midrash, which traces the origin of medicine to Shem, son of Noah, who received it from angels, and transmitted it to the ancient Chaldeans, they in turn passing it on to the Egyptians, Greeks, and Arabs.

Though the birth of medicine is not likely to have taken place among Jews, it is indisputable that physicians of the Jewish race are largely to be credited with the development of medical science at every period. At the time we speak of, Jews in Egypt, northern Africa, Italy, Spain, France, and Germany were physicians in ordinary to caliphs, emperors, and popes, and everywhere they are represented among medical writers. The position occupied in the Arabian world by Israeli, in the Occident was occupied by Sabattaï Donnolo, one of the Salerno school in its early obscure days, the author of a work on *Materia medica*, possibly the oldest original production on medicine in the Hebrew language.

The period of Jewish prosperity in Spain has been called a fairy vision of history. The culture developed under its genial influences pervaded the middle ages, and projected suggestions even into our modern era. One of the most renowned *savants* at the beginning of the period was the statesman Chasdaï ben Shaprut, whose translation of Dioscorides's " Plant Lore " served as the botanical textbook of mediæval Europe. The first poet was Solomon ibn Gabirol, the author of " The Source of Life," a systematic exposition of Neoplatonic philosophy, a book of most curious fortunes. Through the Latin translation, made with the help of an apostate Jew, and bearing the author's name in the mutilated form of Avencebrol, later changed into Avicebron, scholasticism became saturated with its philosophic ideas. The pious fathers of Christian philosophy, Albertus Magnus and Thomas Aquinas, took pains to refute them, while Duns Scotus and Giordano Bruno frequently consulted the work as an authority. In the struggle between the Scotists and the Thomists it had a prominent place as late as the fourteenth century, the contestants taking it to be the work of some great Christian philosopher standing on the threshold of the Occident and at the portals of philosophy. So it happened that the author came down through the centuries, recognized by none, forgotten by his own, until, in our time, behind the Moorish-Christian mask of Avencebrol, Solomon Munk discovered the Jewish thinker and poet Solomon ibn Gabirol.

The work *De Causis*, attributed to David, a forgotten Jewish philosopher, must be classed with Gabirol's "Source of Life," on account of its Neoplatonism and its paramount influence upon scholasticism. In fact, only by means of a searching analysis of these two works can insight be gained into the development and aberrations of the dogmatic system of mediæval philosophy.

Other sciences, too, especially mathematics, flourished among them. One century after he wrote them, the works of Abraham ibn Ezra, renowned as an astronomer and mathematician, were translated into Latin by Italians, among whom his prestige was so great that, as may still be seen, he was painted among the expounders of mathematical science in an Italian church fresco representing the seven liberal arts. Under the name Abraham Judæus, later corrupted into Avenare, he is met with throughout the middle ages. Abraham ben Chiya, another distinguished scientist, known by the name Savasorda, compiled the first systematic outline of astronomy, and in his geographical treatise, he explained the sphericity of the earth, while the Latin translation of his geometry, based on Arabic sources, proves him to have made considerable additions to the stock of knowledge in this branch. Moses

Maimuni's intellectual vigor, and his influence upon the schoolmen through his medical, and more particularly his religio-philosophical works, are too well known to need more than passing mention.

Even in southern France and in Germany, whither the light of culture did not spread so rapidly as in Spain, Jews participated in the development of the sciences. Solomon ben Isaac, called Rashi, the great exegete, was looked up to as an authority by others beside his brethren in faith. Nicolas de Lyra, one of the most distinguished Christian Bible exegetes, confesses that his simple explanations of Scriptural passages are derived pre-eminently from Rashi's Bible commentary, and among scientific men it is acknowledged that precisely in the matter of exegesis this French monk exercised decisive influence upon Martin Luther. So it happens that in places Luther's Bible translation reveals Rashi seen through Nicolas de Lyra's spectacles.

In the quickened intellectual life of Provence Jews also took active part. David Kimchi has come to be regarded as the teacher *par excellence* of Hebrew grammar and lexicography, and Judah ibn Tibbon, one of the most notable of translators, in his testament addressed to his son made a complete presentation of contemporary science, a cyclopædia of the Arabic and the Hebrew language and literature, grammar, poetry, botany, zoology, natural history, and particularly religious philosophy, the studies of the Bible and the Talmud.

The golden age of letters was followed by a less

creative period, a significant turning-point in the history of Judaism as of spiritual progress in general. The contest between tradition and philosophy affected every mind. Literature was widely cultivated; each of its departments found devotees. The European languages were studied, and connections established between the literatures of the nations. Hardly a spiritual current runs through the middle ages without, in some way, affecting Jewish culture. It is the irony of history that puts among the forty proscribers of the Talmud assembled at Paris in the thirteenth century the Dominican Albertus Magnus, who, in his successful efforts to divert scholastic philosophy into new channels, depended entirely upon the writings and translations of the very Jews he was helping to persecute. Schoolmen were too little conversant with Greek to read Aristotle in the original, and so had to content themselves with accepting the Judæo-Arabic construction put upon the Greek sage's teachings.

Besides acting as intermediaries, Jews made original contributions to scholastic philosophy. For instance, Maimonides, the first to reconcile Aristotle's teachings with biblical theology, was the originator of the method adopted by schoolmen in the case of Aristotelian principles at variance with their dogmas. Frederick II., the liberal emperor, employed Jewish scholars and translators at his court; among them Jacob ben Abba-Mari ben Anatoli, to whom an annuity was paid for translating Aristotelian works. Michael Scotus, the imperial astrologer, was his intimate friend. His contemporaries were chiefly popular philosophers or mystics, excepting only the prominent Provençal Jacob ben Machir, or Profatius Judæus, as he was called, a member of the Tibbon family of translators. His observations on the inclination of the earth's axis were used later by Copernicus as the basis of further investigations. He was a famous teacher at the Montpellier academy, which reminds me to mention that Jews were prominently identified with the founding and the success of the medical schools at Montpellier and Salerno, they, indeed, being almost the only physicians in all parts of the known world. Salerno, in turn, suggests Italy, where at that period translations were made from Latin into Hebrew. Hillel ben Samuel, for instance, the same who carried on a lively philosophic correspondence with another distinguished Jew, Maestro Isaac Gayo, the pope's physician, translated some of Thomas Aquinas's writings, Bruno di Lungoburgo's book on surgery, and various other works, from Latin into Hebrew.

These successors of the great intellects of the golden age of neo-Hebraic literature, thoroughly conversant with Arabic literature, busied themselves with rendering accessible to literary Europe the treasury of Indian and Greek fables. Their translations and compilations have peculiar value in the history of literary development. During the middle ages, when the memory of ancient literature had perished, they were the means of preserving the romances, fairy tales, and fables that have descended, by way of Spain and Arabia, from classical antiquity and the many-hued Oriental world to our modern literatures. Between the eleventh and the thirteenth century, the foundations were laid for our narrative literature, demonstrating the importance of delight in fable lore, stories of travel, and all sorts of narratives, for to it we owe the creation of new and the transformation of old, literary forms.

In Germany at that time, a Jewish minnesinger and strolling minstrel, Süsskind von Trimberg, went up and down the land, from castle to castle, with the poets' guild; while Santob di Carrion, a Jewish troubadour, ventured to impart counsel and moral lessons to the Castilian king Don Pedro before his assembled people. A century later, another Jew, Samson Pnie, of Strasburg, lent his assistance to the two German poets at work upon the continuation of *Parzival*. The historians of German literature have not laid sufficient stress upon the share of the Jews, heavily oppressed and persecuted though they were, in the creation of national epics and romances of chivalry from the thirteenth to the fifteenth century. German Jews, being more than is generally recognized diligent readers of the poets, were well acquainted with the drift of mediæval poetry, and to this familiarity a new department of Jewish literature owed its rise and development. It is said that a Hebrew version of the Arthurian cycle was made as early as the thirteenth century, and at the end of the period we run across epic poems on Bible characters, composed in the *Nibelungen* metre, in imitation of old German legend lore and national poetry.

If German Jews found heart for literary interests, it may be assumed as a matter of course that Spanish and Provençal Jews participated in the advancement of their respective national literatures and in Troubadour poetry. In these countries, too, the new taste for popular literature, especially in the form of fables, was made to serve moral ends. A Jew, Berachya ben Natronaï, was the precursor of Marie de France, the famous French fabulist, and La Fontaine and Lessing are indebted to him for some of their material. As in the case of Aristotelian philosophy and of Greek and Arabic medical science, Jews assumed the rôle of mediators in the transmission of fables. Indian fables reached their Arabic guise either directly or by way of Persian and Greek; thence they passed into Hebrew and Latin translations, and through these last forms became the property of the European languages. For instance, the Hebrew translation of the old Sanskrit fox fables was the one of greatest service in literary evolution. The translator of the fox fables is credited also with the translation of the romance of "The Seven Wise Masters," under the title *Mishlê Sandabar*. These two works gave the impetus to a great series in Occidental literature, and it seems altogether probable that Europe's first acquaintance with them dates from their Hebrew translation.

In Arabic poetry, too, many a Jew deservedly attained to celebrity. Abraham ibn Sahl won such renown that the Arabs, notorious for parsimony, gave ten gold pieces for one of his songs. Other poets have come down to us by name, and Joseph Ezobi, whom Reuchlin calls *Judæorum poeta dulcissimus*, went so far as to extol Arabic beyond Hebrew poetry. He was the first to pronounce the dictum famous in Buffon's repetition: "The style is the man himself." Provence, the land of song, produced Kalonymos ben Kalonymos (Maestro Calo), known to his brethren in faith not only as a poet, but also as a scholar, whose Hebrew translations from the Arabic are of most important works on philosophy, medicine, and mathematics. As Anatoli had worked under Emperor Frederick II., so Kalonymos was attached to Robert of Naples, patron of Jewish scholars. At the same time with the Spanish and the German minstrel, there flourished in Rome Immanuel ben Solomon, the friend of Dante, upon whose death he wrote an Italian sonnet, and whose *Divina Commedia* inspired a part of his poetical works also describing a visit to paradise and hell.

With the assiduous cultivation of romantic poetry, which was gradually usurping the place of moral romances and novels, grew the importance of Oriental legends and traditions, so pregnant with literary suggestions. This is attested by the use made of the Hebrew translation of Indian fables mentioned before, and of the famous collection of tales, the *Disciplina clericalis* by the baptized Jew Petrus Alphonsus. The Jews naturally introduced many of their own peculiar traditions, and thus can be explained the presence of tales from the Talmud and the Midrash in our modern fairy tale books.

It is necessary to note again that the Jews in turn submitted to the influence of foreign literatures. Immanuel Romi, for example, at his best, is an exponent of Provençal versification and scholastic philosophy, while his lapses testify to the self-complacency and levity characteristic of the times. Yehuda Romano, one of his contemporaries, is said to have been teacher to the king of Naples. He was the first Jew to attain to a critical appreciation of the vagaries of scholasticism, but his claim to mention rests upon his translations from the Latin.

As Jews assisted at the birth of Arabic, French, and German, so they have a share in the beginnings of Spanish, literature. Jews must be credited with the first "Chronicle of the Cid," with the romance, *Comte Lyonnais*, *Palanus*, with the first collection of tales, the first chess poems, and the first troubadour songs. Again, the oldest collection of the last into a *cancionera* was made by the Jew Juan Alfonso de Bæna.

Even distant Persia has proofs to show of Jewish ability and energy in those days. One Jew composed an epic on a biblical subject in the Persian language, another translated the Psalms into the vernacular.

The most prominent Jewish exponent of philosophy in this age of strenuous interest in metaphysical speculations and contests was Levi ben Gerson (Leon di Bannolas), theologian, scientist, physician, and astronomer. One of his ancestors, Gerson ben Solomon, had written a work typical of the state of the natural sciences in his day. Levi ben Gerson's chief work became famous not among Jews alone. It was referred to in words of praise by Pico della Mirandola, Reuchlin, Kepler, and other Christian thinkers. He was the inventor of an astronomical instrument, a description of which was translated into Latin at the express command of Pope Clement VI., and carefully studied by Kepler. Besides, Levi ben Gerson was the author of an arithmetical work. In those days, in fact up to the seventeenth century, there was but a faint dividing line between astronomy and mathematics, as between medicine and natural history. John of Seville was a notable mathematician, the compiler of a practical arithmetic, the first to make mention of decimal fractions, which possibly may have been his invention, and in the Zohar, the text-book of mediæval Jewish mysticism, which appeared centuries before Copernicus's time, the cause of the succession of day and night is stated to be the earth's revolution on its axis.

In this great translation period scarcely a single branch of human science escaped the mental avidity of Jews. They found worthy of translation such essays as "Rules for the Shoeing and Care of Horses in Royal Stables" and "The Art of Carving and Serving at Princely Boards." Translations of works on scholasticism now took rank beside those from Greek and Arabic philosophers, and to translations from the Arabic into Hebrew were added translations from and into Latin, or even into the vernacular idiom wherever literary forms had developed. The bold assertion can be made good that not a single prominent work of ancient science was left untranslated. On the other hand it is hard to speculate what would have been the fate of these treasures of antiquity without Jewish intermediation. Doubtless an important factor in the work was the encouragement given Jewish scholars by enlightened rulers, such as Emperor Frederick II., Charles and Robert of Anjou, Jayme I. of Aragon, and Alfonso X. of Castile, and by popes, and private patrons of learning. Mention has been made of Jewish contributions to the work of the medical schools of Montpellier and Salerno. Under Jayme I. Christian and Jewish savants of Barcelona worked together harmoniously to promote the cause of civilization and culture in their native land. The first to use the Catalan dialect for literary purposes was the Jew Yehuda ben Astruc, and under Alfonso (X.) the Wise, Jews again attained to prominence in the king's favorite science of astronomy. The Alfonsine Tables were chiefly the work of Isaac ibn Sid, a Toledo *chazan* (precentor). In general, the results reached by Jewish scholarship at Alfonso's court were of the utmost importance, having been largely instrumental in establishing in the age of Tycho de Brahe and Kepler the fundamental principles of astronomy and a correct view of the orbits of the heavenly bodies. Equal suggestiveness characterizes Jewish research in mathematics, a science to which, rising above the level of intermediaries and translators, Jews made original contributions of importance, the first being Isaac Israeli's "The Foundation of the Universe." Basing his observations on Maimuni's and Abraham ben Chiya's statement of the sphericity of the earth, Israeli showed that the heavenly bodies do not seem to occupy the place in which they would appear to an observer at the centre of the earth, and that the two positions differ by a certain angle, since known as parallax in the terminology of science. To Judah Hakohen, a scholar in correspondence with Alfonso the Wise, is ascribed the arrangement of the stars in forty-eight constellations, and to another Jew, Esthori Hafarchi, we owe the first topographical description of Palestine, whither he emigrated when the Jews were expelled from France by Philip the Fair.

Meanwhile the condition of the Jews, viewed from without and from within, had become most pitiable. The Kabbala lured into her charmed circle the strongest Jewish minds. Scientific aspirations seemed completely extinguished. Even the study of the Talmud was abandoning simple, undistorted methods of interpretation, and espousing the hair-splitting dialectics of the northern French school. Synagogue poetry was languishing, and general culture found no votaries among Jews. Occasionally only the religious disputations between Jews and Christians induced some few to court acquaintance with secular branches of learning. In the fourteenth century Chasdaï Crecas was the only philosopher with an original system, which in its arguments on free will and the nature of God anticipated the views of one greater than himself, who, however, had a different purpose in view. That later and greater philosopher, to whom the world is indebted for the evangel of modern life, was likewise a Jew, a descendant of Spanish-Jewish fugitives. His name is Baruch Spinoza.

However sad their fortunes, the literature of the Jews never entirely eschewed the consideration of subjects of general interest. This receives curious confirmation from the re-introduction of Solomon Gabirol's peculiar views into Jewish religious philosophy, by way of Christian scholasticism, as formulated especially by Thomas Aquinas, the *Doctor angelicus*.

The Renaissance and the humanistic movement also reveal Jewish influences at work. The spirit of liberty abroad in the earth passed through the halls of Israel, clearing the path thenceforth to be trodden by men. Again the learned were compelled to engage the good offices of the Jews, the custodians of biblical antiquity. The invention of the printing press acted as a wonderful stimulus to the development of Jewish literature. The first products of the new machine were Hebrew works issued in Italy and Spain. Among the promoters of the Renaissance, and one of the most thorough students of religio-philosophical systems, was Elias del Medigo, the friend of Pico della Mirandola, and the umpire chosen by the quarrelling factions in the University of Padua. John Reuchlin, chief of the humanists, was taught Hebrew by Obadiah Sforno, a *savant* of profound scholarship, who dedicated his "Commentary on Ecclesiastes" to Henry II. of France. Abraham de Balmes was a teacher at the universities of Padua and Salerno, and physician in ordinary to Cardinal Dominico Grimani. The Kabbala was made accessible to the heroes of the Renaissance by Jochanan Alemanno, of Mantua, and there is pathos in the urgency with which Reuchlin entreats Jacob Margoles, rabbi of Nuremberg, to send him Kabbalistic writings in addition to those in his possession. Reuchlin's good offices to the Jews—his defense of them against the attacks of obscurantists—are a matter of general knowledge. Among the teachers of the humanists who revealed to them the treasures of biblical literature the most prominent was Elias Levita, the introducer, through his disciples Sebastian Münster and Paul Fagius, of Hebrew studies into Germany. He may be accounted a true humanist, a genuine exponent of the Renaissance. His Jewish coadjutors were Judah Abrabanel (Leo Hebræus), whose chief work was *Dialoghi di Amore*, an exposition of the Neoplatonism then current in Italy; Jacob Mantino, physician to Pope Paul III.; Bonet di Lattes, known as a writer on astronomical subjects, and the inventor of an astronomical instrument; and a number of others.

While in Italy the Spanish-Jewish exiles fell into line in the Renaissance movement, the large numbers of them that sought refuge in Portugal turned their attention chiefly to astronomical research and to voyages of discovery and adventure, the national enterprises of their protectors. João II. employed Jews in investigations tending to make reasonably safe the voyages, on trackless seas, under unknown skies, for the discovery of long and ardently sought passages to distant lands. In his commission charged with the construction of an instrument to indicate accurately the course of a vessel, the German knight Martin Behaim was assisted by Jews—astronomers, metaphysicians, and physicians—chief among them Joseph Vecinho, distinguished for his part in the designing of the artificial globe, and Pedro di Carvallho, navigator, whose claim to praise rests upon his improvement of Leib's *Astrologium*, and to censure, upon his abetment of the king when he refused the request of the bold Genoese Columbus to fit out a squadron for the discovery of wholly unknown lands. But when Columbus's plans found long deferred realization in Spain, a Jewish youth, Luis de Torres, embarked among the ninety adventurers who accompanied him. Vasco da Gama likewise was aided in his search for a waterway to the Indies by a Jew, the pilot Gaspar, the same who later set down in writing the scientific results of the voyage, and two Jews were despatched to explore the coasts of the Red Sea and the island of Ormus in the Persian Gulf. Again, Vasco da Gama's plans were in part made with the valuable assistance of a Jew, a profound scholar, Abraham Zacuto, sometime professor of astronomy at the University of Salamanca, and after the banishment of Jews from Spain, astronomer and chronographer to Manuel the Great, of Portugal. It was he that advised the king to send out Da Gama's expedition, and from the first the explorer was supported by his counsel and scientific knowledge.

Meritorious achievements, all of them, but they did not shield the Jews against impending banishment. The exiles found asylums in Italy and Holland, and in each country they at once projected themselves into the predominant intellectual movement. A physician, Abraham Portaleone, distinguished himself on the field of antiquarian research; another, David d'Ascoli, wrote a defense of Jews; and a third, David de Pomis, a defense of Jewish physicians. The most famous was Amatus Lusitanus, one of whose important discoveries is said to have brought him close up to that of the circulation of the blood. Before the banishment of Jews from Spain took effect, Antonio di Moro, a Jewish peddler of Cordova, flourished as the last of Spanish troubadours, and Rodrigo da Cota, a neo-Christian of Seville, as the first of Spanish dramatists, the supposed author of *Celestina*, one of the most celebrated of old Spanish dramatic compositions.

The proscribed, in the guise of Marranos, and under the hospitable shelter of their new homes, could not be banished from literary Spain, even in its newest departures. Indeed, for a long time Spanish and Italian literatures were brought into contact with each other only through the instrumentality of Jews. Not quite half a century after the expulsion of Jews from Portugal and their settlement in Italy, a Jew, Solomon Usque, made a Spanish translation of Petrarch (1567), dedicated to Alessandro Farnese, duke of Parma, and wrote Italian odes, dedicated to Cardinal Borromeo.

At the zenith of the Renaissance, Jews won renown as Italian poets, and did valiant work as translators from Latin into Hebrew and Italian. In the later days of the movement, in the Reformation period, illustrious Christian scholars studied Hebrew under Jewish tutorship, and gave it a place on the curriculum of the universities. Luther himself submitted to rabbinical guidance in his biblical studies.

In great numbers the Spanish exiles turned to Turkey, where numerous new communities rapidly arose. There, too, in Constantinople and elsewhere, Jews, like Elias Mizrachi and Elias Kapsali, were the first to pursue scientific research.

We have now reached the days of deepest misery for Judaism. Yet, in the face of unrelenting oppression, Jews win places of esteem as diplomats, custodians and advocates of important interests at royal courts. From the earliest period of their history, Jews manifested special talent for the arts of diplomacy. In the Arabic-Spanish period they exercised great political influence upon Mohammedan caliphs. The Fatimide and Omayyad dynasties employed Jewish representatives and ministers, Samuel ibn Nagdela, for instance, being grand vizir of the caliph of Granada. Christian sovereigns also valued their services: as is well known, Charlemagne sent a Jewish ambassador to Haroun al Rashid; Pope Alexander III. appointed Yechiel ben Abraham as minister of finance; and so late as in the fifteenth century the wise statesman Isaac Abrabanel was minister to Alfonso V., of Portugal, and, wonderful to relate, for eight years to Ferdinand and Isabella, of Spain. At this time Jewish literature was blessed with a patron in the person of Joseph Nasi, duke of Naxos, whom, it is said, Sultan Selim II. wished to crown king of Cyprus. His rival was Solomon Ashkenazi, Turkish ambassador to the Venetian republic, who exercised decisive influence upon the election of a Polish king. And this is not the end of the roll of Jewish diplomats and ministers.

Unfortunately, the Kabbala, whose spell was cast about even the most vigorous of Jewish minds, was the leading intellectual current of those sad days, the prevailing misery but serving to render her allurements more fascinating. But in the hands of such men as Abraham Herrera, who influenced Benedict Spinoza, even Kabbalistic studies were informed with a scientific spirit, and brought into connection with Neoplatonic philosophy.

Mention of Spinoza suggests Holland where Jews were kindly received, and shortly after their arrival they interested themselves in the philosophical pursuits in vogue. The best index to their position in Holland is furnished by Manasseh ben Israel's prominent rôle in the politics and the literary ventures of Amsterdam, and by his negotiations with Oliver Cromwell. We may pardon the pride which made him say, "I have enjoyed the friendship of the wisest and the best of Europe." Uriel Acosta and Baruch Spinoza, though children of the Amsterdam *Judengasse*, were ardent patriots.

The last great Spanish poet was Antonio Enrique de Gomez, the Jewish Calderon, burnt in effigy at Seville; while the last Portuguese poet of note was Antonio Jose de Silva, who perished at the stake for his faith, leaving his dramas as a precious possession to Portuguese literature.

Even in the dreariest days of decadence, when the study of the Talmud seemed to engross their attention, Jews prosecuted scientific inquiries, as witness Moses Isserles's translation of *Theorica*, an astronomical treatise by Peurbach, the Vienna humanist.

With the migration of Jews eastward, *Judendeutsch*, a Jewish-German dialect, with its literature, was introduced into Slavic countries. It is a fact not generally known that this jargon is the depository of certain Middle High German expressions and elements no longer used in the modern German, and that philologists are forced to resort to the study of the Polish-Jewish patois to reconstruct the old idiom. In 1523, the year of Luther's Pentateuch translation, a Jewish-German Bible dictionary was published at Cracow, and in 1540 appeared the first Jewish-German translation of the Pentateuch. The Germans strongly influenced the popular literature of the Jews. The two nationalities seized the same subjects, often imitating the same models, or using the same translations. The German "Till

Eulenspiegel" was printed in 1500, the Jewish-German in 1600. Besides incorporating German folklore, Jewish-German writings borrowed from German romances, assimilated foreign literatures, did not neglect the traditions of the Jews themselves, and embraced even folk-songs, some of which have perpetuated themselves until the modern era.

Mention of the well-known fact that the Hebrew studies prosecuted by Christians in the eighteenth century were carried on under Jewish influence brings us to the threshold of the modern era, the period of the Jewish Renaissance. Here we are on well-worn ground. Since Jews have been permitted to enter at will upon the multifarious pursuits growing out of modern culture, their importance as factors of civilization is universally acknowledged, and it would be wearisome, and would far transgress the limits of a lecture, to enumerate their achievements.

In trying to show what share the Jew has had in the world's civilization, I have naturally concerned myself chiefly with literature, for literature is the mirror of culture. It would be a mistake, however, to suppose that the Jew has been inactive in other spheres. His contributions, for instance, to the modern development of international commerce, cannot be overlooked. Commerce in its modern extension was the creation of the mercantile republics of mediæval Italy—Venice, Florence, Genoa, and Pisa—and in them Jews determined and regulated its course. When Ravenna contemplated a union with Venice, and formulated the conditions for the alliance, one of them was the demand that rich Jews be sent thither to open a bank for the relief of distress. Jews were the first to obtain the privilege of establishing banks in the Italian cities, and the first to discover the advantages of a system of checks and bills of exchange, of unique value in the development of modern commerce.

Even in art, a sphere from which their rigorous laws might seem to have the effect of banishing them, they were not wholly inactive. They always numbered among themselves handicraftsmen. In Venice, in the sixteenth century, we find celebrated Jewish wood engravers. Jacob Weil's rules for slaughtering were published with vignettes by Hans Holbein, and one of Manasseh ben Israel's works was adorned with a frontispiece by Rembrandt. In our own generation Jews have won fame as painters and sculptors, while music has been their staunch companion, deserting them not even in the darkest days of the Ghetto.

These certainly are abundant proofs that the Jew has a share in all the phases and stages of culture, from its first germs unto its latest complex development—a consoling, elevating reflection. A learned historian of literature, a Christian, in discussing this subject, was prompted to say: " Our first knowledge of philosophy, botany, astronomy, and cosmography, as well as the grammar of the holy language and the results of biblical study, we owe primarily to Jews." Another historian, also a Christian, closes a review of Jewish national traits with the words: " Looking back over the course of history, we find that in the gloom, bareness, and intellectual sloth of the middle ages, Jews maintained a rational system of agriculture, and built up international commerce, upon which rests the well-being of the nations."

Truly, there are reasons for pride on our part, but no less do great obligations devolve upon us. I cannot refrain from exhortation. In justice we should confess that Jews drew their love of learning and ability to advance the work of civilization from Jewish writings. Furthermore, it is a fact that these Jewish writings no longer excite the interest, or claim the devotion of Jews. I maintain that it is the duty of the members of our Order to take this neglected, lightly esteemed literature under their protection, and secure for it the appreciation and encouragement that are the offspring of knowledge.

Modern Judaism presents a curious spectacle. The tiniest of national groups in Eastern Europe, conceiving the idea of establishing its independence, proceeds forthwith to create a literature, if need be, inventing and forging. Judaism possesses countless treasures of inestimable worth, amassed by research and experience in the course of thousands of years, and her latter-day children brush them aside with indifference, even with scorn, leaving it to the sons of the stranger, yea, their adversaries, to gather and cherish them.

When Goethe in his old age conceived and outlined a scheme of universal literature, the first place was assigned to Jewish literature. In his pantheon of the world's poetry, the first tone uttered was to be that of "David's royal song and harp." But, in general, Jewish literature is still looked upon as the Cinderella of the world's literatures. Surely, the day will come when justice will be done, Cinderella's claim be acknowledged equal to that of her royal sisters, and together they will enter the spacious halls of the magnificent palace of literature.

Among the prayers prescribed for the Day of Atonement is one of subordinate importance which affects me most solemnly. When the shadows of evening lengthen, and the light of the sun wanes, the Jew reads the *Neïlah* service with fervor, as though he would "burst open the portals of heaven with his tears," and the inmost depths of my nature are stirred with melancholy pride by the prayer of the pious Jew. He supplicates not for his house and his family, not for Zion dismantled, not for the restoration of the Temple, not for the advent of the Messiah, not for respite from suffering. All his sighs and hopes, all his yearning and aspiration, are concentrated in the one thought: "Our splendor and our glory have departed, our treasures have been snatched from us; there remains nothing to us but this Law alone." If this is true; if naught else is left of our former state; if this Law, this science, this literature, are our sole treasure and best inheritance, then let us cherish and cultivate them so as to have a legacy to bequeath to our children to stand them in good stead against the coming of the *Neïlah* of humanity, the day when brethren will "dwell together in unity."

Perhaps that day is not far distant. Methinks I hear the rustling of a new springtide of humanity; methinks I discern the morning flush of new world-stirring ideas, and before my mind's eye rises a bridge, over which pass all the nations of the earth, Israel in their midst, holding aloft his ensign with the inscription, "The Lord is my banner!"—the one which he bore on every battlefield of thought, and which was never suffered to fall into the enemy's hand. It is a mighty procession moving onward and upward to a glorious goal: "Humanity, Liberty, Love!"

WOMEN IN JEWISH LITERATURE

Among the songs of the Bible there are two, belonging to the oldest monuments of poetry, which have preserved the power to inspire and elevate as when they were first uttered: the hymn of praise and thanksgiving sung by Moses and his sister Miriam, and the impassioned song of Deborah, the heroine in Israel.

Miriam and Deborah are the first Israelitish women whose melody thrilled and even now thrills us—Miriam, the inspired prophetess, pouring forth her people's joy and sorrow, and Deborah, *Esheth Lapidoth*, the Bible calls her, "the woman of the flaming heart," an old writer ingeniously interprets the Scriptural name. They are the chosen exemplars of all women who, stepping across the narrow confines of home, have lifted up a voice, or wielded a pen, for Israel. The time is not yet when woman in literature can be discussed without an introductory justification. The prejudice is still deep-rooted which insists that domestic activity is woman's only legitimate career, that to enter the literary arena is unwomanly, that inspired songs may drop only from male lips. Woman's heart should, indeed, be the abode of the angels of gentleness, modesty, kindness, and patience. But no contradiction is involved in the belief that her mind is endowed with force and ability on occasion to grasp the spokes of fortune's wheel, or produce works which need not shrink from public criticism. Deborah herself felt that it would have better become a man to fulfil the mission with which she was charged—that a cozy home had been a more seemly place for her than the camp upon Mount Tabor. She says: "Desolate were the open towns in Israel, they were desolate. . . . Was there a shield seen or a spear among forty thousand in Israel? . . . I—unto the Lord will I sing." Not until the fields of Israel were desert, forsaken of able-bodied men, did the woman Deborah arise for the glory of God. She refused to pose as a heroine, rejected the crown of victory, nor coveted the poet's laurel, meet recognition of her triumphal song. Modestly she chose the simplest yet most beautiful of names. She summoned the warriors to battle; the word of God was proclaimed by her lips; she pronounced judgment, and right prevailed; her courage sustained her on the battlefield, and victory followed in her footsteps—yet neither judge, nor poetess, nor singer, nor prophetess will she call herself, but only *Em beyisrael,* "a mother in Israel."[1]

This heroine, this "mother in Israel," in all the wanderings and vicissitudes of the Jewish people, was the exemplar of its women and maidens, the especial model of Israelitish poetesses and writers.

The student of Jewish literature is like an astronomer. While the casual observer faintly discerns

Judges v. 7.

single stars dotted in the expanse of blue overhead, he takes in the whole sweep of the heavens, readily following the movements of the stars of every magnitude. The history of the Jewish race, its mere preservation during the long drawn out period of suffering—sad days of national dissolution and sombre middle age centuries—is a perplexing puzzle, unless regarded with the eye of faith. But that this race, cuffed, crushed, pursued, hounded from spot to spot, should have given birth to men, yea, even women ranking high in the realm of letters, is wholly inexplicable, unless the explanation of the unique phenomenon is sought in the wondrous gift of inspiration operative in Israel even after the last seer ceased to speak.

Judaism has preserved the Jews! Judaism, that is, the Law with its development and ramifications of a great religious thought, was the sustaining power of the Jewish people under its burden of misery, suffering, torture, and oppression, enabling it to survive its tormentors. The Jews were the nation of hope. Like hope this people is eternal. The storms of fanaticism and race hatred may rage and roar, the race cannot be destroyed. Precisely in the days of its abject degradation, when its suffering was dire, how marvellous the conduct of this people! The conquered were greater than their conquerors. From their spiritual height they looked down compassionately on their victorious but ignorant adversaries, who, feeling the condescension of the victims, drove their irons deeper. The little nation grew only the stronger, and its religion, the flower of hope and trust, developed the more sturdily for its icy covering. Jews were mowed down by fire and sword, but Judaism continued to live. From the ashes of every pyre sprang the Jewish Law in unfading youth—that indestructible, ineradicable mentality and hope, which opponents are wont to call unconquerable Jewish defiance.

The men of this great little race were preserved by the Law, the spirit, and the influences and effects of this same Law transformed weak women into God-inspired martyrs, dowered the daughters of Israel with courage to sacrifice life for the glory of the God-idea confessed by their ancestors during thousands of years. Purity of morals, confiding domesticity, were the safeguards against storm and stress. The outside world presented a hostile front to the Jew of the middle ages. Every step beyond Ghetto precincts was beset with peril. So his home became his world, his sanctuary, in whose intimate seclusion the blossom of pure family love unfolded. While spiritual darkness brooded over the nations, the great Messianic God-idea took refuge from the icy chill of the middle ages in his humble rooms, where it was cherished against the coming of a glorious future.

"Every Jew has the making of a Messiah in him," says a clever modern author,[1] "and every Jewess of a *mater dolorosa*," of which the first part is only an epigram, the second, a truth, an historic fact. Me-

[1] M. Hess, *Rom und Jerusalem*, p. 2.

diæval Judaism knew many "sorrowful mothers," whose heroism passes our latter-day conception. Greece and Rome tell tales upon tales of womanly bravery under suffering and pain—Jewish history buries in silence the names of its thousands of woman and maiden martyrs, joyously giving up life in the vindication of their faith. Perhaps, had one woman been too weak to resist, too cowardly to court and embrace death, her name might have been preserved. Such, too, fail to appear in the Jewish annals, which contain but few women's names of any kind. Inspired devotion of strength and life to Judaism was as natural with a Jewess as quiet, unostentatious activity in her home. No need, therefore, to make mention of act or name.

Jewish woman, then, has neither found, nor sought, and does not need, a Frauenlob, historian or poet, to proclaim her praise in the gates, to touch the strings of his lyre in her honor. Her life, in its simplicity and gentleness, its patience and exalted devotion, is itself a Song of Songs, more beautiful than poet ever composed, a hymn more joyous than any ever sung, on the prophetess's sublime and touching text, *Em beyisrael*, "a mother in Israel."

As Miriam and Deborah are representative of womanhood during Israel's national life, so later times, the Talmudic periods, produced women with great and admirable qualities. Prominent among them was Beruriah, the gentle wife of Rabbi Meïr, the Beruriah whose heart is laid bare in the following touching story from the Talmud:[1]

[1] Midrash *Yalkut* on Proverbs.

One Sabbath her husband had been in the academy all day teaching the crowds that eagerly flocked to his lectures. During his absence from home, his two sons, distinguished for beauty and learning, died suddenly of a malignant disease. Beruriah bore the dear bodies into her sleeping chamber, and spread a white cloth over them. When the rabbi returned in the evening, and asked for his boys that, according to wont, he might bless them, his wife said, " They have gone to the house of God."

She brought the wine-cup, and he recited the concluding prayer of the Sabbath, drinking from the cup, and, in obedience to a hallowed custom, passing it to his wife. Again he asked, " Why are my sons not here to drink from the blessed cup?" " They cannot be far off," answered the patient sufferer, and suspecting naught, Rabbi Meïr was happy and cheerful. When he had finished his meal, Beruriah said: " Rabbi, allow me to ask you a question." With his permission, she continued: " Some time ago a treasure was entrusted to me, and now the owner demands it. Shall I give it up?" " Surely, my wife should not find it necessary to ask this question," said the rabbi. " Can you hesitate about returning property to its rightful owner?" " True," she replied, " but I thought best not to return it until I had advised you thereof." And she led him into the chamber to the bed, and withdrew the cloth from the bodies. " O, my sons, my sons," lamented the father with a loud voice, " light of my eyes, lamp of my soul. I was your father, but you taught me

the Law." Her eyes suffused with tears, Beruriah seized her grief-stricken husband's hand, and spoke: "Rabbi, did you not teach me to return without reluctance that which has been entrusted to our safe-keeping? See, 'the Lord gave, and the Lord hath taken away; blessed be the name of the Lord.'"
"'Blessed be the name of the Lord,'" repeated the rabbi, accepting her consolation, "and blessed, too, be His name for your sake; for, it is written: 'Who can find a virtuous woman? for far above pearls is her value. . . . She openeth her mouth with wisdom, and the law of kindness is upon her tongue.'"

Surrounded by the halo of motherhood, richly dowered with intellectual gifts, distinguished for learning, gentleness, and refinement, Beruriah is a truly poetic figure. Incensed at the evil-doing of the unrighteous, her husband prayed for their destruction. "How can you ask that, Rabbi?" Beruriah interrupted him; "do not the Scriptures say: 'May *sins* cease from off the earth, and the wicked will be no more'? When *sin* ceases, there will be no more *sinners*. Pray rather, my rabbi, that they repent, and amend their ways."[1]

That a woman could attain to Beruriah's mental poise, and make her voice heard and heeded in the councils of the teachers of the Law, and that the rabbis considered her sayings and doings worthy of record, would of itself, without the evidence of numerous other learned women of Talmud fame, prove, were proof necessary, the honorable position

[1] *Berachoth*, 10a.

occupied by Jewish women in those days. Long before Schiller, the Talmud said:[1] "Honor women, because they bring blessing." Of Abraham it is said: "It was well with him, because of his wife Sarah." Again: "More glorious is the promise made to women, than that to men: In Isaiah (xxxii. 9) we read: 'Ye women that are at ease, hear my voice!' for, with women it lies to inspire their husbands and sons with zeal for the study of the Law, the most meritorious of deeds." Everywhere the Talmud sounds the praise of the virtuous woman of Proverbs and of the blessings of a happy family life.

A single Talmudic sentence, namely, "He who teaches his daughter the Law, teaches her what is unworthy," torn from its context, and falsely interpreted, has given rise to most absurd theories with regard to the views of Talmudic times on the matter of woman's education. It should be taken into consideration that its author, who is responsible also for the sentiment that "woman's place is at the distaff," was the husband of Ima Shalom, a clever, highly cultured, but irascible woman, who was on intimate terms with Jewish Christians, and was wont to interfere in the disputations carried on by men—in short, a representative Talmudic blue-stocking, with all the attributes with which fancy would be prone to invest such a one.[2]

Elsewhere the Talmud tells about Rabbi Nachman's wife Yaltha, the proud and learned daughter of a princely line. Her guest, the poor itinerant

[1] *Baba Metsiah*, 59a. [2] *Sota*, 20a.

preacher Rabbi Ulla, expressed the opinion that according to the Law it was not necessary to pass the wine-cup over which the blessing has been said to women. The opinion, surely not the withheld wine, so angered his hostess, that she shivered four hundred wine-pitchers, letting their contents flow over the ground.[1] If the rabbis had such incidents in mind, crabbed utterances were not unjustifiable. Perhaps every rabbinical antagonist to woman's higher education was himself the victim of a learned wife, who regaled him, after his toilsome research at the academy, with unpalatable soup, or, worse still, with Talmudic discussions. Instances are abundant of erudite rabbis tormented by their wives. One, we are told, refused to cook for her husband, and another, day after day, prepared a certain dish, knowing that he would not touch it.

But this is pleasantry. It would betray total ignorance of the Talmud and the rabbis to impute to them the scorn of woman prevalent at that time. The Talmud and its sages never weary of singing the praise of women, and at every occasion inculcate respect for them, and devotion to their service. The compiler of the Jerusalem Talmud, Rabbi Jochanan, whose life is crowned with the aureole of romance, pays a delicate tribute to woman by the question: " Who directed the first prayer of thanksgiving to God? A woman, Leah, when she cried out in the fulness of her joy: ' Now again will I praise the Lord.' "

[1] *Berachoth*, 51*b*.

Under the influence of such ideal views, and in obedience to such standards, Jewish woman led a modest, retired life of domestic activity, the helpmeet and solace of her husband, the joy of his age, the treasure of his liberty, his comforter in sorrow. For, when the portentous catastrophe overwhelmed the Jewish nation, when Jerusalem and the Temple lay in ruins, when the noblest of the people were slain, and the remnant of Israel was made to wander forth out of his land into a hostile world, to fulfil his mission as a witness to the truth of monotheism, then Jewish woman, too, was found ready to assume the burdens imposed by distressful days.

Israel, broken up into unresisting fragments, began his two thousand years' journey through the desert of time, despoiled of all possessions except his Law and his family. Of these treasures Titus and his legions could not rob him. From the ruins of the Jewish state blossomed forth the spirit of Jewish life and law in vigorous renewal. Judaism rose rejuvenated on the crumbling temples of Jupiter, immaculate in doctrine, incorruptible in practice. Israel's spiritual guides realized that adherence to the Law is the only safeguard against annihilation and oblivion. From that time forth, the men became the guardians of the *Law*, the women the guardians of the purity of *life*, both working harmoniously for the preservation of Judaism.

The muse of history recorded no names of Jewish women from the destruction of the Temple to the eleventh century. Yet the student cannot fail to assign the remarkable preservation of the race to woman's gentle, quiet, though paramount influence by the side of the earnest tenacity of men. Among Jews leisure, among non-Jews knowledge, was lacking to preserve names for the instruction of posterity. Before Jews could record their suffering, the oppressor's hand again fell, its grasp more relentless than ever. For many centuries blood and tears constitute the chronicle of Jewish life, and at the sources of these streams of blood and rivers of tears, the genius of Jewish history sits lamenting.

Whenever the sun of tolerance broke through the clouds of oppression, and for even a brief period shone upon the martyr race, its marvellous development under persecution and in despite of unspeakable suffering at once stood revealed. During these occasional breaks in the darkness, women appeared whose erudition was so profound as to earn special mention. As was said above, the first names of women distinguished for beauty and intellect come down to us from the eleventh century, and even then only Italy, Provence, Andalusia, and the Orient, were favored, Jews in these countries living unmolested and in comparative freedom, and zealously devoting their leisure to the study of the Talmud and secular branches of learning. In praise of Italy it was said: "Out of Bari goes forth the Law, and the word of the Lord from Otranto." It is, therefore, not surprising to read in Jewish sources of the maiden Paula, of the family Deï Mansi (Anawim), the daughter of Abraham, and later the wife of Yechiel deï Mansi, who, in 1288, copied her father's abstruse Talmudic commentary, adding ingenious explanations, the result of independent research. But one grows somewhat sceptical over the account, by a Jewish tourist, Rabbi Petachya of Ratisbon, of Bath Halevi, daughter of Rabbi Samuel ben Ali in Bagdad, equally well-read in the Bible and the Talmud, and famous for her beauty. She lectured on the Talmud to a large number of students, and, to prevent their falling in love with her, she sat behind lattice-work or in a glass cabinet, that she might be heard but not seen. The dry tourist-chronicler fails to report whether her disciples approved of the preventive measure, and whether in the end it turned out to have been effectual. At all events, the example of the learned maiden found an imitator. Almost a century later we meet with Miriam Shapiro, of Constance, a beautiful Jewish girl, who likewise delivered public lectures on the Talmud sitting behind a curtain, that the attention of her inquisitive pupils might not be distracted by sight of her from their studies.

Of the learned El Muallima we are told that she transplanted Karaite doctrines from the Orient to Castile, where she propagated them. The daughter of the prince of poets, Yehuda Halevi, is accredited with a soulful religious poem hitherto attributed to her father, and Rabbi Joseph ibn Nagdela's wife was esteemed the most learned and representative woman in Granada. Even in the choir of Arabic-Andalusian poets we hear the voice of a Jewish songstress, Kasmune, the daughter of the poet Ishmael. Only a few blossoms of her delicate poetry have been preserved.[1] Catching sight of her young face in the mirror, she called out:

> "A vine I see, and though 'tis time to glean,
>   No hand is yet stretched forth to cull the fruit.
> Alas! my youth doth pass in sorrow keen,
>   A nameless 'him' my eyes in vain salute."

Her pet gazelle, raised by herself, she addresses thus:

> "In only thee, my timid, fleet gazelle,
>   Dark-eyed like thee, I see my counterpart;
> We both live lone, without companion dwell,
>   Accepting fate's decree with patient heart."

Of other women we are told whose learning and piety inspired respect, not only in Talmudic authorities, but, more than that, in their sisters in faith. Especially in the family of Rashi (Rabbi Solomon ben Isaac), immortal through his commentaries on the Bible and the Talmud, a number of women distinguished themselves. His daughter Rachel (Bellejeune), on one occasion when her father was sick, wrote out for Rabbi Abraham Cohen of Mayence an opinion on religious questions in dispute. Rashi's two granddaughters, Anna and Miriam, were equally famous. In questions relating to the dietary laws, they were cited as authorities, and their decisions accepted as final.

[1] Cmp. W. Bacher in *Frankel-Graetz Monatsschrift*, Vol. XX., p. 186.

Zunz calls the wife of Rabbi Joseph ben Jochanan of Paris "almost a rabbi"; and Dolce, wife of the learned Rabbi Eleazar of Worms, supported her family with the work of her hands, was a thorough student of the dietary laws, taught women on Jewish subjects, and on Sabbath delivered public lectures. She wore the twofold crown of learning and martyrdom. On December 6, 1213, fanatic crusaders rushed into the rabbi's house, and most cruelly killed her and her two daughters, Bella and Anna.

Israel having again fallen on evil times, the rarity of women writers during the next two centuries needs no explanation. In the sixteenth century their names reappear on the records, not only as Talmudic scholars, but also as writers of history in the German language. Litte of Ratisbon composed a history of King David in the celebrated "Book of Samuel," a poem in the *Nibelungen* stanza, and we are told that Rachel Ackermann of Vienna was banished for having written a piquant novel, "Court Secrets."

These tentative efforts led the way to busy and widespread activity by Jewish women in various branches of literature at a somewhat later period, when the so-called *Judendeutsch*, also known as *Altweiberdeutsch* (old women's German), came into general use. Rebekah Tiktiner, daughter of Rabbi Meïr Tiktiner, attained to a reputation considerable enough to suggest her scholarly work to J. G. Zeltner, a Rostock professor, as the subject of an essay published in 1719. Her book, *Meneketh Ribka*, deals with the duties of woman. Edel Mendels of Cracow epitomized "Yosippon" (History of the Jews after Josephus); Bella Chasan, who died a martyr's death, composed two instructive works on Jewish history, in their time widely read; Glikel Hamel of Hamburg wrote her memoirs, describing her contemporaries and the remarkable events of her life; Hannah Ashkenasi was the author of addresses on moral subjects; and Ella Götz translated the Hebrew prayers into Jewish-German.

Litte of Ratisbon found imitators. Rosa Fischels of Cracow was the first to put the psalms into Jewish-German rhymes (1586). She turned the whole psalter "into simple German very prettily, modestly, and withal pleasantly for women and maidens to read." The authoress acknowledges that it was her aim to imitate the rhyme and melody of the "Book of Samuel" by her famed predecessor. Occasionally her paraphrase rises to the height of true poetry, as in the first and last verses of Psalm xcvi:

"Sing to God a new song, sing to God all the land, sing to God, praise His name, show forth His ready help from day to day. . . . The field and all thereon shall show great joy; they will sing with all their leaves, the trees of the wood and the grove, before the Lord God who will come to judge the earth far and near. He judgeth the earth with righteousness and the nations with truth."

Rosa Fischels was followed by a succession of women writers: Taube Pan in Prague, a poetess; Bella Hurwitz, who wrote a history of the House of David, and, in association with Rachel Rausnitz, an account of the settlement of Jews in Prague; and a number of scholarly women famous among their co-religionists for knowledge of the Talmud, piety, and broad, secular culture.

In a rapid review like this of woman's achievements on the field of Jewish scholarship, the results recorded must appear meagre, owing partly to the paucity of available data, partly to the nature of the inquiry. Abstruse learning, pure science, original research, are by no means woman's portion. Such occupations demand complete surrender on the part of the student, uninterrupted attention to the subject pursued, and delicately organized woman is not capable of such absorption. Woman's perceptions are subtle, and she rests satisfied with her intuitions; while man strives to transmute his feelings, deeper than hers, into action. The external appeals to woman who comprehends easily and quickly, and, therefore, does not penetrate beneath the surface. Man, on the other hand, strives to pierce to the essence of things, apprehends more slowly, but thinks more profoundly, and tests carefully before he accepts. Hence we so rarely meet woman in the field of science, while her work in the domain of poetry and the humanities is abundant and attractive. Jewish women form no exception to the rule: a survey of Jewish poetry will show woman's share in its productions to have been considerable and of high quality. While there was little or no possibility to prosecute historic or scientific inquiry during the harrowing days of persecution, the well-spring of Jewish poetry never ran dry. Poetry followed the race into exile, and clave to it through all vicissitudes, its solacement in suffering, the holy mediatrix between its past and future. "The Orient dwells an exile in the Occident, and its tears of longing for home are the fountain-head of Jewish poetry," says a Christian scholar. And at the altar of this poetry, whose sweetness and purity sanctified home life, and spread a sense of morality in a time when brutality and corruptness were general, the women singers of Israel offered the gifts of their muse. While the culture of that time culminated in the service of love (*Minnedienst*), in woman worship, so offensive to modern taste, Jewish poetry was pervaded by a pure, ideal conception of love and womanhood, testifying to the high ethical principles of its devotees.

Judaism and Jewish poetry know naught of the sensual love so assiduously fostered by the cult of the Virgin. "Love," says a celebrated historian of literature, "was glorified in all shapes and guises, and represented as the highest aim of life. Woman's virtues, yea, even her vices, were invested with exaggerated importance. Woman became accustomed to think that she could be neither faithful nor faithless without turning the world topsy-turvy. She shared the fate of all objects of excessive adulation: flattery corrupted her. Thus it came about that love of woman overshadowed every other social force and every form of family affection, and so spent its power. The Jews were the only ones sane enough to subordinate sexual love to reverence for motherhood. Alexander Weill makes a Jewish mother say: 'Is it proper for a good Jewish mother to concern herself about love? Love is revolting idolatry. A Jewess may love only God, her husband, and her children.' Granny (*Alt-Babele*) in one of Kompert's tales says: 'God could not be everywhere, so he created mothers.' In Jewish novels, maternal love is made the basis of family life, its passion and its mystery. A Jewish mother! What an image the words conjure up! Her face is calm, though pale; a melancholy smile rests upon her lips, and her soulful eyes seem to hide in their depths the vision of a remote future."

This is a correct view. Jewish poetry is interpenetrated with the breath of intellectual love, that is, love growing out of the recognition of duty, no less ideal than sensual love. In the heart of the Jew love is an infinite force. Too mighty to be confined to the narrow limits of personal passion, it extends so as to include future generations.

Thus it happened that while in Christian poetry woman was the subject of song and sonnet, in Jewish poetry she herself sang and composed, and her productions are worthy of ranking beside the best poetic creations of each generation.

The earliest blossoms of Jewish poetry by women unfolded in the spring-like atmosphere of the Renaissance under the blue sky of Italy, the home of the immortal trio, Dante, Petrarch, and Boccaccio.

The first Jewish women writers of Italian verse were Deborah Ascarelli and Sara Copia Sullam, who, arrayed in the full panoply of the culture of their day, and as thoroughly equipped with Jewish knowledge, devoted their talents and their zeal to the service of their nation.

Deborah Ascarelli of Rome, the pride of her sex, was the wife of the respected rabbi Giuseppe Ascarelli, and lived at Venice in the beginning of the seventeenth century. She made a graceful Italian translation of Moses Rieti's *Sefer ha-Hechal*, a Hebrew poem written in imitation of the *Divina Commedia*, and enjoying much favor at Rome. As early as 1609, David della Rocca published a second edition of her translation, dedicating it to the charming authoress. To put the highly wrought, artificial poetry of the Hebrew Dante into mellifluous Italian verse was by no means easy. While Rieti's poetry is not distinguished by the vigor and fulness of the older classical productions of neo-Hebraic poetry, his rhythm is smooth, pleasant, and polished. Yet her rendition is admirable. Besides, she won fame as a writer of hymns in praise of the God of her people, who so wondrously rescued it from all manner of distress.

> "Let other poets of victory's trophies tell,
> Thy song will e'er thy people's praises swell,"

says a Jewish Italian poet enchanted by her talent.

A still more gifted poetess was Sara Copia Sullam, a particular star in Judah's galaxy.[1] The only child of a wealthy Venetian at the end of the sixteenth century, she was indulged in her love of study, and afforded every opportunity to advance in the arts and sciences. "She revelled in the realm of beauty, and crystallized her enthusiasm in graceful, sweet, maidenly verses. Young, lovely, of generous impulses and keen intellectual powers, her ambition set upon lofty attainments, a favorite of the muses, Sara Copia charmed youth and age."

These graces of mind became her misfortune. An old Italian priest, Ansaldo Çeba, in Genoa, published an Italian epic with the Esther of the Bible as the heroine. Sara was delighted with the choice of the subject. It was natural that a high-minded, sensitive girl with lofty ideals, stung to the quick by the injustice and contumely suffered by her people, should rejoice extravagantly in the praise lavished upon a heroine of her nation. Carried away by enthusiasm she wrote the poet, a stranger to her, a letter overflowing with gratitude for the pure delight his poem had yielded her. Her passionate warmth, betraying at once the accomplished poetess and the gifted thinker, did not fail to fascinate the old priest, who immediately resolved to capture this beautiful soul for the church. His desire brought about a lively correspondence, our chief source of information about Sara Copia. Her conversion became a passion with the highstrung priest, taking complete

[1] Cmp. E. David, *Sara Copia Sullam, une héroïne juive au XVIIe siècle.*

possession of him during the last years of his life. He brought to bear upon her case every trick of dialectics and flattery at his command. All in vain. The greatest successes of which he could boast were her promise to read the New Testament, and her consent to his praying for her conversion. Sara's arguments in favor of Judaism arouse the reader's admiration for the sharpness of intellect displayed, her poetic genius, and her intimate acquaintance with Jewish sources as well as philosophic systems.

Ansaldo never abandoned the hope of gaining her over to Christianity. Unable to convince her reason, he attacked her heart. Though evincing singular love and veneration for her old admirer, Sara could not be moved from steadfast adherence to her faith. She sent him her picture with the words: "This is the picture of one who carries yours deeply graven on her heart, and, with finger pointing to her bosom, tells the world: 'Here dwells my idol, bow before him.'"

With old age creeping upon him with its palsy touch, he continued to think of nothing but Sara's conversion, and assailed her in prose and verse. One of his imploring letters closes thus:

> "Life's fair, bright morn bathes thee in light,
>   Thy cheeks are softly flushed with youthful zest.
> For me the night sets in; my limbs
>   Are cold, but ardent love glows in my breast."

Sara having compared his poems with those of Amphion and Orpheus, he answered her:

"To Amphion the stones lent ear
  When soft he touched his lute ;
And beasts came trooping nigh to hear
  When Orpheus played his flute.

How long, O Sara, wilt thou liken me
  To those great singers of the olden days?
My God and faith I sought to give to thee,
  In vain I proved the error of thy ways.
Their song had charms more potent than my own,
Or art thou harder than a beast or stone?"

The query long remained unanswered, for just then the poetess was harassed by many trials. Serious illness prostrated her, then her beloved father died, and finally she was unjustly charged by the envious among her co-religionists with neglect of Jewish observances, and denial of the divine origin of the Law. She found no difficulty in refuting the malicious accusation, but she was stung to the quick by the calumnious attack, the pain it inflicted vanishing only in the presence of a grave danger. Balthasar Bonifacio, an obscure author, in a brochure published for that purpose, accused her of rejecting the doctrine of the immortality of the soul, a most serious charge, which, if sustained, would have thrown her into the clutches of the Inquisition. In two days she wrote a brilliant defense completely exonerating herself and exposing the spitefulness of the attack, a masterful production by reason of its vigorous dialectics, incisive satire, and noble enthusiasm for the cause of religion. Together with some few of her sonnets, this is all that has come down to us of her writings. She opened her vindication with the following sonnet:

"O Lord, Thou know'st my inmost hope and thought,
 Thou know'st whene'er before Thy judgment throne
 I shed salt tears, and uttered many a moan,
'Twas not for vanities that I besought.
O turn on me Thy look with mercy fraught,
 And see how envious malice makes me groan!
 The pall upon my heart by error thrown
Remove; illume me with Thy radiant thought.
At truth let not the wicked scorner mock,
 O Thou, that breath'dst in me a spark divine.
The lying tongue's deceit with silence blight,
Protect me from its venom, Thou, my Rock,
 And show the spiteful sland'rer by this sign
That Thou dost shield me with Thy endless might."

Sara's vindication was complete. Her friend Ceba was kept faithfully informed of all that befell her, but he was absorbed in thoughts of her conversion and his approaching end. He wrote to her that he did not care to receive any more letters from her unless they announced her acceptance of the true faith.

After Ansaldo's death, we hear nothing more about the poetess. She died at the beginning of 1641, and the celebrated rabbi, Leon de Modena, composed her epitaph, a poetic tribute to one whose life redounded to the glory of Judaism.

Our subject now carries us from the luxuriant south to the dunes of the North Sea. Holland was the first to open the doors of its cities hospitably to the three hundred thousand Jews exiled from Spain, and its busy capital Amsterdam became the centre whither tended the intelligent of the Marranos, fleeing before the Holy Inquisition. Physicians, mathematicians, philologists, military men, and diplomats, poets and poetesses, took refuge there. Among the poetesses,[1] the most prominent was Isabella Correa, distinguished for wit as well as poetic endowment, the wife of the Jewish captain and author, Nicolas de Oliver y Fullano, of Majorca. One of her contemporaries, Daniel de Barrios, says that "she was an accomplished linguist, wrote delightful letters, composed exquisite verses, played the lute like a *maestro*, and sang like an angel. Her sparkling black eyes sent piercing darts into every beholder's heart, and she was famed for beauty as well as intellect." She made a noble Spanish translation of *Pastor Fido*, the most popular Italian drama of the day, and published a volume of poems, also in Spanish. Antonio dos Reys sings her praises:

"*Pastor Fido!* no longer art thou read in thy own tongue, since Correa,
    Faithfully rendering thy song, created thee anew in Spanish forms.
  A laurel wreath surmounts her brow,
  Because her right hand had cunning to strike tones from the tragic lyre.
  On the mount of singers, a seat is reserved for her,
  Albeit many a Batavian voice refused consent.
  For, Correa's faith invited scorn from aliens,
  And her own despised her cheerful serenity.
  Now, with greater justice, all bend a reverent knee to Correa, the Jewess,
  Correa, who, it seems, is wholly like Lysia."

[1] For the following, compare Kayserling, *Sephardim*, p. 250 ff.

Donna Isabella Enriquez, a Spanish poetess of great versatility, was her contemporary. She lived first in Madrid, afterwards in Amsterdam, and even in advanced age was surrounded by admirers. At the age of sixty-two, she presented the men of her acquaintance with amulets against love, notwithstanding that she had spoken and written against the use of charms. For instance, when an egg with a crown on the end was found in the house of Isaac Aboab, the celebrated rabbi at Amsterdam, she wrote him the following:

> "See, the terror! Lo! the wonder!
> Basilisk, the fabled viper!
> Superstition names it so.
> Look at it, I pray, with calmness,
> 'Twas thy mind that was at fault.
> God's great goodness is displayed here;
> He, I trow, rewards thy eloquence
> In the monster which thou seest:
> All this rounded whole's thy virtue,
> Wisdom's symbol is the crown!"

Besides Isabella Correa and Isabella Enriquez, we have the names, though not the productions, of Sara de Fonseca Pina y Pimentel, Bienvenida Cohen Belmonte, and Manuela Nunes de Almeida. They have left but faint traces of their work, and fancy can fill in the sketch only with conjectures.

After these Marrano poetesses, silence fell upon the women of Israel for a whole century—a century of oppression and political slavery, of isolation in noisome Ghettos, of Christian scorn and mockery.

The Jews of Germany and Poland, completely crushed beneath the load of sorrow, hibernated until the gentle breath of a new time, levelling Ghetto walls and heralding a dawn when human rights would be recognized, awoke them to activity and achievement.

Mighty is the spirit of the times! It clears a way for itself, boldly pushing aside every stumbling-block in the shape of outworn prejudices and decaying customs. A century dawned, the promise of liberty and tolerance flaming on its horizon, to none so sweet as to the Jew. Who has the heart to cast the first stone upon a much-tried race, tortured throughout the centuries, for surrendering itself to the unwonted joy of living, for drinking deep, intoxicating draughts from the newly discovered fount of liberty, and, alas! for throwing aside, under the burning sun of the new era, the perennial protection of its religion? And may we utterly condemn the daughters of Israel, the "roses of Sharon," and "lilies of the valleys," "unkissed by the dew, lost wanderers cheered by no greeting," who, now that all was sunshine, forgot their people, and disregarded the sanctity of family bonds, their shield and their refuge in the sorrow and peril of the dark ages?

With emotion, with pain, not with resentment, Jewish history tells of those women, who spurned Judaism, knowing only its external appearance, its husk, not its essence, high ethical principles and philosophical truths—of Rahel Varnhagen, Henriette Herz, Regina Fröhlich, Dorothea Mendelssohn,

Sarah and Marianne Meyer, Esther Gad, and many others, first products of German culture in alliance with Jewish wit and brilliancy.

Rahel Levin was the foster-mother of "Young Germany," and leader in the woman's emancipation movement, so fruitful later on of deplorable excesses. Rahel herself never overstepped the limits of "*das Ewig-Weibliche.*" No act of hers ran counter to the most exalted requirements of morality. Her being was pervaded by high seriousness, noble dignity, serene cheerfulness. "She dwelt always in the Holy of holies of thought, and even her most daring wishes for herself and mankind leapt shyly heavenwards like pure sacrificial flames." Nothing more touching can be found in the history of the human heart than her confession before death: "With sublime rapture I dwell upon my origin and the marvellous web woven by fate, binding together the oldest recollections of the human race and its most recent aspirations, connecting scenes separated by the greatest possible intervals of time and space. My Jewish birth which I long considered a stigma, a sore disgrace, has now become a precious inheritance, of which nothing on earth can deprive me."[1]

The fact is that Rahel Levin was a great woman, great even in her aberrations, while her satellites, shining by reflected light, and pretending to perpetuate her spirit, transgressed the bounds of wom-

[1] Cmp. *Rahel, ein Buch des Andenkens für ihre Freunde*, Vol. I., p. 43.

anliness, and opened wide a door to riotous sensuality. Certain opponents of the woman's emancipation movement take malicious satisfaction in rehearsing that it was a Jewess who inaugurated it, prudently neglecting to mention that in the list of Rahel's followers, not one Jewish name appears.

The spirit of Judaism and with it the spirit of morality can never be extinguished. They may flag, or vanish for a time, but their restoration in increased vigor and radiance is certain; for, they bear within themselves the guarantee of a future. Henriette Herz, the apostate daughter of Judaism chewing the cud of Schleiermacher's sentimentality and Schlegel's romanticism, had not yet passed away when England produced Jewish women whose deeds were quickened by the spirit of olden heroism, who walked in the paths of wisdom and faith, and, recoiling from the cowardice that counsels apostasy, would have fought, if need be, suffered, and bled, for their faith. What answer but the blush of shame mantling her cheek could the proud beauty have found, had she been asked by, let us say, Lady Judith Montefiore, to tell what it was that chained her to the ruins of the Jewish race?

Lady Montefiore truly was a heroine, worthy to be named with those who have made our past illustrious, and her peer in intellect and strength of character was Charlotte Montefiore, whose early death was a serious loss to Judaism as well as to her family. Her work, "A Few Words to the Jews by one of themselves," containing that charming tale,

"The Jewel Island," displays intellectual and poetic gifts.

The most prominent of women writers in our era unquestionably is Grace Aguilar, in whom we must admire the rare union of broad culture and profound piety. She was born at Hackney in June of 1816, and early showed extraordinary talent and insatiable thirst for knowledge. In her twelfth year she wrote "Gustavus Vasa," an historical drama evincing such unusual gifts that her parents were induced to devote themselves exclusively to her education. It is a charming picture this, of a young, gifted girl, under the loving care of cultured parents actuated by the sole desire to imbue their daughter with their own taste for natural and artistic beauty and their steadfast love for Judaism, and content to lead a modest existence, away from the bustle and the opportunities of the city, in order to be able to give themselves up wholly to the education and companionship of their beloved, only daughter. Under the influence of a wise friend, Grace Aguilar herself tells us, she supplicated God to enable her to do something by which her people might gain higher esteem with their Christian fellow-citizens.

God hearkened unto her prayer, for her efforts were crowned with success. Her first work was the translation of a book from the Hebrew, "Israel Defended." Next came "The Magic Wreath," a collection of poems, and then her well-known works, "Home Influence," "The Spirit of Judaism," her best production, "The Women of Israel," "The

Jewish Faith," and "History of the Jews in England"—a rich harvest for one whose span of life was short. Her pen was dipped into the blood of her veins and the sap of her nerves; the sacred fire of the prophets burnt in her soul, and she was inspired by olden Jewish enthusiasm and devotion to a trust.

So ardent a spirit could not long be imprisoned within so frail a body. In the very prime of life, just thirty-one years old, Grace Aguilar passed away, as though her beautiful soul were hastening to shake off the mortal coil. She rests in German earth, in the Frankfort Jewish cemetery. Her grave is marked with a simple stone, bearing an equally simple epitaph:

> "Give her of the fruit of her hands,
> And let her own works praise her in the gates."

Her death was deeply lamented far and wide. She was a golden link in the chain of humanity—a bold, courageous, withal thoroughly womanly woman, a God-inspired daughter of her race and faith. "We are persuaded," says a non-Jewish friend of hers, "that had this young woman lived in the times of frightful persecution, she would willingly have mounted the stake for her faith, praying for her murderers with her last breath." That the nobility of a solitary woman, leaping like a flame from heart to heart, may inspire highminded thoughts, and that Grace Aguilar's life became a blessing for her people and for humanity, is illustrated by the following testimonial signed by several hundred Jewish women, presented to her when she was about to leave England:

"Dearest Sister—Our admiration of your talents, our veneration for your character, our gratitude for the eminent services your writings render our sex, our people, our faith, in which the sacred cause of true religion is embodied: all these motives combine to induce us to intrude on your presence, in order to give utterance to sentiments which we are happy to feel and delighted to express. Until you arose, it has, in modern times, never been the case that a Woman in Israel should stand forth the public advocate of the faith of Israel; that with the depth and purity of feelings which is the treasure of woman, and with the strength of mind and extensive knowledge that form the pride of man, she should call on her own to cherish, on others to respect, the truth as it is in Israel.

"You, dearest Sister, have done this, and more. You have taught us to know and appreciate our dignity; to feel and to prove that no female character can be . . . more pure than that of the Jewish maiden, none more pious than that of the woman in Israel. You have vindicated our social and spiritual equality with our brethren in the faith: you have, by your own excellent example, triumphantly refuted the aspersion, that the Jewish religion leaves unmoved the heart of the Jewish woman. Your writings place within our reach those higher motives, those holier consolations, which flow from the spirituality of our religion, which urge the soul to commune with its Maker and direct it to His grace and His mercy as the best guide and protector here and hereafter. . . ."

Her example fell like seed upon fertile soil, for Abigail Lindo, Marian Hartog, Annette Salomon, and especially Anna Maria Goldsmid, a writer of merit, daughter of the well-known Sir Isaac Lyon Goldsmid, may be considered her disciples, the fruit of her sowing.

The Italian poetess, Rachel Morpurgo, a worthy successor of Deborah Ascarelli and Sara Copia Sullam, was contemporaneous with Grace Aguilar, though her senior by twenty-six years. Our interest in her is heightened by her use of the Hebrew language, which she handled with such consummate skill that her writings easily take rank with the best of neo-Hebraic literature. A niece of the famous scholar S. D. Luzzatto, she was born at Triest, April 8, 1790. Until the age of twelve she studied the Bible, then she read Bechaï's "Duties of the Heart" and Rashi's commentary, and from her fourteenth to her sixteenth year she devoted herself to the Talmud and the Zohar—a remarkable course of study, pursued, too, in despite of adverse circumstances. At the same time she was taught the turner's art by Luzzatto's father, and later she learned tailoring. One of her poems having been published without her knowledge, she gives vent to her regret in a sonnet:

"My soul surcharged with grief now loud complains,
  And fears upon my spirit heavily weigh.
    'Thy poem we have heard,' the people say,
    'Who like to thee can sing melodious strains?'
    'They're naught but sparks,' outspeaks my soul in chains,
    'Struck from my life by torture every day.
    But now all perfume's fled—no more my lay
  Shall rise; for, fear of shame my song restrains.'
  A woman's fancies lightly roam, and weave
  Themselves into a fairy web. Should I
  Refrain? Ah! soon enough this pleasure, too,
  Will flee! Verily I cannot conceive
  Why I'm extolled. For woman 'tis to ply
  The spinning wheel—then to herself she's true."

This painful self-consciousness, coupled with the oppression of material cares, forms the sad refrain of Rachel Morpurgo's writings. She is a true poetess: the woes of humanity are reflected in her own sorrows, to which she gave utterance in soulful tones. She, too, became an exemplar for a number of young women. A Pole, Yenta Wohllerner, like Rachel Morpurgo, had to propitiate churlish circumstances before she could publish the gifts of her muse, and Miriam Mosessohn, Bertha Rabbinowicz, and others, emulated her masterly handling of the Hebrew language.

The opening of the new era was marked by the appearance of a triad of Jewesses—Grace Aguilar in England, Rachel Morpurgo in Italy, and Henriette Ottenheimer in Germany. A native of the blessed land of Suabia, Henriette Ottenheimer was consecrated to poetry by intercourse with two masters of song—Uhland and Rückert. Her poems, fragrant blossoms plucked on Suabian fields, for the most part are no more than sweet womanly lyrics, growing strong with the force of enthusiasm only when she dwells upon her people's sacred mission and the heroes of Bible days.

Women like these renew the olden fame of the Jewess, and add achievements to her brilliant record. As for their successors and imitators, our contemporaries, whose literary productions are before us, on them we may not yet pass judgment; their work is still on probation.

One striking circumstance in connection with their activity should be pointed out, because it goes to prove the soundness of judgment, the penetration, and expansiveness characteristic of Jews. While the movement for woman's complete emancipation has counted not a single Jewess among its promoters, its more legitimate successor, the movement to establish woman's right and ability to earn a livelihood in any branch of human endeavor—a right and ability denied only by prejudice, or stupidity—was headed and zealously supported by Jewesses, an assertion which can readily be proved by such names as Lina Morgenstern, known to the public also as an advocate of moderate religious reforms, Jenny Hirsch, Henriette Goldschmidt, and a number of writers on subjects of general and Jewish interest, such as Rachel Meyer, Elise Levi (Henle), Ulla Frank-Wolff, Johanna Goldschmidt, Caroline Deutsch, in Germany; Rebekah Eugenie Foa, Julianna and Pauline Bloch, in France; Estelle and Maria Hertzveld, in Holland, and Emma Lazarus, in America.

One other name should be recorded. Fanny Neuda, the writer of "Hours of Devotion," and a number of juvenile stories, has a double claim upon our recognition, inasmuch as she is an authoress of the Jewish race who has addressed her writings exclusively to Jewish women.

We have followed Jewish women from the days of their first flight into the realm of song through a period of two thousand years up to modern times, when our record would seem to come to a natural conclusion. But I deem it proper to bring to your attention a set of circumstances which would be called phenomenal, were it not, as we all know, that the greatest of all wonders is that true wonders are so common.

It is a well-known fact, spread by literary journals, that the Rothschild family, conspicuous for financial ability, has produced a goodly number of authoresses. But it is less well known, and much more noteworthy, that many of the excellent women of this family have devoted their literary gifts and attainments to the service of Judaism. The palaces of the Rothschilds, the richest family in the world, harbor many a warm heart, whose pulsations are quickened by the thought of Israel's history and poetic heritage. Wealth has not abated a jot of their enthusiasm and loyal love for the faith. The first of the house of Rothschild to make a name for herself as an authoress was Lady Charlotte Rothschild, in London, one of the noblest women of our time, who, standing in the glare of prosperity, did not disdain to take up the cudgels in defense of her people, to go Sabbath after Sabbath to her poor, unfortunate sisters in faith, and expound to them, in the school established by her generosity, the nature and duties of a moral, religious life, in lectures pervaded by the spirit of truth and faith. Two volumes of these addresses have been published in German and English (1864 and 1869), and every page gives evidence of rare piety, considerable scholarship, thorough knowledge of the Bible, and a high degree of culture. Equal enthusiasm for Judaism pervades the two volumes of "Thoughts Suggested by Bible Texts" (1859), by Baroness Louise, another of the English Rothschilds.

Three young women of this house, in which wealth is not hostile to idealism, have distinguished themselves as writers, foremost among them Clementine Rothschild, a gentle, sweet maiden, claimed by death before life with its storms could rob her of the pure ideals of youth. She died in her twentieth year, and her legacy to her family and her faith is contained in "Letters to a Christian Friend on the Fundamental Truths of Judaism," abundantly worthy of the perusal of all women, regardless of creed. This young woman displayed more courage, more enthusiasm, more wit, to be sure also more precise knowledge of Judaism, than thousands of men of our time, young and old, who fancy grandiloquent periods sufficient to solve the great religious problems perplexing mankind.

Finally, mention must be made of Constance and Anna de Rothschild, whose two volume "History and Literature of the Israelites" (1872) created a veritable sensation, and awakened the literary world to the fact that the Rothschild family is distinguished not only for wealth, but also for the talent and religious zeal of its authoresses.

I have ventured to group these women of the Rothschild family together as a conclusion to the history of Jewish women in literature, because I take their work to be an earnest of future accomplishment. Such examples cannot fail to kindle the spark of enthusiasm slumbering in the hearts of Jewish women, and the sacred flame of religious zeal, tended once more by women, will leap from rank to rank in the Jewish army. As it is, a half-century has brought about a remarkable change in feeling towards Judaism. Fifty years ago the following lines by Caroline Deutsch, one of the above-mentioned modern German writers, could not have awakened the same responsive chord as now:

> "Little cruet in the Temple
>   That didst feed the sacrificial flame,
> What a true expressive symbol
>   Art thou of my race, of Israel's fame!
> Thou for days the oil didst furnish
>   To illume the Temple won from foe—
> So for centuries in my people
>   Spirit of resistance ne'er burnt low.

It was cast from home and country,
   Gloom and sorrow were its daily lot;
Yet the torch of faith gleamed steady,
   Courage, like thy oil, forsook it not.
Mocks and jeers were all its portion,
   Death assailed it in ten thousand forms—
Yet this people never faltered,
   Hope, its beacon, led it through all storms.
Poorer than dumb, driven cattle,
   It went forth enslaved from its estate,
All its footsore wand'rings lighted
   By its consciousness of worth innate.
Luckless fortunes could not bend it;
   Unjust laws increased its wondrous faith;
From its heart exhaustless streaming,
   Freedom's light shone on its thorny path.
Oil that burnt in olden Temple,
   Eight days only didst thou give forth light!
Oil of faith sustained this people
   Through the centuries of darkest night!"

We can afford to look forward to the future of Judaism serenely. The signs of the times seem propitious to him whose eye is clear to read them, whose heart not too embittered to understand their message aright.

Our rough and tumble time, delighting in negation and destruction, crushing underfoot the tender blossoms of poetry and faith, living up to its quasi motto, "What will not die of itself, must be put to death," will suddenly come to a stop in its mad career of annihilation. That will mark the dawn of a new era, the first stirrings of a new spring-tide for storm-driven Israel. On the ruins will rise the Jewish home, based on Israel's world-saving conception of family life, which, having enlightened the nations of the earth, will return to the source whence it first issued. Built on this foundation, and resting on the pillars of modern culture, Jewish spirit, and true morality, the Jewish home will once more invite the nations to exclaim: "How beautiful are thy tents, O Jacob, thy dwellings, O Israel!"

May the soft starlight of woman's high ideals continue to gleam on the thorny path of the thinker Israel; may they never depart from Israel, those God-kissed women that draw inspiration at the sacred fount of poesy, and are consecrated by its limpid waters to give praise and thanksgiving to Him that reigns on high; may the poet's words ever remain applicable to the matrons and maidens of Israel:[1]

> "Pure woman stands in life's turmoil
>   A rose in leafy bower;
> Her aspirations and her toil
>   Are tinted like a flower.
>
> Her thoughts are pious, kind, and true,
>   In evil have no part;
> A glimpse of empyrean blue
>   Is seen within her heart."

[1] By Julius Rodenberg.

MOSES MAIMONIDES

"Who is Maimonides? For my part, I confess that I have merely heard the name." This naïve admission was not long since made by a well-known French writer in discussing the subject of a prize-essay, "Upon the Philosophy of Maimonides," announced by the *académie universitaire* of Paris. What short memories the French have for the names of foreign scholars! When the proposed subject was submitted to the French minister of instruction, he probably asked himself the same question; but he was not at a loss for an answer; he simply substituted Spinoza for Maimonides. To be sure, Spinoza's philosophy is somewhat better known than that of Maimonides. But why should a minister of instruction take that into consideration? The minister and the author—both presumably over twenty-five years of age—might have heard this very question propounded and answered some years before. They might have known that their colleague Victor Cousin, to save Descartes from the disgrace of having stood sponsor to Spinozism, had established a far-fetched connection between the Dutch philosopher and the Spanish, pronouncing Spinoza the devoted disciple of Maimonides. Perhaps they might have been expected to know, too, that Solomon Munk, through his French translation of Maimonides' last work, had made it possible for modern thinkers to approach the Jewish philosopher, and that soon after this translation was published, E. Saisset had written an article upon Jewish philosophy in the *Revue des Deux Mondes*, in which he gave a popular and detailed exposition of Maimonides' religious views. All this they did not know, and, had they known it, they surely would not have been so candid as the German thinker, Heinrich Ritter, who, in his "History of Christian Philosophy," frankly admits: "My impression was that mediæval philosophy was not indebted to Jewish metaphysicians for any original line of thought, but M. Munk's discovery convinced me of my mistake."[1]

Who was Maimonides? The question is certainly more justifiable upon German than upon French soil. In France, attention has been invited to his works, while in Germany, save in the circle of the learned, he is almost unknown. Even among Jews, who call him "Rambam," he is celebrated rather than known. It seems, then, that it may not be unprofitable to present an outline of the life and works of this philosopher of the middle ages, whom scholars have sought to connect with Spinoza, with Leibnitz, and even with Kant.[2]

While readers in general possess but little information about Maimonides himself, the period in

[1] Ritter, *Geschichte der christlichen Philosophie*, Vol. I., p. 610 ff.

[2] Joel, *Beiträge zur Geschichte der Philosophie*, Vol. II., p. 9.

which he lived, and which derives much of its brilliancy and importance from him, is well known, and has come to be a favorite subject with modern writers. That period was a very dreamland of culture. Under enlightened caliphs, the Arabs in Spain developed a civilization which, during the whole of the middle ages up to the Renaissance, exercised pregnant influence upon every department of human knowledge. A dreamland, in truth, it appears to be, when we reflect that the descendants of a highly cultured people, the teachers of Europe in many sciences, are now wandering in African wilds, nomads, who know of the glories of their past only through a confused legend, holding out to them the extravagant hope that the banner of the Prophet may again wave from the cathedral of Granada. Yet this Spanish-Arabic period bequeathed to us such magnificent tokens of architectural skill, of scientific research, and of philosophic thought, that far from regarding it as fancy's dream, we know it to be one of the corner-stones of civilization.

Prominent among the great men of this period was the Jew Moses ben Maimon, or as he was called in Arabic, Abu Amran Musa ibn Maimûn Obaid Allah (1135-1204). It may be said that he represented the full measure of the scientific attainments of the age at the close of which he stood— an age whose culture comprised the whole circle of sciences then known, and whose conscious goal was the reconciliation of religion and philosophy. The sturdier the growth of the spirit of inquiry, the more ardent became the longing to reach this goal, the keener became the perception of the problems of life and faith. Arabic and Jewish thinkers zealously sought the path leading to serenity. Though they never entered upon it, their tentative efforts naturally prepared the way for a great comprehensive intellect. Only a genius, master of all the sciences, combining soundness of judgment and clearness of insight with great mental vigor and depth, can succeed in reconciling the divergent principles of theology and speculation, if such reconciliation be within the range of the possible. At Cordova, in 1135, when the sun of Arabic culture reached its zenith, was born Maimonides, the man gifted with this all-embracing mind.

Many incidents in his life, not less interesting than his philosophic development, have come down to us. His father was his first teacher. To escape the persecutions of the Almohades, Maimonides, then thirteen years old, removed to Fez with his family. There religious persecution forced Jews to abjure their faith, and the family of Maimon, like many others, had to comply, outwardly at least, with the requirements of Islam. At Fez Maimonides was on intimate terms with physicians and philosophers. At the same time, both in personal intercourse with them and in his writings, he exhorted his pseudo-Mohammedan brethren to remain true to Judaism. This would have cost him his life, had he not been rescued by the kindly offices of Mohammedan theologians. The feeling of insecurity induced his family to leave Fez and join the Jewish community in Palestine. "They embarked at dead of night. On the sixth day of their voyage on the Mediterranean, a frightful storm arose; mountainous waves tossed the frail ship about like a ball; shipwreck seemed imminent. The pious family besought God's protection. Maimonides vowed that if he were rescued from threatening death, he would, as a thank-offering for himself and his family, spend two days in fasting and distributing alms, and devote another day to solitary communion with God. The storm abated, and after a month's voyage, the vessel ran into the harbor of Accho."[1] The travellers met with a warm welcome, but they tarried only a brief while, and finally settled permanently in Egypt. There, too, disasters befell Maimonides, who found solace only in his implicit reliance on God and his enthusiastic devotion to learning. It was then that Maimonides became the religious guide of his brethren. At the same time he attained to eminence in his medical practice, and devoted himself zealously to the study of philosophy and the natural sciences. Yet he did not escape calumny, and until 1185 fortune refused to smile upon him. In that year a son, afterwards the joy and pride of his heart, was born to him. Then he was appointed physician at the court of Saladin, and so great was his reputation that Richard Coeur de Lion wished to make him his physician in ordinary, but Maimonides refused the offer. Despite the fact that his works raised

[1] Graetz, *Geschichte der Juden*, Vol. VI., p. 298 *f.*

many enemies against him, his influence grew in the congregations of his town and province. From all sides questions were addressed to him, and when religious points were under debate, his opinion usually decided the issue. At his death at the age of seventy great mourning prevailed in Israel. His mortal remains were moved to Tiberias, and a legend reports that Bedouins attacked the funeral train. Finding it impossible to move the coffin from the spot, they joined the Jews, and followed the great man to his last resting-place. The deep reverence accorded him both by the moral sense and the exuberant fancy of his race is best expressed in the brief eulogy of the saying, now become almost a proverb: "From Moses, the Prophet, to Moses ben Maimon, there appeared none like unto Moses."

In three different spheres Maimonides' work produced important results. First in order stand his services to his fellow-believers. For them he compiled the great Codex, the first systematic arrangement, upon the basis of Talmudic tradition, of all the ordinances and tenets of Judaism. He gave them a system of ethics which even now should be prized, because it inculcates the highest possible ethical views and the most ideal conception of man's duties in life. He explained to them, almost seven hundred years ago, Islam's service to mankind, and the mission Christianity was appointed by Providence to accomplish.

His early writings reveal the fundamental principles of his subsequent literary work. An astronomical treatise on the Jewish calendar, written in his early youth, illustrates his love of system, but his peculiar method of thinking and working is best shown in the two works that followed. The first is a commentary on parts of the Talmud, probably meant to present such conclusions of the Babylonian and the Jerusalem Talmud as affect the practices of Judaism. The second is his Arabic commentary on the Mishna. He explains the Mishna simply and clearly from a strictly rabbinical point of view—a point of view which he never relinquished, permitting a deviation only in questions not affecting conduct. Master of the abundant material of Jewish literature, he felt it to be one of the most important tasks of the age to simplify, by methodical treatment, the study of the mass of written and traditional religious laws, accumulated in the course of centuries. It is this work that contains the attempt, praised by some, condemned by others, to establish articles of the Jewish faith, the Bible being used in authentication. Thirteen articles of faith were thus established. The first five naturally define the God-idea: Article 1 declares the existence of God, 2, His unity, 3, His immateriality, 4, His eternity, 5, that unto Him alone, to whom all created life owes its being, human adoration is due; the next four treat of revelation: 6, of revelations made through prophets in general, 7, of the revelation made through Moses, 8, of the divine origin of the Law, 9, of the perfection of the Law, and its eternally binding force; and the rest dwell upon the divine government of the world: 10, Divine Providence, 11, reward and punishment, here and hereafter, 12, Messianic promises and hopes, and 13, resurrection.

Maimonides' high reputation among his own people is attested by his letters and responses, containing detailed answers to vexed religious questions. An especially valuable letter is the one upon "Enforced Apostasy," *Iggereth ha-Sh'mad*. He advises an inquirer what to do when menaced by religious persecutions. Is one to save life by accepting, or to court death by refusing to embrace, the Mohammedan faith? Maimonides' opinion is summed up in the words: "The solution which I always recommend to my friends and those consulting me is, to leave such regions, and to turn to a place in which religion can be practiced without fear of persecution. No considerations of danger, of property, or of family should prevent one from carrying out this purpose. The divine Law stands in higher esteem with the wise than the haphazard gifts of fortune. These pass away, the former remains." His responses as well as his most important works bear the impress of a sane, well-ordered mind, of a lofty intellect, dwelling only upon what is truly great.

Also his second famous work, the above-mentioned Hebrew Codex, *Mishneh Torah*, "Recapitulation of the Law," was written in the interest of his brethren in faith. Its fourteen divisions treat of knowledge, love, the festivals, marriage laws, sanctifications, vows, seeds, Temple-service, sacrifices, purifications, damages, purchase and sale, courts, and judges. "My work is such," says Maimonides, "that my book in connection with the Bible will enable a student to dispense with the Talmud." From whatever point of view this work may be regarded, it must be admitted that Maimonides carried out his plan with signal success, and that it is the only one by which method could have been introduced into the manifold departments of Jewish religious lore. But it is obvious that the thinker had not yet reached the goal of his desires. In consonance with his fundamental principle, a scientific systemization of religious laws had to be followed up by an explanation of revealed religion and Greek-Arabic philosophy, and by the attempt to bring about a reconciliation between them.

Before we enter upon this his greatest book, it is well to dispose of the second phase of his work, his activity as a medical writer. Maimonides treated medicine as a science, a view not usual in those days. The body of facts relating to medicine he classified, as he had systematized the religious laws of the Talmud. In his methodical way, he also edited the writings of Galen, the medical oracle of the middle ages, and his own medical aphorisms and treatises are marked by the same love of system. It seems that he had the intention to prepare a medical codex to serve a purpose similar to that of his religious code. How great a reputation he enjoyed among

Mohammedan physicians is shown by the extravagantly enthusiastic verses of an Arabic poet:

> "Of body's ills doth Galen's art relieve,
> Maimonides cures mind and body both,—
> His wisdom heals disease and ignorance.
> And should the moon invoke his skill and art,
> Her spots, when full her orb, would disappear;
> He'd fill her breach, when time doth inroads make,
> And cure her, too, of pallor caused by earth."

Maimonides' real greatness, however, must be sought in his philosophic work. Despite the wide gap between our intellectual attitude and the philosophic views to which Maimonides gave fullest expression, we can properly appreciate his achievements and his intellectual grasp by judging him with reference to his own time. When we realize that he absorbed all the thought-currents of his time, that he was their faithful expounder, and that, at the same time, he was gifted with an accurate, historic instinct, making him wholly objective, we shall recognize in him "the genius of his peculiar epoch become incarnate." The work containing Maimonides' deepest thought and the sum of his knowledge and erudition was written in Arabic under the name *Dalalat al-Haïrin*. In Hebrew it is known as *Moreh Nebuchim*, in Latin, as *Doctor Perplexorum*, and in English as the "Guide of the Perplexed." To this book we shall now devote our attention. The original Arabic text was supposed, along with many other literary treasures of the middle ages, to be lost, until

Solomon Munk, the blind *savant* with clear vision, discovered it in the library at Paris, and published it. But in its Hebrew translation the book created a stir, which subsided only with its public burning at Montpellier early in the thirteenth century. The Latin translation we owe to Buxtorf; the German is, I believe, incomplete, and can hardly be said to give evidence of ripe scholarship.[1]

The question that naturally suggests itself is: What does the book contain? Does it establish a new system of philosophy? Is it a cyclopædia of the sciences, such as the Arab schools of that day were wont to produce? Neither the one nor the other. The "Guide of the Perplexed" is a system of rational theology upon a philosophic basis, a book not intended for novices, but for thinkers, for such minds as know how to penetrate the profound meaning of tradition, as the author says in a prefatory letter addressed to Joseph ibn Aknin, his favorite disciple. He believes that even those to whom the book appeals are often puzzled and confused by the apparent inconsistencies between the literal interpretation of the Bible and the evidence of reason, that they do not know whether to take Scriptural expressions as symbolic or allegoric, or to accept them in their literal meaning, and that they fall a prey to doubt, and long for a guide. Maimonides is prepared to lead them to an eminence on which religion and philosophy meet in perfect harmony.

[1] "The Guide of the Perplexed," the English translation, consulted in this work, was made by M. Friedländer, Ph. D., (London, Trübner & Co., 1885). [Tr.]

Educated in the school of Arabic philosophers, notably under the influence of Ibn Sina (Avicenna), Maimonides paid hero-worship to Aristotle, the autocrat of the middle ages in the realm of speculation. There is no question that the dominion wielded by the Greek philosopher throughout mediæval times, and the influence which he exercises even now, are chiefly attributable to the Arabs, and beside them, pre-eminently to Maimonides. For him, Aristotle was second in authority only to the Bible. A rational interpretation of the Bible, in his opinion, meant its interpretation from an Aristotelian point of view. Still, he does not consider Aristotle other than a thinker like himself, not by any means the infallible "organ of reason." The moment he discovers that a peripatetic principle is in direct and irreconcilable conflict with his religious convictions, he parts company with it, let the effort cost what it may. For, above all, Maimonides was a faithful Jew, striving to reach a spiritual conception of his religion, and to assign to theology the place in his estimation belonging to it in the realm of science. He stands forth as the most eminent intermediary between Greek-Arabic thought and Christian scholasticism. A century later, the most prominent of the schoolmen endeavored, in the same way as Maimonides, to reconcile divine with human wisdom as manifested by Aristotle. It has been demonstrated that Maimonides was followed by both Albertus Magnus and Thomas Aquinas, and that the new aims of philosophy, conceived at the beginning of the thirteenth century, are, in part, to be traced to the influence of "Rabbi Moses of Egypt," as Maimonides was called by the first of these two celebrated doctors of the Church.

What a marvellous picture is presented by the unfolding of the Aristotelian idea in its passage through the ages! And one of the most attractive figures on the canvas is Maimonides. Let us see how he undertakes to guide the perplexed. His path is marked out for him by the Bible. Its first few verses suffice to puzzle the believing thinker. It says: "Let us make man in our image, after our likeness." What! Is this expression to be taken literally? Impossible! To conceive of God as such that a being can be made in His image, is to conceive of Him as a corporeal substance. But God is an invisible, immaterial Intelligence. Reason teaches this, and the sacred Book itself prohibits image-worship. On this point Aristotle and the Bible are in accord. The inference is that in the Holy Scriptures there are many metaphors and words with a double or allegoric sense. Such is the case with the word "image." It has two meanings, the one usual and obvious, the other figurative. Here the word must be taken in its figurative sense. God is conceived as the highest Reason, and as reason is the specific attribute which characterizes the human mind, it follows that man, by virtue of his possession of reason, resembles God, and the more fully he realizes the ideal of Reason, the closer does he approach the form and likeness of

God. Such is Maimonides' method of reasoning. He does not build up a new system of philosophy, he adopts an existing system. Beginning with Bible exegesis, he leads us, step by step, up to the lofty goal at which philosophy and faith are linked in perfect harmony.

The arguments for the existence, unity, and incorporeity of God divide the Arabic philosophers into two schools. Maimonides naturally espoused the view permitting the most exalted conception of God, that is, the conception of God free from human attributes. He recognizes none but negative attributes; in other words, he defines God by means of negations only. For instance, asserting that the Supreme Being is omniscient or omnipotent, is not investing Him with a positive attribute, it is simply denying imperfection. The student knows that in the history of the doctrine of attributes, the recognition of negative attributes marks a great advance in philosophic reasoning. Maimonides holds that the conception of the Deity as a pure abstraction is the only one truly philosophic. His evidences for the existence, the immateriality, and the unity of God, are conceived in the same spirit. In offering them he follows Aristotle's reasoning closely, adding only one other proof, the cosmological, which he took from his teacher, the Arab Avicenna. He logically reaches this proof by more explicitly defining the God-idea, and, at the same time, taking into consideration the nature of the world of things and their relation to one another. Acquainted with

Ptolemy's "Almagest" and with the investigations of the Arabs, he naturally surpasses his Greek master in astronomical knowledge. In physical science, however, he gives undivided allegiance to the Aristotelian theory of a sublunary and a celestial world of spheres, the former composed of the sublunary elements in constantly shifting, perishable combinations, and the latter, of the stable, unchanging fifth substance (quintessence). But the question, how God moves these spheres, separates Maimonides from his master. His own answer has a Neoplatonic ring. He holds, with Aristotle, that there are as many separate Intelligences as spheres. Each sphere is supposed to aspire to the Intelligence which is the principle of its motion. The Arabic thinkers assumed ten such independent Intelligences, one animating each of the nine permanent spheres, and the tenth, called the "Active Intellect," influencing the sublunary world of matter. The existence of this tenth Intelligence is proved by the transition of our own intellect from possible existence to actuality, and by the varying forms of all transient things, whose matter at one time existed only in a potential state. Whenever the transition from potentiality to actuality occurs, there must be a cause. Inasmuch as the tenth Intelligence (*Sechel Hapoel*, Active Intellect) induces form, it must itself be form, inasmuch as it is the source of intellect, it is itself intellect. This is, of course, obscure to us, but we must remember that Maimonides would not have so charming and individual a personality, were he not part and parcel of his time and the representative of its belief. Maimonides, having for once deviated from the peripatetic system, ventures to take another bold step away from it. He offers an explanation, different from Aristotle's, of the creation of the world. The latter repudiated the *creatio ex nihilo* (creation out of nothing). Like modern philosophers, he pre-supposed the existence of an eternal " First substance " (*materia prima*). His Bible does not permit our rabbi to avail himself of this theory. It was reserved for the modern investigator to demonstrate how the Scriptural word, with some little manipulation, can be so twisted as to be made to harmonize with the theories of natural science. But to such trickery the pure-minded guide will not stoop. Besides, the acceptance of Aristotle's theory would rule out the intervention of miracles in the conduct of the world, and that Maimonides does not care to renounce. Right here his monotheistic convictions force him into direct opposition to the Greek as well as to the Arabic philosophers. Upon this subject, he brooked neither trifling nor compromise with reason. It is precisely his honesty that so exalted his teachings, that they have survived the lapse of centuries, and maintain a place in the pure atmosphere of modern philosophic thought.

According to Maimonides, man has absolute free-will, and God is absolutely just. Whatever good befalls man is reward, all his evil fortune, punishment. What Aristotle attributes to chance, and the Mohammedan philosophers to Divine Will or Divine Wisdom, our rabbi traces to the *merits of man* as its cause. He does not admit any suffering to be unmerited, or that God ordains trials merely to indemnify the sufferer in this or the future world. Man's susceptibility to divine influence is measured by his intellectual endowment. Through his "intellect," he is directly connected with the "Active Intellect," and thus secures the grace of God, who embraces the infinite. Such views naturally lead to a conception of life in consonance with the purest ideals of morality, and they are the goal to which the "Guide" leads the perplexed. He teaches that the acquiring of high intellectual power, and the "possession of such notions as lead to true metaphysical opinions" about God, are "man's final object," and they constitute true human perfection. This it is that "gives him immortality," and confers upon him the dignity of manhood.

The highest degree of perfection, according to Maimonides, is reached by him who devotes all his thoughts and actions to perfecting himself in divine matters, and this highest degree he calls prophecy. He is probably the first philosopher to offer so rationalistic an explanation, and, on that account, it merits our attention. What had previously been regarded as supernatural inspiration, the "Guide" reduces to a psychological theory. "Prophecy," he says, "is, in truth and reality, an emanation sent forth by the Divine Being through the medium of the Active Intellect, in the first instance to man's rational faculty, and then to his imaginative faculty; it is the highest degree . . . of perfection man can attain; it consists in the most perfect development of the imaginative faculty." Maimonides distinguishes eleven degrees of inspiration, and three essential conditions of prophecy: 1. Perfection of the natural constitution of the imaginative faculty, 2. mental perfection, which may partially be acquired by training, and 3. moral perfection. Moses arrived at the highest degree of prophecy, because he understood the knowledge communicated to him without the medium of the imaginative faculty. This spiritual height having been scaled, the "Guide" needs but to take a step to reach revelation, in his estimation also an intellectual process: man's intellect rises to the Supreme Being.

In the third part of his work, Maimonides endeavors to reconcile the conclusions of philosophy with biblical laws and Talmudical traditions. His method is both original and valuable; indeed, this deserves to be considered the most important part of his work. Detailed exposition of his reasoning may prove irksome; we shall, therefore, consider it as briefly as possible.

Maimonides laid down one rule of interpretation which, almost without exception, proves applicable: The words of Holy Writ express different sets of ideas, bearing a certain relation to each other, the one set having reference to physical, the other to spiritual, qualities. By applying this rule, he thinks that nearly all discrepancies between the literal interpretation of the Bible and his own philosophic theories disappear. Having passed over the domain of metaphysical speculation, he finally reaches the consideration of the practical side of the Bible, that is to say, the Mosaic legislation. These last investigations of his are attractive, not only by reason of the satisfactory method pursued, but chiefly from the fact that Maimonides, divesting himself of the conservatism of his contemporaries, ventures to inquire into the reasons of biblical laws. For many of them, he assigns local and historical reasons; many, he thinks, owe their origin to the desire to oppose the superstitious practices of early times and of the Sabeans, a mythical, primitive race; but all, he contends, are binding, and with this solemn asseveration, he puts the seal upon his completed work.

When Maimonides characterized the "Guide of the Perplexed" as "the true science of the Bible," he formed a just estimate of his own work. It has come to be the substructure of a rational theology based upon speculation. Maimonides cannot be said to have been very much ahead of his own age; but it is altogether certain that he attained the acme of the possibilities of the middle ages. In many respects there is a striking likeness between his life and work and those of the Arabic freethinker Averroës, whom we now know so well through Ernest Renan. While the Jewish theologian was composing his great work, the Arabic philosopher was writing his "Commentaries on Aristotle." The two had similar ends in view—the one to enthrone "the

Stagirite" as the autocrat of philosophy in the Mosque, the other, in the Synagogue. We have noted the fact that, some centuries later, the Church also entered the federation subject to Aristotelian rule. Albertus Magnus uses Maimonides, Thomas Aquinas joins him, and upon them depend the other schoolmen. Recent inquirers follow in their train. Philosophy's noblest votary, Benedict Spinoza himself, is influenced by Maimonides. He quotes frequently and at great length the finest passages of the "Guide." Again, Moses Mendelssohn built his system on the foundations offered by Maimonides, and an acute critic assures us that, in certain passages, Kant's religious philosophy breathes the spirit of Maimonides.[1]

The "Guide of the Perplexed" did not, however, meet with so gracious a reception in the Synagogue. There, Maimonides' philosophic system conjured up violent storms. The whole of an epoch, that following Maimonides' death, was absorbed in the conflict between philosophy and tradition. Controversial pamphlets without number have come down to us from those days. Enthusiasts eulogized, zealots decried. Maimonides' ambiguous expressions about bodily resurrection, seeming to indicate that he did not subscribe to the article of the creed on that subject, caused particularly acrimonious polemics. Meïr ben Todros ha-Levi, a Talmudist and poet of Toledo, denounced the equivocation in the following lines:

[1] Joel, *l. c.*

"If those that rise from death again must die,
 For lot like theirs I ne'er should long and sigh.
 If graves their bones shall once again confine,
 I hope to stay where first they bury mine."

Naturally, Maimonides' followers were quick to retort:

"His name, forsooth, is Meïr ' Shining.'
  How false! since *light* he holds in small esteem.
 Our language always contrast loveth,—
  Twi*light*'s the name of ev'ning's doubtful gleam."

Another of Maimonides' opponents was the physician Judah Alfachar, who bore the hereditary title *Prince*. The following pasquinade is attributed to him:

"Forgive, O Amram's son, nor deem it crime,
 That he, deception's master, bears thy name.
 Nabi we call the prophet of truths sublime,
 Like him of Ba'al, who doth the truth defame."

Maimonides, in his supposed reply to the Prince, played upon the word *Chamor*, the Hebrew word for *ass*, the name of a Hivite prince mentioned in the Bible:

"High rank, I wot, we proudly claim
  When sprung from noble ancestor;
 Henceforth my mule a *prince* I'll name
  Since once a prince was called *Chamor*."

It seems altogether certain that this polemic rhyming is the fabrication of a later day, for we know that the controversies about Maimonides' opinions in Spain and Provence broke out only after his death, when his chief work had spread far and wide in its Hebrew translation. The following stanza passed from mouth to mouth in northern France:

> "Be silent, 'Guide,' from further speech refrain!
>   Thus truth to us was never brought.
> Accursed who says that Holy Writ's a trope,
>   And idle dreams what prophets taught."

Whereupon the Provençals returned:

> " Thou fool, I pray thou wilt forbear,
>   Nor enter on this consecrated ground.
> Or trope, or truth—or vision fair,
>   Or only dream—for thee 'tis too profound."

The homage paid to Maimonides' memory in many instances produced most extravagant poetry. The following high-flown lines, outraging the canons of good taste recognized in Hebrew poetry, are supposed to be his epitaph:

> "Here lies a man, yet not a man,
>   And if a man, conceived by angels,
>   By human mother only born to light;
>   Perhaps himself a spirit pure—
>   Not child by man and woman fostered—
>   From God above an emanation bright."

Such hyperbole naturally challenged opposition, and Maimonides' opponents did not hesitate to give voice to their deep indignation, as in the following:

"Alas! that man should dare
  To say, with reckless air,
    That Holy Scripture's but a dream of night;
  That all we read therein
  Has truly never been,
    Is naught but sign of meaning recondite.
  And when God's wondrous deeds
  The haughty scorner reads,
    Contemptuous he cries, 'I trust my sight.'"

A cessation of hostilities came only in the fourteenth century. The "Guide" was then given its due meed of appreciation by the Jews. Later, Maimonides' memory was held in unbounded reverence, and to-day his "Guide of the Perplexed" is a manual of religious philosophy treasured by Judaism.

If we wish once more before parting from this earnest, noble thinker to review his work and attitude, we can best do it by applying to them the standard furnished by his own reply to all adverse critics of his writings: "In brief, such is my disposition. When a thought fills my mind, though I be able to express it so that only a single man among ten thousand, a thinker, is satisfied and elevated by it, while the common crowd condemns it as absurd, I boldly and frankly speak the word that enlightens the wise, never fearing the censure of the ignorant herd."

This was Maimonides—he of pure thought, of noble purpose; imbued with enthusiasm for his faith, with love for science; ruled by the loftiest moral principles; full of disinterested love and the milk of human kindness in his intercourse with those of other faiths and other views; an eagle-eyed thinker, in whom were focused and harmoniously blended the last rays of the declining sun of Arabic-Jewish-Spanish culture.

JEWISH TROUBADOURS AND MINNE-SINGERS

A great tournament at the court of Pedro I.! Deafening fanfares invite courtiers and cavaliers to participate in the festivities. In the brilliant sunshine gleam the lances of the knights, glitter the spears of the hidalgos. Gallant paladins escort black-eyed beauties to the elevated balcony, on which, upon a high-raised throne, under a gilded canopy, surrounded by courtiers, sit Blanche de Bourbon and her illustrious lord Dom Pedro, with Doña Maria de Padilla, the lady of his choice, at his left. Three times the trumpets have sounded, announcing the approach of the troubadours gathered from all parts of Castile to compete with one another in song. Behold! a venerable old man, with silvery white beard flowing down upon his breast, seeks to extricate himself from the crowd. With admiring gaze the people respectfully make way, and enthusiastically greet him: "Rabbi Don Santo! Rabbi Don Santo!"

The troubadour makes a low obeisance before the throne. Dom Pedro nods encouragement, Maria de Padilla smiles graciously, only Doña Blanca's pallid face remains immobile. The hoary bard begins his song:[1]

[1] Cmp. Kayserling, *Sephardim*, p. 23 ff.

> "My noble king and mighty lord,
>   A discourse hear most true;
> 'Tis Santob brings your Grace the word,
>   Of Carrion's town the Jew.
>
> In plainest verse my thought I tell,
>   With gloss and moral free,
> Drawn from Philosophy's pure well,
>   As onward you may see."[1]

A murmur of approval runs through the crowd; grandees and hidalgos press closer to listen. In well-turned verse, fraught with worldly-wise lessons, and indifferent whether his hortations meet with praise or with censure, the poet continues to pour out words of counsel and moral teachings, alike for king, nobles, and people.

Who is this Rabbi Don Santob? We know very little about him, yet, with the help of "bright-eyed fancy," enough to paint his picture. The real name of this Jew from Carrion de los Condes, a city of northern Spain, who lived under Alfonso XI. and Peter the Cruel, was, of course, not Santob, but Shem-Tob. Under Alfonso the intellectual life of Spain developed to a considerable degree, and in Spain, as almost everywhere, we find Jews in sympathy with the first intellectual strivings of the nation. They have a share in the development of all Romance languages and literatures. Ibn Alfange, a Moorish Jew, after his conversion a high official, wrote the first "Chronicle of the Cid," the

[1] Translation by **Ticknor.** [Tr.]

oldest source of the oft-repeated biography, thus furnishing material to subsequent Spanish poets and historians. Valentin Barruchius (Baruch), of Toledo, composed, probably in the twelfth century, in pure, choice Latin, the romance *Comte Lyonnais*, *Palanus*, which spread all over Europe, affording modern poets subject-matter for great tragedies, and forming the groundwork for one of the classics of Spanish literature. A little later, Petrus Alphonsus (Moses Sephardi) wrote his *Disciplina Clericalis*, the first collection of tales in the Oriental manner, the model of all future collections of the kind.

Three of the most important works of Spanish literature, then, are products of Jewish authorship. This fact prepares the student to find a Jew among the Castilian troubadours of the fourteenth century, the period of greatest literary activity. The Jewish spirit was by no means antagonistic to the poetry of the Provençal troubadours. In his didactic poem, *Chotham Tochnith* ("The Seal of Perfection," together with "The Flaming Sword"), Abraham Bedersi, that is, of Béziers (1305), challenges his co-religionists to a poetic combat. He details the rules of the tournament, and it is evident that he is well acquainted with all the minutiæ of the *jeu parti* and the *tenso* (song of dispute) of the Provencal singers, and would willingly imitate their *sirventes* (moral and political song). His plaint over the decadence of poetry among the Jews is characteristic: "Where now are the marvels of Hebrew poetry? Mayhap thou'lt find them in the Provençal or Romance. Aye, in Folquet's verses is manna, and from the lips of Cardinal is wafted the perfume of crocus and nard "—Folquet de Lunel and Peire Cardinal being the last great representatives of Provençal troubadour poetry. Later on, neo-Hebraic poets again show acquaintance with the regulations governing song-combats and courts of love. Pious Bible exegetes, like Samuel ben Meïr, do not disdain to speak of the *partimens* of the troubadours, "in which lovers talk to each other, and by turns take up the discourse." One of his school, a *Tossafist*, goes so far as to press into service the day's fashion in explaining the meaning of a verse in the "Song of Songs": "To this day lovers treasure their mistress' locks as love-tokens." It seems, too, that Provençal romances were heard, and their great poets welcomed, in the houses of Jews, who did not scruple occasionally to use their melodies in the synagogue service.

National customs, then, took root in Israel; but that Jewish elements should have become incorporated into Spanish literature is more remarkable, may, indeed, be called marvellous. Yet, from one point of view, it is not astonishing. The whole of mediæval Spanish literature is nothing more than the handmaiden of Christianity. Spanish poetry is completely dominated by Catholicism; it is in reality only an expression of reverence for Christian institutions. An extreme naturally induces a counter-current; so here, by the side of rigid orthodoxy, we meet with latitudinarianism and secular delight in the good things of life. For instance, that jolly rogue, the archpriest of Hita, by way of relaxation from the tenseness of church discipline, takes to composing *dansas* and *baladas* for the rich Jewish bankers of his town. He and his contemporaries have much to say about Jewish generosity—unfortunately, much, too, about Jewish wealth and pomp. Jewish women, a Jewish chronicler relates, are tricked out with finery, as " sumptuously as the pope's mules." It goes without saying that, along with these accounts, we have frequent wailing about defection from the faith and neglect of the Law. Old Akiba is right: " History repeats itself!" (" *Es ist alles schon einmal da gewesen!*").

Such were the times of Santob de Carrion. Our first information about him comes from the Marquis de Santillana, one of the early patrons and leaders of Spanish literature. He says, " In my grandfather's time there was a Jew, Rabbi Santob, who wrote many excellent things, among them *Proverbios Morales* (Moral Proverbs), truly commendable in spirit. A great troubadour, he ranks among the most celebrated poets of Spain." Despite this high praise, the marquis feels constrained to apologize for having quoted a passage from Santob's work. His praise is endorsed by the critics. It is commonly conceded that his *Consejos y Documentos al Rey Dom Pedro* (" Counsel and Instruction to King Dom Pedro "), consisting of six hundred and twenty-eight romances, deserves a place among the best creations of Castilian poetry, which, in form and substance, owes not a little to Rabbi Santob. A valuable manuscript at the Escurial in Madrid contains his *Consejos* and two other works, *La Doctrina Christiana* and *Dansa General*. A careless copyist called the whole collection "Rabbi Santob's Book," so giving rise to the mistake of Spanish critics, who believe that Rabbi Santob, indisputably the author of *Consejos*, became a convert to Christianity, and wrote, after his conversion, the didactic poem on doctrinal Christianity, and perhaps also the first "Dance of Death."[1] It was reserved for the acuteness of German criticism to expose the error of this hypothesis. Of the three works, only *Consejos* belongs to Rabbi Santob, the others were accidentally bound with it. In passing, the interesting circumstance may be noted that in the first "Dance of Death" a bearded rabbi (*Rabbi barbudo*) dances toward the universal goal between a priest and an usurer. Santob de Carrion remained a Jew. His *consejos*, written when he was advanced in age, are pervaded by loyalty to his king, but no less to his faith, which he openly professed at the royal court, and whose spiritual treasures he adroitly turned to poetic uses.

Santob, it is interesting to observe, was not a writer of erotic poetry. He composed poems on moral subjects only, social satires and denunciations of vice. Such are the *consejos*. It is in his capacity as a preacher of morality that Santob is to be

[1] Cmp. F. Wolf, *Studien zur Geschichte der spanischen Nationalliteratur*, p. 236 *ff.*

classed among troubadours. First he addressed himself, with becoming deference, to the king, leading him to consider God's omnipotence:

> "As great, 'twixt heav'n and earth the space—
>   That ether pure and blue—
> So great is God's forgiving grace
>   Your sins to lift from you.
>
> And with His vast and wondrous might
>   He does His deeds of power;
> But yours are puny in His sight,
>   For strength is not man's dower."

At that time it required more than ordinary courage to address a king in this fashion; but Santob was old and poor, and having nothing to lose, could risk losing everything. A democratic strain runs through his verses; he delights in aiming his satires at the rich, the high-born, and the powerful, and takes pride in his poverty and his fame as a poet:

> "I will not have you think me less
>   Than others of my faith,
> Who live on a generous king's largess,
>   Forsworn at every breath.
>
> And if you deem my teachings true,
>   Reject them not with hate,
> Because a minstrel sings to you
>   Who's not of knight's estate.
>
> The fragrant, waving reed grows tall
>   From feeble root and thin,
> And uncouth worms that lowly crawl
>   Most lustrous silk do spin.

> Because beside a thorn it grows
>   The rose is not less fair;
> Though wine from gnarlèd branches flows,
>   'Tis sweet beyond compare.
>
> The goshawk, know, can soar on high,
>   Yet low he nests his brood.
> A Jew true precepts doth apply,
>   Are they therefore less good?
>
> Some Jews there are with slavish mind
>   Who fear, are mute, and meek.
> My soul to truth is so inclined
>   That all I feel I speak.
>
> There often comes a meaning home
>   Through simple verse and plain,
> While in the heavy, bulky tome
>   We find of truth no grain.
>
> Full oft a man with furrowed front,
>   Whom grief hath rendered grave,
> Whose views of life are honest, blunt,
>   Both fool is called and knave."

It is surely not unwarranted to assume that from these confessions the data of Santob's biography may be gathered.

Now as to Santob's relation to Judaism. Doubtless he was a faithful Jew, for the views of life and the world laid down in his poems rest on the Bible, the Talmud, and the Midrash. With the fearlessness of conviction he meets the king and the people, denouncing the follies of both. Some of his romances sound precisely like stories from the Haggada, so skilfully does he clothe his counsel in the gnomic style of the Bible and the Talmud. This characteristic is particularly well shown in his verses on friendship, into which he has woven the phraseology of the Proverbs:

> "What treasure greater than a friend
>   Who close to us hath grown?
> Blind fate no bitt'rer lot can send
>   Than bid us walk alone.
>
> For solitude doth cause a dearth
>   Of fruitful, blessed thought.
> The wise would pray to leave this earth,
>   If none their friendship sought.
>
> Yet sad though loneliness may be,
>   That friendship surely shun
> That feigns to love, and inwardly
>   Betrays affections won."

The poem closes with a prayer for the king, who certainly could not have taken offense at Santob's frankness:

> "May God preserve our lord and king
>   With grace omnipotent,
> Remove from us each evil thing,
>   And blessed peace augment.
>
> The nations loyally allied
>   Our empire to exalt,
> May God, in whom we all confide,
>   From plague keep and assault.

> If God will answer my request,
>   Then will be paid his due—
> Your noble father's last behest—
>   To Santob, Carrion's Jew."

Our troubadour's poetry shows that he was devotedly attached to his prince, enthusiastically loved his country, and was unfalteringly loyal to his faith; that he told the king honest, wholesome truths disguised in verse; that he took no pains to conceal his scorn of those who, with base servility, bowed to the ruling faith, and permitted its yoke to be put upon their necks; that he felt himself the peer of the high in rank, and the wealthy in the goods of this world; that he censured, with incisive criticism, the vices of his Spanish and his Jewish contemporaries—all of which is calculated to inspire us with admiration for the Jewish troubadour, whose manliness enabled him to meet his detractors boldly, as in the verses quoted above:

> "Because beside a thorn it grows,
>   The rose is not less fair;
> Though wine from gnarlèd branches flows,
>   'Tis sweet beyond compare.
>
> A Jew true precepts doth apply,
>   Are they therefore less good?"

History does not tell us whether Pedro rewarded the Jewish troubadour as the latter, if we may judge by the end of his poem, had expected. Our accounts of his life are meagre; even his fellow-believers do not make mention of him. We do know, however, that the poor poet's prayers for his sovereign, his petitions for the weal and the glory of his country were not granted. Pedro lost his life by violence, quarrels about the succession and civil wars convulsed the land, and weakened the royal power. Its decline marked the end of the peace and happiness of the Jew on Castilian soil.

As times grew worse, and persecutions of the Jews in Christian Spain became frequent, many forsook the faith of their fathers, to bask in the sunshine of the Church, who treated proselytes with distinguished favor. The example of the first Jewish troubadour did not find imitators. Among the converts were many poets, notably Juan Alfonso de Bæna, who, in the fifteenth century, collected the oldest troubadour poetry, including his own poems and satires, and the writings of the Jewish physician Don Moses Zarzal, into a *cancionera general*. Like many apostates, he sought to prove his devotion to the new faith by mocking at and reviling his former brethren. The attacked were not slow to answer in kind, and the Christian world of poets and bards joined the latter in deriding the neophytes. Spanish literature was not the loser by these combats, whose description belongs to general literary criticism. Lyric poetry, until then dry, serious, and solemn, was infused by the satirist with flashing wit and whimsical spirit, and throwing off its connection with the drama, developed into an independent species of poetry.

The last like the first of Spanish troubadours was a Jew,[1] Antonio di Montoro (Moro), *el ropero* (the tailor), of Cordova, of whom a contemporary says,

> "A man of repute and lofty fame;
> As poet, he puts many to shame;
> Anton di Montoro is his name."

The tailor-poet was exposed to attacks, too. A high and mighty Spanish *caballero* addresses him as

> "You Cohn, you cur,
> You miserable Jew,
> You wicked usurer."

It must be admitted that he parries these thrusts with weak, apologetic appeals, preserved in his *Respuestas* (Rhymed Answers). He claims his highborn foe's sympathy by telling him that he has sons, grandchildren, a poor, old father, and a marriageable daughter. In extenuation of his cowardice it should be remembered that Antonio di Montoro lived during a reign of terror, under Ferdinand and Isabella, when his race and his faith were exposed to most frightful persecution. All the more noteworthy is it that he had the courage to address the queen in behalf of his faith. He laments plaintively that despite his sixty years he has not been able to eradicate all traces of his descent (*reato de su origen*), and turns his irony against himself:

[1] Cmp. Kayserling, *l. c.* p. 85 *ff.*

> "Ropero, so sad and so forlorn,
>   Now thou feelest pain and scorn.
>   Until sixty years had flown,
>   Thou couldst say to every one,
>   'Nothing wicked have I known.'
>
> Christian convert hast thou turned,
> *Credo* thou to say hast learned;
> Willing art now bold to view
> Plates of ham—no more askew.
> Mass thou hearest,
> Church reverest,
> Genuflexions makest,
> Other alien customs takest.
> Now thou, too, mayst persecute
> Those poor wretches, like a brute."

"Those poor wretches" were his brethren in faith in the fair Spanish land. With a jarring discord ends the history of the Jews in Spain. On the ninth of Ab, 1492, three hundred thousand Jews left the land to which they had given its first and its last troubadour. The irony of fate directed that at the selfsame time Christopher Columbus should embark for unknown lands, and eventually reach America, a new world, the refuge of all who suffer, wherein thought was destined to grow strong enough "to vanquish arrogance and injustice without recourse to arrogance and injustice"—a new illustration of the old verse: "Behold, he slumbereth not, and he sleepeth not—the keeper of Israel."

182 JEWISH TROUBADOURS AND MINNESINGERS

A great tournament at the court of the lords of Trimberg, the Franconian town on the Saale! From high battlements stream the pennons of the noble race, announcing rare festivities to all the country round. The mountain-side is astir with knights equipped with helmet, shield, and lance, and attended by pages and armor-bearers, minnesingers and minstrels. Yonder is Walther von der Vogelweide, engaged in earnest conversation with Wolfram von Eschenbach, Otto von Botenlaube, Hildebold von Schwanegau, and Reinmar von Brennenberg. In that group of notables, curiously enough, we discern a Jew, whose beautiful features reflect harmonious soul life.

"Süsskind von Trimberg," they call him, and when the pleasure of the feast in the lordly hall of the castle is to be heightened by song and music, he too steps forth, with fearlessness and dignity, to sing of freedom of thought, to the prevalence of which in this company the despised Jew owed his admission to a circle of knights and poets:[1]

> "O thought! free gift to humankind!
> By thee both fools and wise are led,
> But who thy paths hath all defined,
> A man he is in heart and head.
> With thee, his weakness being fled,
> He can both stone and steel command,
> Thy pinions bear him o'er the land.

[1] Livius Fürst in *Illustrirte Monatshefte für die gesammten Interessen des Judenthums*, Vol. I., p. 14 ff. Cmp. also, Hagen, *Minnesänger*, Vol. II., p. 258, Vol. IV., p. 536 ff., and W. Goldbaum, *Entlegene Culturen*, p. 275 *ff.*

> O thought that swifter art than light,
>   That mightier art than tempest's roar!
> Didst thou not raise me in thy flight,
>   What were my song, my minstrel lore,
>   And what the gold from *Minne's* store?
> Beyond the heights an eagle vaunts,
> O bear me to the spirit's haunts!"

His song meets with the approval of the knights, who give generous encouragement to the minstrel. Raising his eyes to the proud, beautiful mistress of the castle, he again strikes his lyre and sings:

> "Pure woman is to man a crown,
>   For her he strives to win renown.
> Did she not grace and animate,
> How mean and low the castle great!
> By true companionship, the wife
> Makes blithe and free a man's whole life;
> Her light turns bright the darkest day.
> Her praise and worth I'll sing alway."

The lady inclines her fair head in token of thanks, and the lord of castle Trimberg fills the golden goblet, and hands it, the mark of honor, to the poet, who drains it, and then modestly steps back into the circle of his compeers. Now we have leisure to examine the rare man.—

Rüdiger Manesse, a town councillor of Zürich in the fourteenth century, raised a beautiful monument to bardic art in a manuscript work, executed at his order, containing the songs of one hundred and forty poets, living between the twelfth and the fourteenth century. Among the authors are kings, princes, noblemen of high rank and low, burgher-poets, and the Jew Süsskind von Trimberg. Each poet's productions are accompanied by illustrations, not authentic portraits, but a series of vivid representations of scenes of knight-errantry. There are scenes of war and peace, of combats, the chase, and tourneys with games, songs, and dance. We see the storming of a castle of Love (*Minneburg*)—lovers fleeing, lovers separated, love triumphant. Heinrich von Veldeke reclines upon a bank of roses; Friedrich von Hausen is on board a boat; Walther von der Vogelweide sits musing on a wayside stone; Wolfram von Eschenbach stands armed, with visor closed, next to his caparisoned horse, as though about to mount. Among the portraits of the knights and bards is Süsskind von Trimberg's. How does Rüdiger Manesse represent him? As a long-bearded Jew, on his head a yellow, funnel-shaped hat, the badge of distinction decreed by Pope Innocent III. to be worn by Jews. That is all! and save what we may infer from his six poems preserved by the history of literature, pretty much all, too, known of Süsskind von Trimberg.

Was it the heedlessness of the compiler that associated the Jew with this merry company, in which he was as much out of place as a Gothic spire on a synagogue? Süsskind came by the privilege fairly. Throughout the middle ages the Jews of Germany were permeated with the culture of their native land, and were keenly concerned in the development of its poetry. A still more important cir-

JEWISH TROUBADOURS AND MINNESINGERS 185

cumstance is the spirit of tolerance and humanity that pervades Middle High German poetry. Wolfram von Eschenbach based his *Parzival,* the herald of "Nathan the Wise," on the idea of the brotherhood of man; Walther von der Vogelweide ranged Christians, Jews, and Mohammedans together as children of the one God; and Freidank, reflecting that God lets His sun shine on the confessors of all creeds, went so far as to repudiate the doctrine of the eternal damnation of Jews. This trend of thought, characterizing both Jews and Christians, suffices to explain how, in Germany, and at the very time in which the teachers of the Church were reviling "the mad Jews, who ought to be hewn down like dogs," it was possible for a Jew to be a minnesinger, a minstrel among minstrels, and abundantly accounts for Süsskind von Trimberg's association with knights and ladies. Süsskind, then, doubtless journeyed with his brother-poets from castle to castle; yet our imagination would be leading us astray, were we to accept literally the words of the enthusiastic historian Graetz, and with him believe that "on vine-clad hills, seated in the circle of noble knights and fair dames, a beaker of wine at his side, his lyre in his hand, he sang his polished verses of love's joys and trials, love's hopes and fears, and then awaited the largesses that bought his daily bread."[1]

Süsskind's poems are not at all like the joyous, rollicking songs his mates carolled forth; they are sad and serious, tender and chaste. Of love there is

[1] Graetz, *Geschichte der Juden*, Vol. VI., p. 257.

not a word. A minnesinger and a Jew—irreconcilable opposites! A minnesinger must be a knight wooing his lady-love, whose colors he wears at the tournaments, and for whose sake he undertakes a pilgrimage to the Holy Land. The Jew's minstrelsy is a lament for Zion.

In fact what is *Minne*—this service of love? Is it not at bottom the cult of the Virgin Mary? Is it not, in a subtle, mysterious way, a phase of Christianity itself? How could it have appealed to the Jew Süsskind? True, the Jews, too, have an ideal of love in the "Song of Songs": "Lo, thou art beautiful, my beloved!" it says, but our old sages took the beloved to be the Synagogue. Of this love Princess Sabbath is the ideal, and the passion of the "Song of Songs" is separated from German *Minne* by the great gap between the soul life of the Semite and that of the Christian German. Unbridled sensuousness surges through the songs rising to the chambers of noble ladies. Kabbalistic passion glows in the mysterious love of the Jew. The German minstrel sings of love's sweetness and pain, of summer and its delights, of winter and its woes, now of joy and happiness, again of ill-starred fortunes. And what is the burden of the exiled Hebrew's song? Mysterious allusions, hidden in a tangle of highly polished, artificial, slow-moving rhymes, glorify, not a sweet womanly presence, but a fleeting vision, a shadow, whose elusive charms infatuated the poet in his dreams. Bright, joyous, blithe, unmeasured is the one; serious, gloomy, chaste, gentle, the other.

Yet, Süsskind von Trimberg was at once a Jew and a minnesinger. Who can fathom a poet's soul? Who can follow his thoughts as they fly hither and thither, like the thread in a weaver's shuttle, fashioning themselves into a golden web? The minnesingers enlisted in love's cause, yet none the less in war and the defense of truth, and for the last Süsskind von Trimberg did valiant service. The poems of his earliest period, the blithesome days of youth, have not survived. Those that we have bear the stamp of sorrow and trouble, the gifts of advanced years. With self-contemptuous bitterness, he bewails his sad lot:

> "I seek and nothing find,—
> That makes me sigh and sigh.
> Lord Lackfood presses me,
> Of hunger sure I'll die;
> My wife, my child go supperless,
> My butler is Sir Meagreness."

Süsskind von Trimberg's poems also breathe the spirit of Hebrew literature, and have drawn material from the legend world of the Haggada. For the praise of his faithful wife he borrows the words of Solomon, and the psalm-like rhythm of his best songs recalls the familiar strains of our evening-prayer:

> "Almighty God! That shinest with the sun,
> That slumb'rest not when day grows into night!
> Thou Source of all, of tranquil peace and joy!
> Thou King of glory and majestic light!

> Thou allgood Father! Golden rays of day
> And starry hosts thy praise to sing unite,
> Creator of heav'n and earth, Eternal One,
> That watchest ev'ry creature from Thy height!"

Like Santob, Süsskind was poor; like him, he denounced the rich, was proud and generous. With intrepid candor, he taught knights the meaning of true nobility—of the nobility of soul transcending nobility of birth—and of freedom of thought—freedom fettered by neither stone, nor steel, nor iron; and in the midst of their rioting and feasting, he ventured to put before them the solemn thought of death. His last production as a minnesinger was a prescription for a "virtue-electuary." Then he went to dwell among his brethren, whom, indeed, he had not deserted in the pride of his youth:

> "Why should I wander sadly,
>   My harp within my hand,
> O'er mountain, hill, and valley?
>   What praise do I command?
>
> Full well they know the singer
>   Belongs to race accursed;
> Sweet *Minne* doth no longer
>   Reward me as at first.
>
> Be silent, then, my lyre,
>   We sing 'fore lords in vain.
> I'll leave the minstrels' choir,
>   And roam a Jew again.
>
> My staff and hat I'll grasp, then,
>   And on my breast full low,
> By Jewish custom olden
>   My grizzled beard shall grow.

> My days I'll pass in quiet,—
> Those left to me on earth—
> Nor sing for those who not yet
> Have learned a poet's worth."

Thus spake the Jewish poet, and dropped his lyre into the stream—in song and in life, a worthy son of his time, the disciple of Walther von der Vogelweide, the friend of Wolfram von Eschenbach—disciple and friend of the first to give utterance, in German song, to the idea of the brotherhood of man. Centuries ago, he found the longed-for quiet in Franconia, but no wreath lies on his grave, no stone marks the wanderer's resting-place. His poems have found an abiding home in the memory of posterity, and in the circle of the German minnesingers the Jew Süsskind forms a distinct link.

In a time when the idea of universal human brotherhood seems to be fading from the hearts of men, when they manifest a proneness to forget the share which, despite hatred and persecution, the Jew of every generation has had in German literature, in its romances of chivalry and its national epics, and in all the spiritual achievements of German genius, we may with just pride revive Süsskind's memory.—

On the wings of fancy let us return to our castle on the Saale. After the lapse of many years, the procession of poets again wends its way in the sunshine up the slope to the proud mansion of the Trimbergs. The venerable Walther von der Vogelweide again opens the festival of song. Wolfram von Eschenbach, followed by a band of young disciples, musingly ascends the mountain-side. The ranks grow less serried, and in solitude and sadness, advances a man of noble form, his silvery beard flowing down upon his breast, a long cloak over his shoulder, and the peaked hat, the badge of the mediæval Jew, on his head. In his eye gleams a ray of the poet's grace, and his meditative glance looks into a distant future. Süsskind von Trimberg, to thee our greeting!

HUMOR AND LOVE IN JEWISH POETRY

One of the most remarkable discoveries of the last ten years is that made in Paris by M. Ernest Renan. He maintains as the result of scientific research that the Semitic races, consequently also the Jews, are lacking in humor, in the capacity for laughter. The justice of the reproach might be denied outright, but a statement enunciated with so much scientific assurance involuntarily prompts questioning and investigation.

In such cases the Jews invariably resort to their first text-book, the Bible, whose pages seem to sustain M. Renan. In the Bible laughing is mentioned only twice, when the angel promises a son to Sarah, and again in the history of Samson, judge in Israel, who used foxes' tails as weapons against the Philistines. These are the only passages in which the Bible departs from its serious tone.

But classical antiquity was equally ignorant of humor as a distinct branch of art, as a peculiar attitude of the mind towards the problems of life. Aristophanes lived and could have written only in the days when Athenian institutions began to decay. It is personal discomfort and the trials and harassments of life that drive men to the ever serene, pure regions of humor for balm and healing. Fun and comedy men have at all times understood—the history of Samson contains the germs of a mock-heroic poem—while it was impossible for humor, genuine humor, to find appreciation in the youth of mankind.

In those days of healthy reliance upon the senses, poetic spirits could obtain satisfaction only in love and in the praise of the good world and its Maker. The sombre line of division had not yet been introduced between the physical and the spiritual world, debasing this earth to a vale of tears, and consoling sinful man by the promise of a better land, whose manifold delights were described, but about which there was no precise knowledge, no traveller, as the Talmud aptly puts it, having ever returned to give us information about it. Those were the days of perfect harmony, when man crept close to nature to be taught untroubled joy in living. In such days, despite the storms assailing the young Israelitish nation, a poet, his heart filled with the sunshine of joy, his mind receptive, his eyes open wide to see the flowers unfold, the buds of the fig tree swell, the vine put forth leaves, and the pomegranate blossom unfurl its glowing petals, could carol forth the "Song of Songs," the most perfect, the most beautiful, the purest creation of Hebrew literature and the erotic poetry of all literatures—the song of songs of stormy passion, bidding defiance to ecclesiastical fetters, at once an epic and a drama, full of childlike tenderness and grace of feeling. Neither Greece, nor the rest of the Orient has produced anything to compare with its marvellous union of voluptuous sensuousness and immaculate chastity. Morality, indeed, is its very pulse-beat. It could be sung only in an age when love reigned supreme, and could presume to treat humor as a pretender. So lofty a song was bound to awaken echoes and stimulate imitation, and its music has flowed down through the centuries, weaving a thread of melody about the heart of many a poet.

The centuries of Israelitish history close upon its composition, however, were favorable to neither the poetry of love nor that of humor. But the poetry of love must have continued to exercise puissant magic over hearts and minds, if its supreme poem not only was made part of the holy canon, but was considered by a teacher of the Talmud the most sacred treasure of the compilation.

The blood of the Maccabean heroes victorious over Antiochus Epiphanes again fructified the old soil of Hebrew poetry, and charmed forth fragrant blossoms, the psalms designated as Maccabean by modern criticism. Written in troublous times, they contain a reference to the humor of the future: "When the Lord bringeth back again the captivity of Zion, then shall we be like dreamers, then shall our mouth be filled with laughter, and our tongue with singing."

Many sad days were destined to pass over Israel before that future with its solacement of humor dawned. No poetic work could obtain recognition next to the Bible. The language of the prophets ceased to be the language of the people, and every mind was occupied with interpreting their words and applying them to the religious needs of the hour. The opposition between Jewish and Hellenic-Syrian views became more and more marked. Hellas and Judæa, the two great theories of life supporting the fabric of civilization, for the first time confronted each other. An ancient expounder of the Bible says that to Hellas God gave beauty in the beginning, to Judæa truth, as a sacred heritage. But beauty and truth have ever been inveterate foes; even now they are not reconciled.

In Judæa and Greece, ancient civilization found equally perfect, yet totally different, expression. The Greek worships nature as she is; the Jew dwells upon the origin and development of created things, hence worships their Creator. The former in his speculations proceeds from the multiplicity of phenomena; the latter discerns the unity of the plan. To the former the universe was changeless actuality; to the latter it meant unending development. The world, complete and perfect, was mirrored in the Greek mind; its evolution, in the Jewish. Therefore the Jewish conception of life is harmonious, while among the Greeks grew up the spirit of doubt and speculation, the product of civilization, and the soil upon which humor disports.

Israel's religion so completely satisfied every spiritual craving that no room was left for the growth of the poetic instinct. Intellectual life began to divide into two great streams. The Halacha continued the instruction of the prophets, as the Haggada fostered the spirit of the psalmists. The province of the former was to formulate the Law, of the latter to plant a garden about the bulwark of the Law. While the one addressed itself to reason, the other made an appeal to the heart and the feelings. In the Haggada, a thesaurus of the national poetry by the nameless poets of many centuries, we find epic poems and lyric outbursts, fables, enigmas, and dramatic essays, and here and there in this garden we chance across a little bud of humorous composition.

Of what sort was this humor? In point of fact, what is humor? We must be able to answer the latter question before we may venture to classify the folklore of the Haggada.

To reach the ideal, to bring harmony out of discord, is the recognized task of all art. This is the primary principle to be borne in mind in æsthetic criticism. Tragedy idealizes the world by annihilation, harmonizes all contradictions by dashing them in pieces against each other, and points the way of escape from chaos, across the bridge of death, to the realm beyond, irradiated by the perpetual morning-dawn of freedom and intellect.

Comedy, on the other hand, believes that the incongruities and imperfections of life can be justified, and have their uses. Firmly convinced of the might of truth, it holds that the folly and aberrations of men, their shortcomings and failings, cannot impede its eventual victory. Even in them it sees traces of an eternal, divine principle. While tragedy precipitates the conflict of hostile forces, comedy, rising serene above folly and all indications of transitoriness, reconciles inconsistencies, and lovingly coaxes them into harmony with the true and the absolute.

When man's spirit is thus made to re-enter upon the enjoyment of eternal truth, its heritage, there is, as some one has well said, triumph akin to the joy of the father over the home-coming of a lost son, and the divine, refreshing laughter by which it is greeted is like the meal prepared for the returning favorite. Is Israel to have no seat at the table? Israel, the first to recognize that the eternal truths of life are innate in man, the first to teach, as his chief message, how to reconcile man with himself and the world, whenever these truths suffer temporary obscuration? So viewed, humor is the offspring of love, and also mankind's redeemer, inasmuch as it paralyzes the influence of anger and hatred, emanations from the powers of change and finality, by laying bare the eternal principles and "sweet reasonableness" hidden even in them, and finally stripping them of every adjunct incompatible with the serenity of absolute truth. In whatever mind humor, that is, love and cheerfulness, reigns supreme, the inconsistencies and imperfections of life, all that bears the impress of mutability, will gently and gradually be fused into the harmonious perfection of absolute, eternal truth. Mists sometimes gather about the sun, but unable to extinguish his light, they are forced to serve as his mirror, on which he throws the witching charms of the Fata Morgana. So, when the eternal truths of life are veiled, opportunity is made for humor to play upon and irradiate them. In precise language, humor is a state of perfect self-certainty, in which the mind serenely rises superior to every petty disturbance.

This placidity shed its soft light into the modest academies of the rabbis. Wherever a ray fell, a blossom of Haggadic folklore sprang up. Every occurrence in life recommends itself to their loving scrutiny: pleasures and follies of men, curse turned into blessing, the ordinary course of human events, curiosities of Israel's history and mankind's. As instances of their method, take what Midrashic folk-lore has to say concerning the creation of the two things of perennial interest to poets: wife and wine.

When the Lord God created woman, he formed her not from the head of man, lest she be too proud; not from his eye, lest she be too coquettish; not from his ear, lest she be too curious; not from his mouth, lest she be too talkative; not from his heart, lest she be too sentimental; not from his hands, lest she be too officious; nor from his feet, lest she be an idle gadabout; but from a subordinate part of man's anatomy, to teach her: "Woman, be thou modest!"

With regard to the vine, the Haggada tells us that when Father Noah was about to plant the first one, Satan stepped up to him, leading a lamb, a lion, a pig, and an ape, to teach him that so long as man does not drink wine, he is innocent as a lamb;

if he drinks temperately, he is as strong as a lion; if he indulges too freely, he sinks to the level of swine; and as for the ape, his place in the poetry of wine is as well known to us as to the rabbis of old.

With the approach of the great catastrophe destined to annihilate Israel's national existence, humor and spontaneity vanish, to be superseded by seriousness, melancholy, and bitter plaints, and the centuries of despondency and brooding that followed it were not better calculated to encourage the expression of love and humor. The pall was not lifted until the Haggada performed its mission as a comforter. Under its gentle ministrations, and urged into vitality by the religious needs of the synagogue, the poetic instinct awoke. *Piut* and *Selicha* replaced prophecy and psalmody as religious agents, and thenceforth the springs of consolation were never permitted to run dry. Driven from the shores of the Jordan and the Euphrates, Hebrew poetry found a new home on the Tagus and the Manzanares, where the Jews were blessed with a second golden age. In the interval from the eleventh to the thirteenth century, under genial Arabic influences, Andalusian masters of song built up an ideal world of poetry, wherein love and humor were granted untrammelled liberty.

To the Spanish-Jewish writers poetry was an end in itself. Along with religious songs, perfect in rhythm and form, they produced lyrics on secular subjects, whose grace, beauty, harmony, and wealth of thought rank them with the finest creations of the age. The spirit of the prophets and psalmists revived in these Spanish poets. At their head stands Solomon ibn Gabirol, the Faust of Saragossa, whose poems are the first tinged with *Weltschmerz*, that peculiar ferment characteristic of a modern school of poets.[1] Our accounts of Gabirol's life are meagre, but they leave the clear impression that he was not a favorite of fortune, and passed a bleak childhood and youth. His poems are pervaded by vain longing for the ideal, by lamentations over deceived hopes and unfulfilled aspirations, by painful realization of the imperfection and perishability of all earthly things, and the insignificance and transitoriness of life, in a word, by *Weltschmerz*, in its purest, ideal form, not merely self-deception and irony turned against one's own soul life, but a profoundly solemn emotion, springing from sublime pity for the misery of the world read by the light of personal trials and sorrows. He sang not of a mistress' blue eyes, nor sighed forth melancholy love-notes—the object of his heart's desire was Zion, his muse the fair "rose of Sharon," and his anguish was for the suffering of his scattered people. Strong, wild words fitly express his tempestuous feelings. He is a proud, solitary thinker. Often his *Weltschmerz* wrests scornful criticism of his surroundings from him. On the other hand, he does not lack mild, conciliatory humor, of which his famous drinking-song is a good illustration. His miserly host had

[1] For Gabirol, cmp. A. Geiger, *Salomon Gabirol*, and M. Sachs, *Die religiöse Poesie der Juden in Spanien.*

put a single bottle of wine upon a table surrounded by many guests, who had to have recourse to water to quench their thirst. Wine he calls a septuagenarian, the letters of the Hebrew word for wine (*yayin*) representing seventy, and water a nonagenarian, because *mayim* (water) represents ninety:

WATER SONG

CHORUS:—Of wine, alas! there's not a drop,
  Our host has filled our goblets to the top
    With water.

When monarch wine lies prone,
By water overthrown,
How can a merry song be sung?
For naught there is to wet our tongue
  But water.
    CHORUS:—Of wine, alas! etc.

No sweetmeats can delight
My dainty appetite,
For I, alas! must learn to drink,
However I may writhe and shrink,
  Pure water.
    CHORUS:—Of wine, alas! etc.

Give Moses praise, for he
Made waterless a sea—
Mine host to quench my thirst—the churl!—
Makes streams of clearest water purl,
  Of water.
    CHORUS:—Of wine, alas! etc.

To toads I feel allied,
To frogs by kinship tied;
For water drinking is no joke,
Ere long you all will hear me croak
  Quack water!
    CHORUS:—Of wine, alas! etc.

> May God our host requite;
> May he turn Nazirite,
> Ne'er know intoxication's thrill,
> Nor e'er succeed his thirst to still
> With water!
> CHORUS:—Of wine, alas! etc."

Gabirol was a bold thinker, a great poet wrestling with the deepest problems of human thought, and towering far above his contemporaries and immediate successors. In his time synagogue poetry reached the zenith of perfection, and even in the solemn admonitions of ritualistic literature, humor now and again asserted itself. One of Gabirol's contemporaries or successors, Isaac ben Yehuda ibn Ghayyat, for instance, often made his whole poem turn upon a witticism.

Among the writers of that age, a peculiar style called "mosaic" gradually grew up, and eventually became characteristic of neo-Hebraic poetry and humor. For their subjects and the presentation of their thoughts, they habitually made use of biblical phraseology, either as direct quotations or with an application not intended by the original context. In the latter case, well-known sentences were invested with new meanings, and this poetic-biblical phraseology afforded countless opportunities for the exercise of humor, of which neo-Hebraic poetry availed itself freely. The "mosaics" were collected not only from the Bible; the Targum, the Mishna, and the Talmud were rifled of sententious expressions, woven together, and with the license of art placed in unexpected juxtaposition. An example will make clear the method. In Genesis xviii. 29, God answers Abraham's petition in behalf of Sodom with the words: " I will not do it for the sake of forty," meaning, as everybody knows, that forty men would suffice to save the city from destruction. This passage Isaac ben Yehuda ibn Ghayyat audaciously connects with Deuteronomy xxv. 3, where forty is also mentioned, the forty stripes for misdemeanors of various kinds:

> "If you see men the path of right forsake,
>   To bring them back you must an effort make.
>   Perhaps, if they but hear of stripes, they'll quake,
>   And say, 'I'll do it not for forty's sake.'"

This " mosaic " style, suggesting startling contrasts and surprising applications of Bible thoughts and words, became a fruitful source of Jewish humor. If a theory of literary descent could be established, an illustration might be found in Heine's rapid transitions from tender sentiment to corroding wit, a modern development of the flashing humor of the " mosaic " style.

The " Song of Songs " naturally became a treasure-house of " mosaic " suggestions for the purposes of neo-Hebraic love poetry, which was dominated, however, by Arab influences. The first poet to introduce the sorrow of unhappy love into neo-Hebraic poetry was Moses ibn Ezra. He was in love with his niece, who probably became the wife of one of his brothers, and died early on giving birth to a son. His affection at first was requited, but his brothers opposed the union, and the poet left Spain, embittered and out of sorts with fate, to find peace and consolation in distant lands. Many of his poems are deeply tinged with gloom and pessimism, and the natural inference is that those in which he praises nature, and wine, and "bacchanalian feasts under leafy canopies with merry minstrelsy of birds" belong to the period of his life preceding its unfortunate turning-point, when love still smiled upon him, and hope was strong.

Some of his poems may serve as typical specimens of the love-poetry of those days:

> "With hopeless love my heart is sick,
>   Confession bursts my lips' restraint.
> That thou, my love, dost cast me off,
>   Hath touched me with a death-like taint.
>
> I view the land both near and far,
>   To me it seems a prison vast.
> Throughout its breadth, where'er I look,
>   My eyes are met by doors locked fast.
>
> And though the world stood open wide,
>   Though angel hosts filled ev'ry space,
> To me 'twere destitute of charm
>   Didst thou withdraw thy face."

Here is another:

> "Perchance in days to come,
>   When men and all things change,
> They'll marvel at my love,
>   And call it passing strange.

> Without I seem most calm,
>   But fires rage within—
> 'Gainst me, as none before,
>   Thou didst a grievous sin.
>
> What! tell the world my woe!
>   That were exceeding vain.
> With mocking smile they'd say,
>   'You know, he is not sane!'"

When his lady-love died, he composed the following elegy:

> "In pain she bore the son who her embrace
>   Would never know. Relentless death spread straight
> His nets for her, and she, scarce animate,
> Unto her husband signed: I ask this grace,
> My friend; let not harsh death our love efface;
>   To our babes, its pledges, dedicate
>   Thy faithful care; for vainly they await
> A mother's smile each childish fear to chase.
> And to my uncle, prithee, write. Deep pain
>   I brought his heart. Consumed by love's regret
> He roved, a stranger in his home. I fain
>   Would have him shed a tear, nor love forget.
> He seeketh consolation's cup, but first
> His soul with bitterness must quench its thirst."

Moses ibn Ezra's cup of consolation on not a few occasions seems to have been filled to overflowing with wine. In no other way can the joyousness of his drinking-songs be accounted for. The following are characteristic:

> "Wine cooleth man in summer's heat,
> And warmeth him in winter's sleet.
> My buckler 'tis 'gainst chilling frost,
> My shield when rays of sun exhaust."

> "If men will probe their inmost heart,
>   They must condemn their crafty art:
> For silver pieces they make bold
>   To ask a drink of liquid gold."

To his mistress, naturally, many a stanza of witty praise and coaxing imagery was devoted:

> "My love is like a myrtle tree,
>   When at the dance her hair falls down.
> Her eyes deal death most pitiless,
>   Yet who would dare on her to frown?"

> "Said I to sweetheart: 'Why dost thou resent
>   The homage to thy grace by old men paid?'
> She answered me with question pertinent:
>   'Dost thou prefer a widow to a maid?'"

To his love-poems and drinking-songs must be added his poems of friendship, on true friends, life's crowning gift, and false friends, basest of creatures. He has justly been described as the most subjective of neo-Hebraic poets. His blithe delight in love, exhaling from his poems, transfigured his ready humor, which instinctively pierced to the ludicrous element in every object and occurrence: age dyeing its hair, traitorous friendship, the pride of wealth, or separation of lovers.

Yet in the history of synagogue literature this poet goes by the name *Ha-Sallach*, "penitential poet," on account of his many religious songs, bewailing in elegiac measure the hollowness of life, and the vanity of earthly possessions, and in ardent words advocating humility, repentance, and a contrite heart. The peculiarity of Jewish humor is that it returns to its tragic source.

No mediæval poet so markedly illustrates this characteristic as the prince of neo-Hebraic poetry, Yehuda Halevi, in whose poems the principle of Jewish national poesy attained its completest expression. They are the idealized reflex of the soul of the Jewish people, its poetic emotions, its "making for righteousness," its patriotic love of race, its capacity for martyrdom. Whatever true and beautiful element had developed in Jewish soul life, since the day when Judah's song first rang out in Zion's accents on Spanish soil, greets us in its noblest garb in his poetry. A modern poet[1] says of him:

> "Ay, he was a master singer,
> Brilliant pole star of his age,
> Light and beacon to his people!
> Wondrous mighty was his singing—
>
> Verily a fiery pillar
> Moving on 'fore Israel's legions,
> Restless caravan of sorrow,
> Through the exile's desert plain."

In his early youth the muse of poetry had imprinted a kiss upon Halevi's brow, and the gracious echo of that kiss trembles through all the poet's numbers. Love, too, seems early to have taken up an abode in his susceptible heart, but, as expressed in the poems of his youth, it is not sensuous, earthly love, nor Gabirol's despondency and unselfish grief,

[1] H. Heine, *Romanzero*.

nor even the sentiment of Moses ibn Ezra's artistically conceived and technically perfect love-plaint. It is tender, yet passionate, frankly extolling the happiness of requited love, and as naïvely miserable over separation from his mistress, whom he calls Ophra (fawn). One of his sweetest songs he puts upon her lips:

> "Into my eyes he loving looked,
>   My arms about his neck were twined,
> And in the mirror of my eyes,
>   What but his image did he find?
>
> Upon my dark-hued eyes he pressed
>   His lips with breath of passion rare.
> The rogue! 'Twas not my eyes he kissed;
>   He kissed his picture mirrored there."

Ophra's "Song of Joy" reminds one of the passion of the "Song of Songs":

> "He cometh, O bliss!
> Fly swiftly, ye winds,
> Ye odorous breezes,
> And tell him how long
> I've waited for this!
>
> O happy that night,
> When sunk on thy breast,
> Thy kisses fast falling,
> And drunken with love,
> My troth I did plight.
>
> Again my sweet friend
> Embraceth me close.
> Yes, heaven doth bless us,
> And now thou hast won
> My love without end."

His mistress' charms he describes with attractive grace:

> "My sweetheart's dainty lips are red,
> With ruby's crimson overspread;
> Her teeth are like a string of pearls;
> Adown her neck her clust'ring curls
> In ebon hue vie with the night;
> And o'er her features dances light.
>
> The twinkling stars enthroned above
> Are sisters to my dearest love.
> We men should count it joy complete
> To lay our service at her feet.
> But ah! what rapture in her kiss!
> A forecast 'tis of heav'nly bliss!"

When the hour of parting from Ophra came, the young poet sang:

> "And so we twain must part! Oh linger yet,
> Let me still feed my glance upon thine eyes.
> Forget not, love, the days of our delight,
> And I our nights of bliss shall ever prize.
> In dreams thy shadowy image I shall see,
> Oh even in my dream be kind to me!"[1]

Yehuda Halevi sang not only of love, but also, in true Oriental fashion, and under the influence of his Arabic models, of wine and friendship. On the other hand, he is entirely original in his epithalamiums, charming descriptions of the felicity of young conjugal life and the sweet blessings of pure love. They are pervaded by the intensity of joy,

---

[1] Translation by Emma Lazarus. [Tr.]

and full of roguish allusions to the young wife's shamefacedness, arousing the jest and merriment of her guests, and her delicate shrinking in the presence of longed-for happiness. Characteristically enough his admonitions to feed the fire of love are always followed by a sigh for his people's woes:

> "You twain will soon be one,
>   And all your longing filled.
>   Ah me! will Israel's hope
>   For freedom e'er be stilled?"

It is altogether probable that these blithesome songs belong to the poet's early life. To a friend who remonstrates with him for his love of wine he replies:

> "My years scarce number twenty-one—
>   Wouldst have me now the wine-cup shun?"

which would seem to indicate that love and wine were the pursuits of his youth. One of his prettiest drinking songs is the following:

> "My bowl yields exultation—
>   I soar aloft on song-tipped wing,
>   Each draught is inspiration,
>   My lips sip wine, my mouth must sing.
>
> Dear friends are full of horror,
>   Predict a toper's end for me.
>   They ask: 'How long, O sorrow,
>   Wilt thou remain wine's devotee?'
>
> Why should I not sing praise of drinking?
>   The joys of Eden it makes mine.
>   If age will bring no cowardly shrinking,
>   Full many a year will I drink wine."

But little is known of the events of the poet's career. History's niggardliness, however, has been compensated for by the prodigality of legend, which has woven many a fanciful tale about his life. Of one fact we are certain: when he had passed his fiftieth year, Yehuda Halevi left his native town, his home, his family, his friends, and disciples, to make a pilgrimage to Palestine, the land wherein his heart had always dwelt. His itinerary can be traced in his songs. They lead us to Egypt, to Zoan, to Damascus. In Tyre silence suddenly falls upon the singer. Did he attain the goal he had set out to reach? Did his eye behold the land of his fathers? Or did death overtake the pilgrim singer before his journey's end? Legend which has beautified his life has transfigured his death. It is said, that struck by a Saracen's horse Yehuda Halevi sank down before the very gates of Jerusalem. With its towers and battlements in sight, and his inspired "Lay of Zion" on his lips, his pure soul winged its flight heavenward.

With the death of Yehuda Halevi, the golden age of neo-Hebraic poetry in Spain came to an end, and the period of the epigones was inaugurated. A note of hesitancy is discernible in their productions, and they acknowledge the superiority of their predecessors in the epithet "fathers of song" applied to them. The most noted of the later writers was Yehuda ben Solomon Charisi. Fortune marked him out to be the critic of the great poetic creations of the brilliant epoch just closed, and his fame rests upon the skill with which he acquitted himself of his difficult task. As for his poetry, it lacks the depth, the glow, the virility, and inspiration of the works of the classical period. He was a restless wanderer, a poet tramp, roving in the Orient, in Africa, and in Europe. His most important work is his divan *Tachkemoni*, testifying to his powers as a humorist, and especially to his mastery of the Hebrew language, which he uses with dexterity never excelled. The divan touches upon every possible subject: God and nature, human life and suffering, the relations between men, his personal experiences, and his adventures in foreign parts. The first Makamat[1] writer among Jews, he furnished the model for all poems of the kind that followed; their first genuine humorist, he flashes forth his wit like a stream of light suddenly turned on in the dark. That he measured the worth of his productions by the generous meed of praise given by his contemporaries is a venial offense in the time of the troubadours and minnesingers. Charisi was particularly happy in his use of the "mosaic" style, and his short poems and epigrams are most charming. Deep melancholy is a foil to his humor, but as often his writings are disfigured by levity. The following may serve as samples of his versatile muse. The first is addressed to his grey hair:

> "Those ravens black that rested
>   Erstwhile upon my head,
> Within my heart have nested,
>   Since from my hair they fled."

[1] See note, p. 34. [Tr.]

The second is inscribed to love's tears:

> "Within my heart I held concealed
>   My love so tender and so true;
> But overflowing tears revealed
>   What I would fain have hid from view.
> My heart could evermore repress
> The woe that tell-tale tears confess."

Charisi is at his best when he gives the rein to his humor. Sparks fly; he stops at no caustic witticism, recoils from no satire; he is malice itself, and puts no restraint upon his levity. The "Flea Song" is a typical illustration of his impish mood:

> "You ruthless flea, who desecrate my couch,
>   And draw my blood to sate your appetite,
> You know not rest, on Sabbath day or feast—
>   Your feast it is when you can pinch and bite.
>
> My friends expound the law: to kill a flea
>   Upon the Sabbath day a sin they call;
> But I prefer that other law which says,
>   Be sure a murd'rer's malice to forestall."

That Charisi was a boon companion is evident from the following drinking song:

> "Here under leafy bowers,
>   Where coolest shades descend,
> Crowned with a wreath of flowers,
>   Here will we drink, my friend.
>
> Who drinks of wine, he learns
>   That noble spirits' strength
> But steady increase earns,
>   As years stretch out in length.

A thousand earthly years
　Are hours in God's sight,
A year in heav'n appears
　A minute in its flight.

I would this lot were mine:
　To live by heav'nly count,
And drink and drink old wine
　At youth's eternal fount."

Charisi and his Arabic models found many imitators among Spanish Jews. Solomon ibn Sakbel wrote Hebrew Makamat which may be regarded as an attempt at a satire in the form of a romance. The hero, Asher ben Yehuda, a veritable Don Juan, passes through most remarkable adventures.[1] The introductory Makama, describing life with his mistress in the solitude of a forest, is delicious. Tired of his monotonous life, he joins a company of convivial fellows, who pass their time in carousal. While with them, he receives an enigmatic love letter signed by an unknown woman, and he sets out to find her. On his wanderings, oppressed by love's doubts, he chances into a harem, and is threatened with death by its master. It turns out that the pasha is a beautiful woman, the slave of his mysterious lady-love, and she promises him speedy fulfilment of his wishes. Finally, close to the attainment of his end, he discovers that his beauty is a myth, the whole a practical joke perpetrated by his merry companions. So Asher ben Yehuda in quest of his mistress is led from adventure to adventure.

[1] J. Schor in *He-Chaluz*, Vol. IV., p. 154 *ff.*

Internal evidence testifies against the genuineness of this romance, but at the same time with it appeared two other mock-heroic poems, "The Book of Diversions" (*Sefer Sha'ashuim*) by Joseph ibn Sabara, and "The Gift of Judah the Misogynist" (*Minchath Yehuda Soneh ha-Nashim*) by Judah ibn Sabbataï, a Cordova physician, whose poems Charisi praised as the "fount of poesy." The plot of his "Gift," a satire on women, is as follows:[1] His dying father exacts from Serach, the hero of the romance, a promise never to marry, women in his sight being the cause of all the evil in the world. Curious as the behest is, it is still more curious that Serach uncomplainingly complies, and most curious of all, that he finds three companions willing to retire with him to a distant island, whence their propaganda for celibacy is to proceed. Scarcely has the news of their arrival spread, when a mass meeting of women is called, and a coalition formed against the misogynists. Korbi, an old hag, engages to make Serach faithless to his principles. He soon has a falling out with his fellow-celibates, and succumbs to the fascinations of a fair young temptress. After the wedding he discovers that his enemies, the women, have substituted for his beautiful bride, a hideous old woman, Blackcoal, the daughter of Owl. She at once assumes the reins of government most energetically, and answers her husband's groan of despair by the following curtain lecture:

[1] S. Stein in *Freitagabend*, p. 645 *ff.*

"Up! up! the time for sleep is past!
And no resistance will I brook!
Away with thee, and look to it
That thou bringst me what I ask:
Gowns of costly stuff,
Earrings, chains, and veils;
A house with many windows;
Mortars, lounges, sieves,
Baskets, kettles, pots,
Glasses, settles, brooms,
Beakers, closets, flasks,
Shovels, basins, bowls,
Spindle, distaff, blankets,
Buckets, ewers, barrels,
Skillets, forks, and knives;
Vinaigrettes and mirrors;
Kerchiefs, turbans, reticules,
Crescents, amulets,
Rings and jewelled clasps;
Girdles, buckles, bodices,
Kirtles, caps, and waists;
Garments finely spun,
Rare byssus from the East.
This and more shalt thou procure,
No matter at what cost and sacrifice.
Thou art affrighted? Thou weepest?
My dear, spare all this agitation;
Thou'lt suffer more than this.
The first year shall pass in strife,
The second will see thee a beggar.
A prince erstwhile, thou shalt become a slave;
Instead of a crown, thou shalt wear a wreath of straw."

Serach in abject despair turns for comfort to his three friends, and it is decided to bring suit for divorce in a general assembly. The women appear at the meeting, and demand that the despiser of their sex be forced to keep his ugly wife. One of the trio of friends proposes that the matter be brought before the king. The poet appends no moral to his tale; he leaves it to his readers to say: "And such must be the fate of all woman-haters!"

Judah Sabbataï was evidently far from being a woman-hater himself, but some of his contemporaries failed to understand the point of his witticisms and ridiculous situations. Yedaya Penini, another poet, looked upon it as a serious production, and in his allegory, "Woman's Friend," destitute of poetic inspiration, but brilliant in dialectics, undertook the defense of the fair sex against the misanthropic aspersions of the woman-hater.

Such works are evidence that we have reached the age of the troubadours and minnesingers, the epoch of the Renaissance, when, under the blue sky of Italy, and the fostering care of the trio of masterpoets, Dante, Petrarch, and Boccaccio, the first germs of popular poetry were unfolding. The Italian Jews were carried along by the all-pervading spirit of the times, and had a share in the vigorous mental activity about them. Suggestions derived from the work of the Renaissance leaders fell like electric sparks into Jewish literature and science, lighting them up, and bringing them into rapport with the products of the humanistic movement. Provence, the land of song, gave birth to Kalonymos ben Kalonymos, later a resident of Italy, whose work, "Touchstone" (*Eben Bochan*) is the first true satire in neo-Hebraic poetry. It is a mirror of morals held up before his people, for high and low, rabbis and leaders, poets and scholars, rich and poor, to see their foibles and follies. The satire expresses a humorous, but lofty conception of life, based upon profound morality and sincere faith. It fulfils every requirement of a satire, steering clear of the pitfall caricature, and not obtruding the didactic element. The lesson to be conveyed is involved in, not stated apart from the satire, an emanation from the poet's disposition. His aim is not to ridicule, but to improve, instruct, influence. One of the most amusing chapters is that on woman's superior advantages, which make him bewail his having been born a man:[1]

"Truly, God's hand lies heavy on him
Who has been created a man:
Full many a trial he must patiently bear,
And scorn and contumely of every kind.
His life is like a field laid waste—
Fortunate he is if it lasts not too long!
Were I, for instance, a woman,
How smooth and pleasant were my course.
A circle of intimate friends
Would call me gentle, graceful, modest.
Comfortably I'd sit with them and sew,
With one or two mayhap at the spinning wheel.
On moonlight nights
Gathered for cozy confidences,
About the hearthfire, or in the dark,
We'd tell each other what the people say,
The gossip of the town, the scandals,

[1] H. A. Meisel, *Der Prüfstein des Kalonymos.*

Discuss the fashions and the last election.
I surely would rise above the average—
I would be an artist needlewoman,
Broidering on silk and velvet
The flowers of the field,
And other patterns, copied from models,
So rich in color as to make them seem nature—
Petals, trees, blossoms, plants, and pots,
And castles, pillars, temples, angel heads,
And whatever else can be imitated with needle by her
Who guides it with art and skill.
Sometimes, too, though 'tis not so attractive,
I should consent to play the cook—
No less important task of woman 'tis
To watch the kitchen most carefully.
I should not be ruffled
By dust and ashes on the hearth, by soot on stoves and pots;
Nor would I hesitate to swing the axe
And chop the firewood,
And not to feed and rake the fire up,
Despite the ashy dust that fills the nostrils.
My particular delight it would be
To taste of all the dishes served.
And if some merry, joyous festival approached,
Then would I display my taste.
I would choose most brilliant gems for ear and hand,
For neck and breast, for hair and gown,
Most precious stuffs of silk and velvet,
Whatever in clothes and jewels would increase my charms.
And on the festal day, I would loud rejoice,
Sing, and sway myself, and dance with vim.
When I reached a maiden's prime,
With all my charms at their height,
What happiness, were heaven to favor me,
Permit me to draw a prize in life's lottery,
A youth of handsome mien, brave and true,
With heart filled with love for me.

If he declared his passion,
I would return his love with all my might.
Then as his wife, I would live a princess,
Reclining on the softest pillows,
My beauty heightened by velvet, silk, and tulle,
By pearls and golden ornaments,
Which he with lavish love would bring to me,
To add to his delight and mine."

After enumerating additional advantages enjoyed by the gentler sex, the poet comes to the conclusion that protesting against fate is vain, and closes his chapter thus:

" Well, then, I'll resign myself to fate,
  And seek consolation in the thought that life comes to an end.
Our sages tell us everywhere
That for all things we must praise God,
With loud rejoicing for all good,
In submission for evil fortune.
So I will force my lips,
However they may resist, to say the olden blessing:
My Lord and God accept my thanks
That thou has made of me a man."

One of Kalonymos's friends was Immanuel ben Solomon of Rome, called the "Heine of the middle ages," and sometimes the "Jewish Voltaire." Neither comparison is apt. On the one hand, they give him too high a place as a writer, on the other, they do not adequately indicate his characteristic qualities. His most important work, the *Mechabberoth*, is a collection of disjointed pieces, full of bold witticisms, poetic thoughts, and linguistic charms. It is composed of poems, Makamat, parodies, novels, epigrams, distichs, and sonnets—all essentially humorous. The poet presents things as they are, leaving it to reality to create ridiculous situations. He is witty rather than humorous. Rarely only a spark of kindliness or the glow of poetry transfigures his wit. He is uniformly objective, scintillating, cold, often frivolous, and not always chaste. To produce a comic effect, to make his readers laugh is his sole desire. Friend and admirer of Dante, he attained to a high degree of skill in the sonnet. In neo-Hebraic poetry, his works mark the beginning of a new epoch. Indelicate witticisms and levity, until then sporadic in Jewish literature, were by him introduced as a regular feature. The poetry of the earlier writers had dwelt upon the power of love, their muse was modest and chaste, a "rose of Sharon," a "lily of the valleys." Immanuel's was of coarser fibre; his witty sallies remind one of Italian rather than Hebrew models. A recent critic of Hebrew poetry speaks of his Makamat as a pendant to "Tristan and Isolde,"—in both sensuality triumphs over spirituality. He is at his best in his sonnets, and of these the finest are in poetic prose. Female beauty is an unfailing source of inspiration to him, but of trust in womankind he has none:

> "No woman ever faithful hold,
> Unless she ugly be and old."

The full measure of mockery he poured out upon a deceived husband, and the most cutting sarcasm at his command against an enemy is a comparison to crabbed, ugly women:

> "I loathe him with the hot and honest hate
> That fills a rake 'gainst maids he cannot bait,
> With which an ugly hag her glass reviles,
> And prostitutes the youths who 'scape their wiles."

His devotion to woman's beauty is altogether in the spirit of his Italian contemporaries. One of his most pleasing sonnets is dedicated to his lady-love's eyes:[1]

> "My sweet gazelle! From thy bewitching eyes
> A glance thrills all my soul with wild delight.
> Unfathomed depths beam forth a world so bright—
> With rays of sun its sparkling splendor vies—
> One look within a mortal deifies.
> Thy lips, the gates wherethrough dawn wings its flight,
> Adorn a face suffused with rosy light,
> Whose radiance puts to shame the vaulted skies.
> Two brilliant stars are they from heaven sent—
> Their charm I cannot otherwise explain—
> By God but for a little instant lent,
> Who gracious doth their lustrous glory deign,
> To teach those on pursuit of beauty bent,
> Beside those eyes all other beauty's vain."

Immanuel's most congenial work, however, is as a satirist. One of his best known poems is a chain of distichs, drawing a comparison between two maidens, Tamar the beautiful, and Beria the homely:

[1] Livius Fürst in *Illustrirte Monatshefte*, Vol. I., p. 105 ff.

" Tamar raises her eyelids, and stars appear in the sky;
  Her glance drops to earth, and flowers clothe the knoll whereon she stands.
Beria looks up, and basilisks die of terror;
Be not amazed; 'tis a sight that would Satan affright.
Tamar's divine form human language cannot describe;
The gods themselves believe her heaven's offspring.
Beria's presence is desirable only in the time of vintage,
When the Evil One can be banished by naught but grimaces.
Tamar! Had Moses seen thee he had never made the serpent of copper,
With thy image he had healed mankind.
Beria! Pain seizes me, physic soothes,
I catch sight of thee, and it returns with full force.
Tamar, with ringlets adorned, greets early the sun,
Who quickly hides, ashamed of his bald pate.
Beria! were I to meet thee on New Year's Day in the morning,
An omen 'twere of an inauspicious year.
Tamar smiles, and heals the heart's bleeding wounds;
She raises her head, the stars slink out of sight.
Beria it were well to transport to heaven,
Then surely heaven would take refuge on earth.
Tamar resembles the moon in all respects but one—
Her resplendent beauty never suffers obscuration.
Beria partakes of the nature of the gods; 'tis said,
None beholds the gods without most awful repentance.
Tamar, were the Virgin like thee, never would the sun
Pass out of Virgo to shine in Libra.
Beria, dost know why the Messiah tarries to bring deliverance to men?
Redemption time has long arrived, but he hides from thee."

With amazement we see the Hebrew muse, so serious aforetimes, participate in truly bacchanalian dances under Immanuel's guidance. It is curious that while, on the one hand, he shrinks from no frivolous utterance or indecent allusion, on the other, he is dominated by deep earnestness and genuine warmth of feeling, when he undertakes to defend or expound the fundamentals of faith. It is characteristic of the trend of his thought that he epitomizes the "Song of Songs" in the sentence: "Love is the pivot of the *Torah*." By a bold hypothesis it is assumed that in Daniel, his guide in Paradise (in the twenty-eighth canto of his poem), he impersonated and glorified his great friend Dante. If true, this would be an interesting indication of the intimate relations existing between a Jew and a circle devoted to the development of the national genius in literature and language, and the stimulating of the sense of nature and truth in opposition to the fantastic visions and grotesque ideals of the past.

Everywhere, not only in Italy, the Renaissance and the humanistic movement attract Jews. Among early Castilian troubadours there is a Jew, and the last troubadour of Spain again is a Jew. Naturally Italian Jews are more profoundly than others affected by the renascence of science and art. David ben Yehuda, Messer Leon, is the author of an epic, *Shebach Nashim* ("Praise of Women"), in which occurs an interesting reference to Petrarch's Laura, whom, in opposition to the consensus of opinion among his contemporaries, he considers, not a figment of the imagination, but a woman of flesh and blood. Praise and criticism of women are favorite themes in the poetic polemics of the sixteenth century. For instance, Jacob ben Elias, of Fano, in his "Shields of Heroes," a small collection of songs in stanzas of three verses, ventures to attack the weaker sex, for which Judah Tommo of Porta Leone at once takes up the cudgels in his "Women's Shield." At the same time a genuine song combat broke out between Abraham of Sarteano and Elias of Genzano. The latter is the champion of the purity of womanhood, impugned by the former, who in fifty tercets exposes the wickedness of woman in the most infamous of her sex, from Lilith to Jezebel, from Semiramis to Medea. An anonymous combatant lends force to his strictures by an arraignment of the lax morals of the women of their own time, while a fourth knight of song, evidently intending to conciliate the parties, begins his "New Song," only a fragment of which has reached us, with praise, and ends it with blame, of woman. Such productions, too, are a result of the Renaissance, of its romantic current, which, as it affected Catholicism, did not fail to leave its mark upon the Jews, among whom romanticists must have had many a battle to fight with adherents of traditional views.

Meantime, neo-Hebraic poetry had "fallen into the sear, the yellow leaf." Poetry drooped under the icy breath of rationalism, and vanished into the abyss of the Kabbala. At most we occasionally hear of a polemic poem, a keen-edged epigram. For the rest, there was only a monotonous succession of religious poems, repeating the old formulas, dry bones of habit and tradition, no longer informed with true poetic, religious spirit. Yet the source of love and humor in Jewish poetry had not run dry. It must be admitted that the sentimentalism of the minneservice, peculiar to the middle ages, never took root in Jewish soil. Pale resignation, morbid despair, longing for death, unmanly indulgence in regret, all the paraphernalia of chivalrous love, extolled in every key in the poetry of the middle ages, were foreign to the sane Jewish mind. Women, the object of unreasoning adulation, shared the fate of all sovereign powers: homage worked their ruin. They became accustomed to think that the weal and woe of the world depended upon their constancy or disloyalty. Jews alone were healthy enough to subordinate sexual love to reverence for maternity. Holding an exalted idea of love, they realized that its power extends far beyond the lives of two persons, and affects the well-being of generations unborn. Such love, intellectual love, which Benedict Spinoza was the first to define from a scientific and philosophic point of view, looks far down the vistas of the future, and gives providential thought to the race.

While humor and romanticism everywhere in the middle ages appeared as irreconcilable contrasts, by Jews they were brought into harmonious relationship. When humor was banished from poetry, it took refuge in Jewish-German literature, that spiritual undercurrent produced by the claims of fancy as opposed to the aggressive, all absorbing demands of reason. Not to the high and mighty, but to the lowly in spirit, the little ones of the earth, to women and children, it made its appeal, and from them its influence spread throughout the nation, bringing refreshment and sustenance to weary, starved minds, hope to the oppressed, and consolation to the afflicted. Consolation, indeed, was sorely needed by the Jews on their peregrinations during the middle ages. Sad, inexpressibly sad, was their condition. With fatal exclusiveness they devoted themselves to the study of the Talmud. Secular learning was deprecated; antagonism to science and vagaries characterized their intellectual life; philosophy was formally interdicted; the Hebrew language neglected; all their wealth and force of intellect lavished upon the study of the Law, and even here every faculty—reason, ingenuity, speculation—busied itself only with highly artificial solutions of equally artificial problems, far-fetched complications, and vexatious contradictions invented to be harmonized. Under such grievous circumstances, oppression growing with malice, Jewish minds and hearts were robbed of humor, and the exercise of love was made a difficult task. Is it astonishing that in such days a rabbi in the remote Slavonic East should have issued an injunction restraining his sisters in faith from reading romances on the Sabbath—romances composed by some other rabbi in Provence or Italy five hundred years before?

Sorrow and suffering are not endless. A new day

broke for the Jews. The walls of the Ghetto fell, dry bones joined each other for new life, and a fresh spirit passed over the House of Israel. Enervation and decadence were succeeded by regeneration, quickened by the spirit of the times, by the ideas of freedom and equality universally advocated. The forces which culminated in their revival had existed as germs in the preceding century. Silently they had grown, operating through every spiritual medium, poetry, oratory, philosophy, political agitation. In the sunshine of the eighteenth century they finally matured, and at its close the rejuvenation of the Jewish race was an accomplished fact in every European country. Eagerly its sons entered into the new intellectual and literary movements of the nations permitted to enjoy another period of efflorescence, and Jewish humor has conquered a place for itself in modern literature.

Our brief journey through the realm of love and humor must certainly convince us that in sunny days humor rarely, love never, forsook Israel. Our old itinerant preachers (*Maggidim*), strolling from town to town, were in the habit of closing their sermons with a parable (*Mashai*), which opened the way to exhortation. The manner of our fathers recommends itself to me, and following in their footsteps, I venture to close my pilgrimage through the ages with a *Mashal*. It transports us to the sunny Orient, to the little seaport town of Jabneh, about six miles from Jerusalem, in the time immediately succeeding the destruction of the Temple.

Thither with a remnant of his disciples, Jochanan ben Zakkaï, one of the wisest of our rabbis, fled to escape the misery incident to the downfall of Jerusalem. He knew that the Temple would never again rise from its ashes. He knew as well that the essence of Judaism has no organic connection with the Temple or the Holy City. He foresaw that its mission is to spread abroad among the nations of the earth, and of this future he spoke to the disciples gathered about him in the academy at Jabneh. We can imagine him asking them to define the fundamental principle of Judaism, and receiving a multiplicity of answers, varying with the character and temper of the young missionaries. To one, possibly, Judaism seemed to rest upon faith in God, to another upon the Sabbath, to a third upon the *Torah*, to a fourth upon the Decalogue. Such views could not have satisfied the spiritual cravings of the aged teacher. When Jochanan ben Zakkaï rises to give utterance to his opinion, we feel as though the narrow walls of the academy at Jabneh were miraculously widening out to enclose the world, while the figure of the venerable rabbi grows to the noble proportions of a divine seer, whose piercing eye rends the veil of futurity, and reads the remote verdict of history: "My disciples, my friends, the fundamental principle of Judaism is love!"

THE JEWISH STAGE

Perhaps no people has held so peculiar a position with regard to the drama as the Jews. Little more than two centuries have passed since a Jewish poet ventured to write a drama, and now, if division by race be admissible in literary matters, Jews indisputably rank among the first of those interested in the drama, both in its composition and presentation.

Originally, the Hebrew mind felt no attraction towards the drama. Hebrew poetry attained to neither dramatic nor epic creations, because the all-pervading monotheistic principle of the nation paralyzed the free and easy marshalling of gods and heroes of the Greek drama. Nevertheless, traces of dramatic poetry appear in the oldest literature. The "Song of Songs" by many is regarded as a dramatic idyl in seven scenes, with Shulammith as the heroine, and the king, the ostensible author, as the hero. But this and similar efforts are only faint approaches to dramatic composition, inducing no imitations.

Greek and Roman theatrical representations, the first they knew, must have awakened lively interest in the Jews. It was only after Alexander the Great's triumphal march through the East, and the establishment of Roman supremacy over Judæa, that a foothold was gained in Palestine by the institutions called theatre by the ancients; that is, *stadia;* circuses for wrestling, fencing, and combats between men and animals; and the stage for tragedies and other plays. To the horror of pious zealots, the Jewish Hellenists, in other words, Jews imbued with the secular culture of the day, built a gymnasium for the wrestling and fencing contests of the Jewish youth of Jerusalem, soon to be further defiled by the circus and the *stadium*. According to Flavius Josephus, Herod erected a theatre at Jerusalem twenty-eight years before the present era, and in the vicinity of the city, an amphitheatre where Greek players acted, and sang to the accompaniment of the lyre or flute.

The first, and at his time probably the only, Jewish dramatist was the Greek poet Ezekielos (Ezekiel), who flourished in about 150 before the common era. In his play, "The Exodus from Egypt," modelled after Euripides, Moses, as we know him in the Bible, is the hero. Otherwise the play is thoroughly Hellenic, showing the Greek tendency to become didactic and reflective and use the heroes of sacred legend as human types. Besides, two fragments of Jewish-Hellenic dramas, in trimeter verse, have come down to us, the one treating of the unity of God, the other of the serpent in Paradise.

To the mass of the Jewish people, particularly to the expounders and scholars of the Law, theatrical performances seemed a desecration, a sin. A violent struggle ensued between the *Beth ha-Midrash* and the stage, between the teachers of the Law and lovers of art, between Rabbinism and Hellenism. Mindful of Bible laws inculcating humanity to beasts and men, the rabbis could not fail to deprecate gladiatorial contests, and in their simple-mindedness they must have revolted from the themes of the Greek playwright, dishonesty, violence triumphant, and conjugal infidelity being then as now favorite subjects of dramatic representations. The immorality of the stage was, if possible, more conspicuous in those days than in ours.

This was the point of view assumed by the rabbis in their exhortations to the people, and a conspiracy against King Herod was the result. The plotters one evening appeared at the theatre, but their designs were frustrated by the absence of the king and his suite. The plot betrayed itself, and one of the members of the conspiracy was seized and torn into pieces by the mob. The most uncompromising rabbis pronounced a curse over frequenters of the theatre, and raised abstinence from its pleasures to the dignity of a meritorious action, inasmuch as it was the scene of idolatrous practices, and its *habitués* violated the admonition contained in the first verse of the psalms. "Cursed be they who visit the theatre and the circus, and despise our laws," one of them exclaims.[1] Another interprets the words of the prophet: "I sat not in the assembly of the mirthful, and was rejoiced," by the prayer: "Lord of the universe, never have I visited a theatre

[1] *Aboda Sara* 18*b*.

or a circus to enjoy myself in the company of scorners."

Despite rampant antagonism, the stage worked its way into the affection and consideration of the Jewish public, and we hear of Jewish youths devoting themselves to the drama and becoming actors. Only one has come down to us by name: the celebrated Alityros in Rome, the favorite of Emperor Nero and his wife Poppæa. Josephus speaks of him as "a player, and a Jew, well favored by Nero." When the Jewish historian landed at Puteoli, a captive, Alityros presented him to the empress, who secured his liberation. Beyond a doubt, the Jewish *beaux esprits* of Rome warmly supported the theatre; indeed, Roman satirists levelled their shafts against the zeal displayed in the service of art by Jewish patrons.

A reaction followed. Theatrical representations were pursued by Talmudic Judaism with the same bitter animosity as by Christianity. Not a matter of surprise, if account is taken of the licentiousness of the stage, so depraved as to evoke sharp reproof even from a Cicero, and the hostility of playwrights to Jews and Christians, whom they held up as a butt for the ridicule of the Roman populace. Talmudic literature has preserved several examples of the buffooneries launched against Judaism. Rabbi Abbayu tells the following:[1] A camel covered with a mourning blanket is brought upon the stage, and gives rise to a conversation. "Why is

[1] Midrash on Lamentations, ch. 3, v. 13 *ff.*

the camel trapped in mourning?" "Because the Jews, who are observing the sabbatical year, abstain from vegetables, and refuse to eat even herbs. They eat only thistles, and the camel is mourning because he is deprived of his favorite food."

Another time a buffoon appears on the stage with head shaved close. "Why is the clown mourning?" "Because oil is so dear." "Why is oil dear?" "On account of the Jews. On the Sabbath day they consume everything they earn during the week. Not a stick of wood is left to make fire whereby to cook their meals. They are forced to burn their beds for fuel, and sleep on the floor at night. To get rid of the dirt, they use an immense quantity of oil. Therefore, oil is dear, and the clown cannot grease his hair with pomade." Certainly no one will deny that the patrons of the Roman theatre were less critical than a modern audience.

Teachers of the Law had but one answer to make to such attacks—a rigorous injunction against theatre-going. On this subject rabbis and Church Fathers were of one mind. The rabbi's declaration, that he who enters a circus commits murder, is offspring of the same holy zeal that dictates Tertullian's solemn indignation: "In no respect, neither by speaking, nor by seeing, nor by hearing, have we part in the mad antics of the circus, the obscenity of the theatre, or the abominations of the arena." Such expressions prepare one for the passion of another remonstrant who, on a Sabbath, explained to his audience that earthquakes are the signs of God's fierce wrath when He looks down upon earth, and sees theatres and circuses flourish, while His sanctuary lies in ruins.[1]

Anathemas against the stage were vain. One teacher of the Law, in the middle of the second century, went so far as to permit attendance at the circus and the *stadium* for the very curious reason that the spectator may haply render assistance to the charioteers in the event of an accident on the race track, or may testify to their death at court, and thus enable their widows to marry again. Another pious rabbi expresses the hope that theatres and circuses at Rome at some future time may "be converted into academies of virtue and morality."

Such liberal views were naturally of extremely rare occurrence. Many centuries passed before Jews in general were able to overcome antipathy to the stage and all connected with it. Pagan Rome with its artistic creations was to sink, and the new Christian drama, springing from the ruins of the old theatre, but making the religious its central idea, was to develop and invite imitation before the first germ of interest in dramatic subjects ventured to show itself in Jewish circles. The first Jewish contribution to the drama dates from the ninth century. The story of Haman, arch-enemy of the Jews, was dramatized in celebration of *Purim*, the Jewish carnival. The central figure was Haman's effigy which was

[1] Jerusalem Talmud, *Berachoth*, 9.

burnt, amid song, music, and general merrymaking, on a small pyre, over which the participants jumped a number of times in gleeful rejoicing over the downfall of their worst enemy—extravagance pardonable in a people which, on every other day of the year, tottered under a load of distress and oppression.

This dramatic effort was only a sporadic phenomenon. Real, uninterrupted participation in dramatic art by Jews cannot be recorded until fully six hundred years later. Meantime the Spanish drama, the first to adapt Bible subjects to the uses of the stage, had reached its highest development. By reason of its choice of subjects it proved so attractive to Jews that scarcely fifty years after the appearance of the first Spanish-Jewish playwright, a Spanish satirist deplores, in cutting verse, the Judaizing of dramatic poetry. In fact, the first original drama in Spanish literature, the celebrated *Celestina*, is attributed to a Jew, the Marrano Rodrigo da Cota. "Esther," the first distinctly Jewish play in Spanish, was written in 1567 by Solomon Usque in Ferrara in collaboration with Lazaro Graziano. The subject treated centuries before in a roughshod manner naturally suggested itself to a genuine dramatist, who chose it in order to invest it with the dignity conferred by poetic art. This first essay in the domain of the Jewish drama was followed by a succession of dramatic creations by Jews, who, exiled from Spain, cherished the memory of their beloved country, and, carrying to their new homes in

Italy and Holland, love for its language and literature, wrote all their works, dramas included, in Spanish after Spanish models. So fruitful was their activity that shortly after the exile we hear of a "Jewish Calderon," the author of more than twenty-two plays, some long held to be the work of Calderon himself, and therefore received with acclamation in Madrid. The real author, whose place in Spanish literature is assured, was Antonio Enriquez di Gomez, a Marrano, burnt in effigy at Seville after his escape from the clutches of the Inquisition. His dramas in part deal with biblical subjects. Samson is obviously the mouthpiece of his own sentiments:

> "O God, my God, the time draws quickly nigh!
> Now let a ray of thy great strength descend!
> Make firm my hand to execute the deed
> That alien rule upon our soil shall end!"

Towards the end of the seventeenth century, the Portuguese language usurped the place of Spanish among Jews, and straightway we hear of a Jewish dramatist, Antonio Jose de Silva (1705-1739), one of the most illustrious of Portuguese poets, whose dramas still hold their own on the repertory of the Portuguese stage. He was burnt at the stake, a martyr to his faith, which he solemnly confessed in the hour of his execution: "I am a follower of a faith God-given according to your own teachings. God once loved this religion. I believe He still loves it, but because you maintain that He no longer turns upon it the light of His countenance, you condemn to death those convinced that God has not withdrawn His grace from what He once favored." It is by no means an improbable combination of circumstances that on the evening of the day whereon Antonio Jose de Silva expired at the stake, an operetta written by the victim himself was played at the great theatre of Lisbon in celebration of the auto-da-fé.

Jewish literature as such derived little increase from this poetic activity among Jews. In the period under discussion a single Hebrew drama was produced which can lay claim to somewhat more praise than is the due of mediocrity. *Asireh ha-Tikwah*, "The Prisoners of Hope," printed in 1673, deserves notice because it was the first drama published in Hebrew, and its author, Joseph Pensa de la Vega, was the last of Spanish, as Antonio de Silva was the last of Portuguese, Jewish poets. The three act play is an allegory, treating of the victory of freewill, represented by a king, over evil inclinations, personified by the handsome lad Cupid. Though imbued with the solemnity of his responsibilities as a ruler, the king is lured from the path of right by various persons and circumstances, chief among them Cupid, his coquettish queen, and his sinful propensities. The opposing good forces are represented by the figures of harmony, Providence, and truth, and they eventually lead the erring wanderer back to the road of salvation. The *dramatis personæ* of this first Hebrew drama are abstractions, devoid of dramatic life, mere allegorical personifications, but the underlying idea is poetic, and the Hebrew style pure, euphonious, and rhythmical. Yet it is impossible to echo the enthusiasm which greeted the work of the seventeen year old author in the Jewish academies of Holland. Twenty-one poets sang its praises in Latin, Hebrew, and Spanish verse. The following couplet may serve as a specimen of their eulogies:

> "At length Israel's muse assumes the tragic cothurn,
> And happily wends her way through the metre's mazes."

Pensa, though the first to publish, was not the first Hebrew dramatist to write. The distinction of priority belongs to Moses Zacuto, who wrote his Hebrew play, *Yesod Olam*[1] ("The Foundation of the World") a quarter of a century earlier. His subject is the persecution inflicted by idolaters upon Abraham on account of his faith, and the groundwork is the Haggadistic narrative about Abraham's bold opposition to idolatrous practices, and his courage even unto death in the service of the true God. According to Talmudic interpretation a righteous character of this description is one of the cornerstones of the universe. It must be admitted that Zacuto's work is a drama with a purpose. The poet wished to fortify his exiled, harassed people with the inspiration and hope that flow from the contempla-

[1] Cmp. Berliner, *Yesod Olam, das älteste bekannte dramatische Gedicht in hebräischer Sprache.*

tion of a strong, bold personality. But the admission does not detract from the genuine merits of the poem. On the other hand, this first dramatic effort naturally is crude, lacking in the poetic forms supplied by highly developed art. Dialogues, prayers, and choruses follow each other without regularity, and in varying metres, not destitute, however, of poetic sentiment and lyric beauties. Often the rhythm rises to a high degree of excellence, even elevation. Like Pensa, Zacuto was the disciple of great masters, and a comparison of either with Lope de Vega and Calderon will reveal the same southern warmth, stilted pathos, exuberance of fancy, wealth of imagery, excessive playing upon words, peculiar turns and phrases, erratic style, and other qualities characteristic of Spanish dramatic poetry in that period.

Another century elapsed before the muse of the Hebrew drama escaped from leading strings. Moses Chayyim Luzzatto (1707-1747) of Padua was a poet of true dramatic gifts, and had he lived at another time he might have attained to absolute greatness of performance. Unluckily, the sentimental, impressionable youth became hopelessly enmeshed in the snares of mysticism. In his seventeenth year he composed a biblical drama, " Samson and the Philistines," the preserved fragments of which are faultless in metre. His next effort was an allegorical drama, *Migdal Oz* (" Tower of Victory "), the style and moral of which show unmistakable signs of Italian inspiration, derived particularly from Guarini and his *Pastor Fido*, models not wholly commendable at a time when Maffei's *Merope* was exerting wholesome influence upon the Italian drama in the direction of simplicity and dignity. Nothing, however, could wean Luzzatto from adherence to Spanish-Italian romanticism. His happiest creation is the dramatic parable, *Layesharim Tehillah* ("Praise unto the Righteous!"). The poetry of the Bible here celebrates its resurrection. The rhythm and exuberance of the Psalms are reproduced in the tone and color of its language. "All the fragrant flowers of biblical poetry are massed in a single bed. Yet the language is more than a mosaic of biblical phrases. It is an enamel of the most superb and the rarest of elegant expressions in the Bible. The peculiarities of the historical writings are carefully avoided, while all modifications of style peculiar to poetry are gathered together to constitute what may fairly be called a vocabulary of poetic diction."[1]

The allegory *Layesharim Tehillah* is full of charming traits, but lacks warmth, naturalness, and human interest, the indispensable elements of dramatic action. The first act treats of the iniquity of men who prize deceit beyond virtue, and closes with the retirement of the pious sage to solitude. The second act describes the hopes of the righteous man and his fate, and the third sounds the praise of truth and justice. The thread of the story is slight, and the characters are pale phantoms, instead of warm-blooded men. Yet the work must be pronounced a

[1] Delitzsch, *Zur Geschichte der jüdischen Poesie*, p. 88.

gem of neo-Hebraic poetry, an earnest of the great creations its author might have produced, if in early youth he had not been caught in the swirling waters, and dragged down into the abysmal depths of Kabbalistic mysticism. Despite his vagaries his poems were full of suggestiveness and stimulation to many of his race, who were inspired to work along the lines laid down by him. He may be considered to have inaugurated another epoch of classical Hebrew literature, interpenetrated with the modern spirit, which the Jewish dramas of his day are vigorously successful in clothing in a Hebrew garb.

In the popular literature in Jewish-German growing up almost unnoticed beside classical Hebrew literature, we find popular plays, comedies, chiefly farces for the *Purim* carnival. The first of them, "The Sale of Joseph" (*Mekirath Yoseph*, 1710), treats the biblical narrative in the form and spirit of the German farcical clown dialogues, Pickelhering (Merry-Andrew), borrowed from the latter, being Potiphar's servant and counsellor. No dramatic or poetic value of any kind attaches to the play. It is as trivial as any of its models, the German clown comedies, and possesses interest only as an index to the taste of the public, which surely received it with delight. Strangely enough the principal scene between Joseph and Selicha, Potiphar's wife, is highly discreet. In a monologue, she gives passionate utterance to her love. Then Joseph appears, and she addresses him thus:

> " Be welcome, Joseph, dearest one,
> My slave who all my heart has won !
> I beg of thee grant my request !
> So oft have I to thee confessed,
> My love for thee is passing great.
> In vain for answering love I wait.
> Have not so tyrannous a mind,
> Be not so churlish, so unkind—
> I bear thee such affection, see,
> Why wilt thou not give love to me ? "

Joseph answers:

> " I owe my lady what she asks,
> Yet this is not among my tasks.
> I pray, my mistress, change thy mind ;
> Thou canst so many like me find.
> How could I dare transgress my state,
> And my great trust so violate ?
> My lord hath charged me with his house,
> Excepting only his dear spouse ;
> Yet she, it seems, needs watching too.
> Now, mistress, fare thee well, adieu ! "

Selicha then says:

> " O heaven now what shall I do ?
> He'll list not to my vows so true.
> Come, Pickelhering, tell me quick,
> What I shall do his love to prick ?
> I'll die if I no means can find
> To bend his humor to my mind.
> I'll give thee gold, thou mayst depend,
> If thou'lt but help me to my end."

Pickelhering appears, and says:

> " My lady, here I am, thy slave,
> My wisest counsel thou shalt have.

> Thou must lay violent hand on him,
> And say: 'Unless thou'lt grant my whim,
> I'll drive thee hence from out my court,
> And with thy woes I'll have my sport,
> Nor will I stay thy punishment,
> Till drop by drop thy blood is spent.'
> Perhaps he will amend his way,
> If thou such cruel words wilt say."

Selicha follows his advice, but being thwarted, again appeals to Pickelhering, who says:

> "My lady fair, pray hark to me,
> My counsel now shall fruitful be.
> A garbled story shalt thou tell
> The king, and say: 'Hear what befell:
> Thy servant Joseph did presume
> To enter in my private room,
> When no one was about the house
> Who could protect thy helpless spouse.
> See here his mantle left behind.
> Seize him, my lord, the miscreant find.'"

Potiphar appears, Selicha tells her tale, and Pickelhering is sent in quest of Joseph, who steps upon the scene to be greeted by his master's far from gentle reproaches:

> "Thou gallowsbird, thou good-for-naught!
> Thou whom so true and good I thought!
> 'Twere just to take thy life from thee.
> But no! still harsher this decree:
> In dungeon chained shalt thou repine,
> Where neither sun nor moon can shine.
> Forever there bewail thy lot unheard;
> Now leave my sight, begone, thou gallowsbird.'"

This ends the scene. Of course, at the last, Joseph escapes his doom, and, to the great joy of the sympathetic public, is raised to high dignities and honors.

This farce was presented at Frankfort-on-the-Main by Jewish students of the city, aided by some from Hamburg and Prague, with extravagant display of scenery. Tradition ascribes the authorship to a certain Beermann.

"Ahasverus" is of similar coarse character, so coarse, indeed, that the directors of the Frankfort Jewish community, exercising their rights as literary censors, forbade its performance, and had the printed copies burnt. A somewhat more refined comedy is *Acta Esther et Achashverosh*, published at Prague in 1720, and enacted there by the pupils of the celebrated rabbi David Oppenheim, "on a regular stage with drums and other instruments." "The Deeds of King David and Goliath," and a travesty, "Haman's Will and Death" also belong to the category of Purim farces.

By an abrupt transition we pass from their consideration to the Hebrew classical drama modelled after the pattern of Moses Chayyim Luzzatto's. Greatest attention was bestowed upon historical dramas, notably those on the trials and fortunes of Marranos, the favorite subjects treated by David Franco Mendez, Samuel Romanelli, and others. Although their language is an almost pure classical Hebrew, the plot is conceived wholly in the spirit of modern times. At the end of the eighteenth century, a large number of writers turned to Bible heroes and heroines for dramatic uses, and since then Jewish interest in the drama has never flagged. The luxuriant fruitfulness of these late Jewish playwrights, standing in the sunlight of modern days, fully compensates for the sterility of the Jewish dramatic muse during the centuries of darkness.

The first Jewish dramatist to use German was Benedict David Arnstein, of Vienna, author of a large number of plays, comedies and melodramas, some of which have been put upon the boards of the Vienna imperial theatre (*Burgtheater*). He was succeeded by L. M. Büschenthal, whose drama, "King Solomon's Seal," was performed at the royal theatre of Berlin. Since his time poets of Jewish race have enriched dramatic literature in all its departments. Their works belong to general literature, and need not be individualized in this essay.

In the province of dramatic music, too, Jews have made a prominent position for themselves. It suffices to mention Meyerbeer and Offenbach, representatives of two widely divergent departments of the art. Again, to assert the prominence of Jews as actors is uttering a truism. Adolf Jellinek, one of the closest students of the racial characteristics of Jews, thinks that they are singularly well equipped for the theatrical profession by reason of their marked subjectivity, which always induces objective, disinterested devotion to a purpose, and their cosmopolitanism, which enables them to transport themselves with ease into a new world of thought.[1]

[1] Jellinek, *Der jüdische Stamm*, p. 64.

"It is natural that a race whose religious, literary, and linguistic development in hundreds of instances proves unique talent to adapt itself with marvellous facility to the intellectual life of various countries and nations, should bring forth individuals gifted with power to project themselves into a character created by art, and impersonate it with admirable accuracy in the smallest detail. What the race as a whole has for centuries been doing spontaneously and by virtue of innate characteristics, can surely be done with greater perfection by some of its members under the consciously accepted guidance of the laws of art." Many Jewish race peculiarities—quick perception, vivacity, declamatory pathos, perfervid imagination—are prime qualifications for the actor's career, and such names as Bogumil Davison, Adolf Sonnenthal, Rachel Felix, and Sarah Bernhardt abundantly illustrate the general proposition.

Strenuous efforts to ascertain the name of the first Jewish actor in Germany have been unavailing. Possibly it was the unnamed artist for whom, at his brother's instance, Lessing interceded at the Mannheim national theatre.

Legion is the name of the Jewish artists of this century who have attained to prominence in every department of the dramatic art, in every country, even the remotest, on the globe. Travellers in Russia tell of the crowds that evening after evening flock to the Jewish-German theatres at Odessa, Kiev, and Warsaw. The plays performed are adaptations of the best dramatic works of all modern nations. We outside of Russia have been made acquainted with the character of these performances by the melodrama "Shulammith," enacted at various theatres by a Jewish-German *opera bouffe* company from Warsaw, and the writer once—can he ever forget it?—saw "Hamlet" played by jargon actors. When Hamlet offers advice to Ophelia in the words: "Get thee to a nunnery!" she promptly retorts: *Mit Eizes bin ich versehen, mein Prinz!* (With good advice I am well supplied, my lord!).

The actor recalled by the recent centennial celebration of the first performance of "The Magic Flute" must have been among the first Jews to adopt the stage as a profession. The first presentation, at once establishing the success of the opera, took place at Prague. According to the *Prager Neue Zeitung* an incident connected with that original performance was of greater interest than the opera itself: "On the tenth of last month, the new piece, 'The Magic Flute,' was produced. I hastened to the theatre, and found that the part of Sarastro was taken by a well-formed young man with a caressing voice who, as I was told to my great surprise, was a Jew—yes, a Jew. He was visibly embarrassed when he first appeared, proving that he was a human being subject to the ordinary laws of nature and to the average mortal's weaknesses. Noticing his stage-fright, the audience tried to encourage him by applause. It succeeded, for he sang and spoke his lines with grace and dignity. At the end he was called out and applauded vigorously.

In short, I found the Prague public very different from its reputation with us. It knows how to appreciate merit even when possessed by an Israelite, and I am inclined to think that it criticises harshly only when there is just reason for complaint. Hartung, the Jewish actor, will soon appear in other rôles, and doubtless will justify the applause of the public."

To return, in conclusion, to the classical drama in Hebrew. Though patterned after the best classical models, and enriched by the noble creations of S. L. Romanelli, M. E. Letteris, the translator of *Faust*, A. Gottloeber, and others, Hebrew dramas belong to the large class of plays for the closet, unsuited for the stage. This dramatic literature contains not only original creations; the masterpieces of all literatures—the works of Shakespere, Racine, Molière, Goethe, Schiller, and Lessing—have been put into the language of the prophets and the psalmists, and, infected by the vigor of their thought, the ancient tongue has been re-animated with the vitality of undying youth.

THE JEW'S QUEST IN AFRICA

Citizens of ancient Greece conversing during the *entr'actes* of a first performance at the national theatre of Olympia were almost sure to ask each other, after the new play had been discussed: "What news from Africa?" Through Aristotle the proverb has come down to us: "Africa always brings us something new." Hence the question: *Quid novi ex Africa?*[1]

If ever two old rabbis in the *Beth ha-Midrash* at Cyrene stole a chat in the intervals of their lectures, the same question probably passed between them. For, Africa has always claimed the interest of the cultured. Jewish-German legend books place the scenes of their most mysterious myths in the "Dark Continent," and I remember distinctly how we youngsters on Sabbath afternoons used to crowd round our dear old grandmother, who, great bowed spectacles on her nose, would read to us from "Yosippon." On many such occasions an unruly listener, with a view to hurrying the distribution of the "Sabbathfruit," would endanger the stability of the dish by vigorous tugging at the table-cloth, and elicit the reproof suggested by our reading: "You

[1] Aristotle, *Hist. Anim.*, 8, 28.   Nicephorus Gregoras, *Hist. Byzant.*, p. 805.

are a veritable Sambation!"—Aristotle, Pliny, Olympia, Cyrene, "Yosippon," and grandam—all unite to whet our appetite for African novelties.

Never has interest in the subject been more active than in our generation, and the question, "What is the quest of the Jews in Africa?" might be applied literally to the achievements of individual Jewish travellers. But our inquiry shall not be into the fortunes of African explorers of Jewish extraction; not into Emin Pasha's journey to Wadelai and Magungo; not into the advisability of colonizing Russian Jews in Africa; nor even into the rôle played by a part of northern Africa in the development of Jewish literature and culture: briefly, "The Jew's quest in Africa" is for the remnants of the ten lost tribes.

For more than eight hundred years, Israel, entrenched on his own soil, bade defiance to every enemy. After the death of Solomon (978 B. C. E.), the kingdom was divided, its power declining in consequence. The world-monarchy Assyria became an adversary to be feared after Ahaz, king of Judah, invited it to assist him against Pekah. Tiglath-Pileser conquered a part of the kingdom of Israel, and, in about the middle of the eighth century, carried off its subjects captive into Assyria. In the reign of Hosea, Shalmaneser finished what his predecessor had begun (722), utterly destroying the kingdom of the north in the two hundred and fifty-eighth year of its independence. Before the catastrophe, a part of its inhabitants had emigrated to

Arabia, so that there were properly speaking only nine tribes, called by their prophets, chief among them Hosea and Amos, Ephraim from the most powerful member of the confederacy. Another part went to Adiabene, a district on the boundary between Assyria and Media, and thence scattered in all directions through the kingdom of the Medes and Persians.

The prophets of the exile still hope for their return. Isaiah says:[1] "The Lord will put forth His hand again the second time to acquire the remnant of his people, which shall remain, from Asshur, and from Egypt, and from Pathros, and from Cush, and from Elam, and from Shinar, and from Chamath, and from the islands of the sea. And he will lift up an ensign unto the nations, and will assemble the outcasts of Israel; and the dispersed of Judah will he collect together from the four corners of the earth. . . . Ephraim shall not envy Judah, and Judah shall not assail Ephraim. . . . And the Lord will utterly destroy the tongue of the Egyptian sea. . . . And there shall be a highway for the remnant of his people, which shall remain from Asshur, like as it was to Israel on the day that they came up out of the land of Egypt." In Jeremiah[2] we read: "Behold I will bring them from the north country, and I will gather them from the farthest ends of the earth . . . for I am become a father to Israel, and Ephraim is my first-born." Referring to this passage, the Talmud maintains that the prophet Jeremiah led the lost tribes back to Palestine.

[1] Isaiah xi. 11-16.   [2] Jeremiah xxxi. 8-9.

The second Isaiah[1] says "to the prisoners, Go forth; to those that are in darkness, Show yourselves." "Ye shall be gathered up one by one. . . . And it shall come to pass on that day that the great cornet shall be blown, and then shall come those that are lost in the land of Asshur, and those who are outcasts in the land of Egypt, and they shall prostrate themselves before the Lord on the holy mount at Jerusalem."

And Ezekiel:[2] "Thou son of man, take unto thyself one stick of wood, and write upon it, 'For Judah, and for the children of Israel his companions'; then take another stick, and write upon it, 'For Joseph, the stick of Ephraim, and for all the house of Israel his companions': and join them one to the other unto thee as one stick; and they shall become one in thy hand."

These prophetical passages show that at the time of the establishment of the second commonwealth the new homes of the ten tribes were accurately known. After that, for more than five hundred years, history is silent on the subject. From frequent allusions in the prophetical writings, we may gather that efforts were made to re-unite Judah and the tribes of Israel, and it seems highly probable that they were successful, such of the ten tribes as had not adopted the idolatrous practices of the heathen returning with the exiles of Judah. In the Samaritan book of Joshua, it is put down that many out of the tribes of Israel migrated to the north of

[1] Isaiah xlix. 9 and xxvii. 13.   [2] Ezekiel xxxvii. 16-17.

Palestine at the time when Zerubbabel and Ezra brought the train of Babylonian exiles to Jerusalem.

In Talmudic literature we occasionally run across a slight reference to the ten tribes, as, for instance, Mar Sutra's statement that they journeyed to Iberia, at that time synonymous with Spain, though the rabbi probably had northern Africa in mind. Another passage relates that the Babylonian scholars decided that no one could tell whether he was descended from Reuben or from Simon, the presumption in their mind evidently being that the ten tribes had become amalgamated with Judah and Benjamin. If they are right, if from the time of Jeremiah to the Syrian domination, a slow process of assimilation was incorporating the scattered of the ten tribes into the returned remnant of Judah and Benjamin, then the ten lost tribes have no existence, and we are dealing with a myth. But the question is still mooted. The prophets and the rabbis continually dwell upon the hope of reunion. The Pesikta is the first authority to locate the exile home of the ten tribes on the Sambation. A peculiarly interesting conversation on the future of the ten tribes between two learned doctors of the Law, Rabbi Akiba and Rabbi Eliezer, has been preserved. Rabbi Eliezer maintains: "The Eternal has removed the ten tribes from their soil, and cast them forth into another land, as irrevocably as this day goes never to return." Rabbi Akiba, the enthusiastic nationalist, thinks very differently: "No, day sinks, and passes into night only to rise again in renewed brilliance. So the ten tribes, lost in darkness, will reappear in refulgent light."

It is not unlikely that Akiba's journeys, extending into Africa, and undertaken to bring about the restoration of the independence of Judæa, had as their subsidiary, unavowed purpose, the discovery of the ten lost tribes. The "Dark Continent" played no unimportant rôle in Talmudic writings, special interest attaching to their narratives of the African adventures of Alexander the Great.[1] On one occasion, it is said, the wise men of Africa appeared in a body before the king, and offered him gifts of gold. He refused them, being desirous only of becoming acquainted with the customs, statutes, and law, of the land. They, therefore, gave him an account of a lawsuit which was exciting much attention at the time: A man had bought a field from his friend and neighbor, and while digging it up, had found a treasure which he refused to keep, as he considered it the property of the original owner of the field. The latter maintained that he had sold the land and all on and within it, and, therefore, had no claim upon the treasure. The doctors of the law put an end to the dispute by the decision that the son of the one contestant was to take to wife the daughter of the other, the treasure to be their marriage portion. Alexander marvelled greatly at this decision. "With us," he said, "the government would have had the litigants killed, and would have confiscated the

[1] Cmp. Spiegel, *Die Alexandersagen bei den Orientalen.*

treasure." Hereupon one of the wise men exclaimed: "Does the sun shine in your land? Have you dumb beasts where you live? If so, surely it is for them that God sends down the rain, and lets the sun shine!"

In biblical literature, too, frequent mention is made of Africa. The first explorer of the "Dark Continent" was the patriarch Abraham, who journeyed from Ur of the Chaldees through Mesopotamia, across the deserts and mountains of Asia, to Zoan, the metropolis of ancient Egypt. When Moses fled from before Pharaoh, he found refuge, according to a Talmudic legend, in the Soudan, where he became ruler of the land for forty years, and later on, Egypt was the asylum for the greater number of Jewish rebels and fugitives. As early as the reign of King Solomon, ships freighted with silver sailed to Africa, and Jewish sailors in part manned the Phoenician vessels despatched to the coasts of the Red Sea to be loaded with the gold dust of Africa, whose usual name in Hebrew was *Ophir*, meaning gold dust. In the Talmud Africa is generally spoken of as "the South," owing to its lying south of Palestine. One of its proverbs runs thus: "He who would be wise, must go to the South." The story of Alexander the Great and the African lawyers is probably a sample of the wisdom lauded. Nor were the doctors of the Talmud ignorant of the physical features of the country. A scoffer asked, "Why have Africans such broad feet." "Because they live on marshy soil, and must go barefoot," was the ready answer given by Hillel the Great.

In the course of a discussion about the appearance of the cherubim, Akiba pointed out that in Africa a little child is called "cherub." Thence he inferred that the faces of cherubim resembled those of little children. On his travels in Africa, the same rabbi was appealed to by a mighty negro king: "See, I am black, and my wife is black. How is it that my children are white?" Akiba asked him whether there were pictures in his palace. "Yes," answered the monarch, "my sleeping chamber is adorned with pictures of white men." "That solves the puzzle," said Akiba. Evidently civilization had taken root in Africa more than eighteen hundred years ago.

To return to the lost tribes: No land on the globe has been considered too small, none too distant, for their asylum. The first country to suggest itself was the one closest to Palestine, Arabia, the bridge between Asia and Africa. In the first centuries of this era, two great kingdoms, Yathrib and Chaibar, flourished there, and it is altogether probable that Jews were constantly emigrating thither. As early as the time of Alexander the Great, thousands were transported to Arabia, particularly to Yemen, where entire tribes accepted the Jewish faith. Recent research has made us familiar with the kingdom of Tabba (500) and the Himyarites. Their inscriptions and the royal monuments of the old African-Jewish population prove that Jewish immigrants must have been numerous here, as in southern Arabia. When Mohammed unfurled the banner of the Prophet, and began his march through the desert, his followers counted not a few Jews. In similar numbers they spread to northern Africa, where, towards the end of the first thousand years of the Christian era, they boasted large communities, and played a prominent rôle in Jewish literature, as is attested by the important contributions to Jewish law, grammar, poetry, and medicine, by such men as Isaac Israeli, Chananel, Jacob ben Nissim, Dunash ben Labrat, Yehuda Chayyug, and later, Isaac Alfassi. When this north-African Jewish literature was at its zenith, interest in the whereabouts of the ten tribes revived, first mention of them being made in the last quarter of the ninth century. One day there appeared in the academy at Kairwan an adventurer calling himself Eldad, and representing himself to be a member of the tribe of Dan. Marvellous tales he told the wondering rabbis of his own adventures, which read like a Jewish Odyssey, and of the independent government established by Jews in Africa, of which he claimed to be a subject. Upon its borders, he reported, live the Levitical singers, the descendants of Moses, who, in the days of Babylonish captivity, hung their harps upon the willows, refusing to sing the songs of Zion upon the soil of the stranger, and willing to sacrifice limb and life rather than yield to the importunities of their oppressors. A cloud had enveloped and raised them aloft, bearing them to the land of Chavila (Ethiopia). To protect them from their enemies, their refuge in a trice was girdled by the famous Sambation, a stream, not of waters, but of rapidly whirling stones and sand, tumultuously flowing during six days, and resting on the Sabbath, when the country was secured against foreign invasion by a dense cloud of dust. With their neighbors, the sons of Moses have intercourse only from the banks of the stream, which it is impossible to pass.[1]

This clever fellow, who had travelled far and wide, and knew men and customs, gave an account also of a shipwreck which he had survived, and of his miraculous escape from cannibals, who devoured his companions, but, finding him too lean for their taste, threw him into a dungeon. Homer's Odyssey involuntarily suggests itself to the reader. In Spain we lose trace of the singular adventurer, who must have produced no little excitement in the Jewish world of his day.

Search for the ten tribes had now re-established itself as a subject of perennial interest. In the hope of the fulfilment of the biblical promise: "The sceptre shall not depart from Judah, nor a lawgiver from between his feet, until he comes to Shiloh," even the most famous Jewish traveller of the middle ages, Benjamin of Tudela, did not disdain to follow up the "traces of salvation." Nor has interest waned in our generation. Whenever we hear of a Jewish community whose settlement in its home is tinged with mystery, we straightway seek to establish its connection with the ten lost tribes. They

[1] Cmp. A. Epstein, *Eldad ha-Dani*, p. x.

have been placed in Armenia, Syria, and Mesopotamia, where the Nestorian Christians, calling themselves sons of Israel, live to the number of two hundred thousand, observing the dietary laws and the Sabbath, and offering up sacrifices. They have been sought in Afghanistan, India, and Western Asia, the land of the "Beni Israel," with Jewish features, Jewish names, such as Solomon, David, and Benjamin, and Jewish laws, such as that of the Levirate marriage. One chain of hills in their country bears the name "Solomon's Mountains," another "Amram Chain," and the most warlike tribe is called Ephraim, while the chief tenet of their law is "eye for eye, tooth for tooth." Search for the lost has been carried still further, to the coast of China, to the settlements of Cochin and Malabar, where white and black Jews write their law upon scrolls of red goatskin.

Westward the quest has reached America: Manasseh ben Israel and Mordecai Noah, the latter of whom hoped to establish a Jewish commonwealth at Ararat near Buffalo, in the beginning of this century, believed that they had discovered traces of the lost tribes among the Indians. The Spaniards in Mexico identified them with the red men of Anahuac and Yucatan, a theory suggested probably by the resemblance between the Jewish and the Indian aquiline nose. These would-be ethnologists obviously did not take into account the Mongolian descent of the Indian tribes and their pre-historic migration from Asia to America across Behring Strait.

Europe has not escaped the imputation of being the refuge of the lost tribes. When Alfonso XI. expelled the Saracens from Toledo, the Jews of the city asked permission to remain on the plea that they were not descendants of the murderers of Jesus, but of those ten tribes whom Nebuchadnezzar had sent to Tarshish as colonists. The petition was granted, and their explanation filed among the royal archives at Toledo.

The English have taken absorbing interest in the fate of the lost tribes, maintaining by most elaborate arguments their identity with the inhabitants of Scandinavia and England. The English people have always had a strong biblical bias. To this day they live in the Bible, and are flattered by the hypothesis that the Anglo-Saxons and kindred tribes, who crossed over to Britain under Hengist and Horsa in the fifth century, were direct descendants of Abraham, their very name *Sakkasuna*, that is, sons of Isaac, vouching for the truth of the theory. The radical falseness of the etymology is patent. The gist of their argument is that the tribe of Dan settled near the source of the Jordan, becoming the maritime member of the Israelitish confederacy, and calling forth from Deborah the rebuke that the sons of Dan tarried in ships when the land stood in need of defenders. And now comes the most extravagant of the vagaries of the etymological reasoner: he suggests a connection between Dan, Danube, Danaï, and Danes, and so establishes the English nation's descent from the tribes of Israel.

In the third decade of this century, when Shalmaneser's obelisk was found with the inscription "Tribute of Jehu, son of Omri," English investigators, seeking to connect it with the Cimbric Chersonese in Jutland, at once took it for "Yehu ibn Umry." An Irish legend has it that Princess Tephi came to Ireland from the East, and married King Heremon, or Fergus, of Scotland. In her suite was the prophet Ollam Folla, and his scribe Bereg. The princess was the daughter of Zedekiah, the prophet none other than Jeremiah, and the scribe, as a matter of course, Baruch. The usefulness of this finespun analogy becomes apparent when we recall that Queen Victoria boasts descent from Fergus of Scotland, and so is furnished with a line of descent which would justify pride if it rested on fact instead of fancy. On the other hand, imagine the dismay of Heinrich von Treitschke, Saxon *par excellence*, were it proved that he is a son of the ten lost tribes!

"Salvation is of the Jews!" is the motto of a considerable movement connected with the lost tribes in England and America. More than thirty weekly and monthly journals are discharging a volley of eloquence in the propaganda of the new doctrine, and lecturers and societies keep interest in it alive. An apostolic believer in the Israelitish descent of the British has recently turned up in the person of a bishop, and the identity of the ancient and the modern people has been raised to the dignity of a dogma of the Christian Church by a sect which, according to a recent utterance of an Indianapolis preacher, holds the close advent of Judgment Day. Yet, the ten lost tribes may be a myth!

One thing seems certain: If scattered remnants do exist here and there, they must be sought in Africa, in that part, moreover, most accessible to travellers, that is to say, Abyssinia, situated in the central portion of the great, high tableland of eastern Africa between the basin of the Nile and the shores of the Red and the Arabian Sea—a tremendous, rocky, fortress-like plateau, intersected closely with a network of river-beds, the Switzerland of Africa, as many please to call it. Alexander the Great colonized many thousands of Jews in Egypt, on the southern and northern coasts of the Mediterranean, and in south-eastern Africa. Thence they penetrated into the interior of Abyssinia, where they founded a mighty kingdom extending to the river Sobat. Abyssinian legends have another version of the history of this realm. It is said that the Queen of Sheba bore King Solomon a son, named Menelek, whom he sent to Abyssinia with a numerous retinue to found an independent kingdom. In point of fact, Judaism seems to have been the dominant religion in Abyssinia until 340 of the Christian era, and the *Golah* of Cush (the exiles in Abyssinia) is frequently referred to in mediæval Hebrew literature.

The Jewish kingdom flourished until a great revolution broke out in the ninth century under Queen Judith (Sague), who conquered Axum, and reigned over Abyssinia for forty years. The Jewish ascendancy lasted three hundred and fifty years. Rüppell,[1] a noted African explorer, gives the names of Jewish dynasties from the ninth to the thirteenth century. In the wars of the latter and the following century, the Jews lost their kingdom, keeping only the province of Semen, guarded by inaccessible mountains. Benjamin of Tudela describes it as "a land full of mountains, upon whose rocky summits they have perched their towns and castles, holding independent sway to the mortal terror of their neighbors." Combats, persecutions, and banishments lasted until the end of the eighteenth century. Anarchy reigned, overwhelming Gideon and Judith, the last of the Jewish dynasty, and proving equally fatal to the Christian empire, whose Negus Theodore likewise traced his descent from Solomon. So, after a thousand years of mutual hostility, the two ancient native dynasties, claiming descent from David and Solomon, perished together, but the memory of the Jewish princes has not died out in the land.

The Abyssinian Jews are called Falashas, the exiled.[2] They live secluded in the province west of Takazzeh, and their number is estimated by some travellers to be two hundred and fifty thousand, while my friend Dr. Edward Glaser judges them to be only twenty-five thousand strong. Into the dreary wastes inhabited by these people, German and English missionaries have found their way to spread among them the blessings of Christianity. The purity of these blessings may be inferred from

[1] Rüppell, *Reisen in Nubien*, p. 416.
[2] Cmp. Epstein, *l. c.*, p. 141.

the names of the missionaries: Flad, Schiller, Brandeis, Stern, and Rosenbaum.

Information about the misery of the Falashas penetrated to Europe, and induced the *Alliance Israélite Universelle* to despatch a Jewish messenger to Abyssinia. Choice fell upon Joseph Halévy, professor of Oriental languages at Paris, one of the most thorough of Jewish scholars, than whom none could be better qualified for the mission. It was a memorable moment when Halévy, returned from his great journey to Abyssinia, addressed the meeting of the *Alliance* on July 30, 1868, as follows:[1] " The ancient land of Ethiopia has at last disclosed the secret concerning the people of whom we hitherto knew naught but the name. In the midst of the most varied fortunes they clung to the Law proclaimed on Sinai, and constant misery has not drained them of the vitality which enables nations to fulfil the best requirements of modern society."

Adverse circumstances robbed Halévy of a great part of the material gathered on his trip. What he rescued and published is enough to give us a more detailed and accurate account of the Falashas than we have hitherto possessed. He reports that they address their prayers to one God, the God of Abraham, Isaac, and Jacob; that they feel pride in belonging to the old, yet ever young tribe which has exercised dominant influence upon the fate of men; that love for the Holy Land fills their hearts; and that the memory of Israel's glorious past is their

[1] *Alliance* Report for 1868.

spiritual stay. One of the articles of their faith is the restoration of Jewish nationality.

The Falashas speak two languages, that of the land, the Amharic, a branch of the ancient Geez, and the Agau, a not yet classified dialect. Their names are chiefly biblical. While in dress they are like their neighbors, the widest difference prevails between their manners and customs and those of the other inhabitants of the land. In the midst of a slothful, debauched people, they are distinguished for simplicity, diligence, and ambition. Their houses for the most part are situated near running water; hence, their cleanly habits. At the head of each village is a synagogue called *Mesgid*, whose Holy of holies may be entered only by the priest on the Day of Atonement, while the people pray in the court without. Next to the synagogue live the monks (*Nesirim*). The priests offer up sacrifices, as in ancient times, daily except on the Day of Atonement, the most important being that for the repose of the dead. On the space surrounding the synagogue stand the houses of the priests, who, in addition to their religious functions, fill the office of teachers of the young. The Falashas are well acquainted with the Bible, but wholly ignorant of the Hebrew language. Their ritual has been published by Joseph Halévy, who has added a Hebrew translation, showing its almost perfect identity with the traditional form of Jewish prayer. About their devotional exercises Halévy says: "From the holy precincts the prayers of the faithful rise aloft to heaven. From midnight on, we hear the clear, rhythmical, melancholy intonation of the precentor, the congregation responding in a monotonous recitative. Praise of the Eternal, salvation of Israel, love of Zion, hope of a happy future for all mankind—these form the burden of their prayers, calling forth sighs and tears, exclamations of hope and joy. Break of day still finds the worshippers assembled, and every evening without fail, as the sun sinks to rest, their loud prayer (beginning with *Abba! Abba!* Lord! Lord!) twice wakes the echoes."[1]

Their well kept houses are presided over by their women, diligent and modest. Polygamy is unknown. There are agriculturists and artisans, representatives of every handicraft: smiths, tailors, potters, weavers, and builders. Commerce is not esteemed, trading with slaves being held in special abhorrence. Their laws permit the keeping of a slave for only six years. If at the expiration of that period he embraces their religion, he is free. They are brave warriors, thousands of them having fought in the army of Negus Theodore.

It must be confessed that intellectually they are undeveloped. They have a sort of Midrash, which apparently has been handed down from generation to generation by word of mouth. The misfortunes they have endured have predisposed them to mysticism, and magicians and soothsayers are numerous and active among them. But they are eager for information.

[1] Halévy, *Les prières des Falashas*, Introduction.

King Theodore protected them, until missionaries poisoned his mind against the Falashas. In 1868 he summoned a deputation of their elders, and commanded them to accept Christianity. Upon their refusal the king ordered his soldiers to fire on the rebels. Hundreds of heads were raised, and the men, baring their breasts, cried out: "Strike, O our King, but ask us not to perjure ourselves." Moved to admiration by their intrepidity, the king loaded the deputies with presents, and dismissed them in peace.

The missionaries—Europe does not yet know how often the path of these pious men is marked by tears and blood—must be held guilty of many of the bitter trials of the Falashas. In the sixties they succeeded in exciting Messianic expectations. Suddenly, from district to district, leapt the news that the Messiah was approaching to lead Israel back to Palestine. A touching letter addressed by the elders of the Falashas to the representatives of the Jewish community at Jerusalem, whom it never reached, was found by a traveller, and deserves to be quoted:

"Has the time not yet come when we must return to the Holy Land and Holy City? For, we are poor and miserable. We have neither judges nor prophets. If the time has arrived, we pray you send us the glad tidings. Great fear has fallen upon us that we may miss the opportunity to return. Many say that the time is here for us to be reunited with you in the Holy City, to bring sacrifices in the Temple of our Holy Land. For the sake of the love we bear you, send us a message. Peace with you and all dwelling in the land given by the Lord to Moses on Sinai!"

Filled with the hope of redemption, large numbers of the Falashas, at their head venerable old men holding aloft banners and singing pious songs, at that time left their homes. Ignorant of the road to be taken, they set their faces eastward, hoping to reach the shores of the Red Sea. The distance was greater than they could travel. At Axum they came to a stop disabled, and after three years the last man had succumbed to misery and privation.

The distress of the Falashas is extreme, but they count it sweet alleviation if their sight is not troubled by missionaries. At a time when the attention of the civilized world is directed to Africa, European Jews should not be found wanting in care for their unfortunate brethren in faith in the "Dark Continent." Abundant reasons recommend them to our loving-kindness. They are Jews—they would suffer a thousand deaths rather than renounce the covenant sealed on Sinai. They are unfortunate; since the civil war, they have suffered severely under all manner of persecution. Mysticism and ignorance prevail among them—the whole community possesses a single copy of the Pentateuch. Finally, they show eager desire for spiritual regeneration. When Halévy took leave of them, a handsome youth threw himself at his feet, and said: "My lord, take me with you to the land of the Franks. Gladly will I undergo the hardships of the journey. I want neither silver nor gold—all I crave is knowledge!" Halévy brought the young Falasha to Paris, and he proved an indefatigable student, who acquired a wealth of knowledge before his early death.

Despite the incubus of African barbarism, this little Jewish tribe on the banks of the legend-famed Sabbath stream has survived with Jewish vitality unbroken and purity uncontaminated. With longing the Falashas are awaiting a future when they will be permitted to join the councils of their Israelitish brethren in all quarters of the globe, and confess, in unison with them and all redeemed, enlightened men, that " the Lord is one, and His name one."

The steadfastness of their faith imposes upon us the obligation to bring them redemption. We must unbar for them not only Jerusalem, but the whole world, that they may recognize, as we do, the eternal truth preached by prophet and extolled by psalmist, that on the glad day when the unity of God is acknowledged, all the nations of the earth will form a single confederacy, banded together for love and peace.

The open-eyed student of Jewish history, in which the Falashas form a very small chapter, cannot fail to note with reverence the power and sacredness of its genius. The race, the faith, the confession, all is unparalleled. Everything about it is wonderful—from Abraham at Ur of the Chaldees shattering his father's idols and proclaiming the unity of God, down to Moses teaching awed mankind the highest ethical lessons from the midst of the thunders and flames of Sinai; to the heroes and seers, whose radiant visions are mankind's solace; to the sweet singers of Israel extolling the virtues of men in hymns and songs; to the Maccabean heroes struggling to throw off the Syrian yoke; to venerable rabbis proof against the siren notes of Hellenism; to the gracious bards and profound thinkers of Andalusia. The genius of Jewish history is never at rest. From the edge of the wilderness it sweeps on to the lands of civilization, where thousands of martyrs seal the confession of God's unity with death on ruddy pyres; on through tears and blood, over nations, across thrones, until the sun of culture, risen to its zenith, sends its rays even into the dark Ghetto, where a drama enacts itself, melancholy, curious, whose last act is being played under our very eyes. Branch after branch is dropping from the timeworn, weatherbeaten trunk. The ground is thickly strewn with dry leaves. Vitality that resisted rain and storm seems to be blasted by sunshine. Yet we need not despair. The genius of Jewish history has the balsam of consolation to offer. It bids us read in the old documents of Israel's spiritual struggles, and calls to our attention particularly a parable in the Midrash, written when the need for its telling was as sore as to-day: A wagon loaded with glistening axes was driven through the woods. Plaintive cries arose from the trees: "Woe, woe, there is no escape for us, we are doomed to swift destruction." A solitary oak towering high above the other trees stood calm, motionless. Many a spring had decked its twigs with tender, succulent green. At last it speaks; all are silent, and listen respectfully: "Possess yourselves in peace. All the axes in the world cannot harm you, if you do not provide them with handles."

So every weapon shaped to the injury of the ancient tree of Judaism will recoil ineffectual, unless her sons and adherents themselves furnish the haft. There is consolation in the thought. Even in sad days it feeds the hope that the time will come, whereof the prophet spoke, when "all thy children shall be disciples of the Lord; and great shall be the peace of thy children."

A JEWISH KING IN POLAND

There is a legend that a Jewish king once reigned in Poland. It never occurs to my mind without at the same time conjuring before me two figures. The one is that charming creation of Ghetto fancy, old Malkoh "with the stout heart," in Aaron Bernstein's *Mendel Gibbor*, who introduces herself with the proud boast: *Wir sennen von königlichem Geblüt* ("We are of royal descent"). The other is a less ideal, less attractive Jew, whom I overheard in the Casimir, the Jewish quarter at Cracow, in altercation with another Jew. The matter seemed of vital interest to the disputants. The one affirmed, the other denied as vigorously, and finally silenced his opponent with the contemptuous argument: "Well, and if it comes about, it will last just as long as Saul Wahl's *Malchus* (reign)."

Legend has always been the companion of history. For each age it creates a typical figure, in which are fixed, for the information of future times, the fleeting, subtle emotions as well as the permanent effects produced by historical events, and this constitutes the value of legendary lore in tracing the development and characteristics of a people. At the same time its magic charms connect the links in the chain of generations.

The legend about Saul Wahl to be known and appreciated must first be told as it exists, then traced through its successive stages, its historical kernel disentangled from the accretions of legend-makers, Saul, the man of flesh and blood discovered, and the ethical lessons it has to teach derived.

In 1734, more than a century after Saul's supposed reign, his great-grandson, Rabbi Pinchas, resident successively in Leitnik, Boskowitz, Wallerstein, Schwarzburg, Marktbreit, and Anspach, related the story of his ancestor: "Rabbi Samuel Judah's son was the great Saul Wahl of blessed memory. All learned in such matters well know that his surname *Wahl* (choice) was given him, because he was chosen king in Poland by the unanimous vote of the noble electors of the land. I was told by my father and teacher, of blessed memory, that the choice fell upon him in this wise: Saul Wahl was a favorite with Polish noblemen, and highly esteemed for his shrewdness and ability. The king of Poland had died. Now it was customary for the great nobles of Poland to assemble for the election of a new king on a given day, on which it was imperative that a valid decision be reached. When the day came, many opinions were found to prevail among the electors, which could not be reconciled. Evening fell, and they realized the impossibility of electing a king on the legally appointed day. Loth to transgress their own rule, the nobles agreed to make Saul Wahl king for the rest of that day and the following night, and thus conform with the letter of the law. And so it was. Forthwith all paid him homage, crying out in their own language: 'Long live our lord and king!' Saul, loaded with royal honors, reigned that night. I heard from my father that they gave into his keeping all the documents in the royal archives, to which every king may add what commands he lists, and Wahl inscribed many laws and decrees of import favorable to Jews. My father knew some of them; one was that the murderer of a Jew, like the murderer of a nobleman, was to suffer the death penalty. Life was to be taken for life, and no ransom allowed—a law which, in Poland, had applied only to the case of Christians of the nobility. The next day the electors came to an agreement, and chose a ruler for Poland.—That this matter may be remembered, I will not fail to set forth the reasons why Saul Wahl enjoyed such respect with the noblemen of Poland, which is the more remarkable as his father, Rabbi Samuel Judah, was rabbi first at Padua and then at Venice, and so lived in Italy. My father told me how it came about. In his youth, during his father's lifetime, Saul Wahl conceived a desire to travel in foreign parts. He left his paternal home in Padua, and journeying from town to town, from land to land, he at last reached Brzesc in Lithuania. There he married the daughter of David Drucker, and his pittance being small, he led but a wretched life.

It happened at this time that the famous, wealthy prince, Radziwill, the favorite of the king, undertook a great journey to see divers lands, as is the custom of noblemen. They travel far and wide to become acquainted with different fashions and governments. So this prince journeyed in great state from land to land, until his purse was empty. He knew not what to do, for he would not discover his plight to the nobles of the land in which he happened to be; indeed, he did not care to let them know who he was. Now, he chanced to be in Padua, and he resolved to unbosom himself to the rabbi, tell him that he was a great noble of the Polish land, and borrow somewhat to relieve his pressing need. Such is the manner of Polish noblemen. They permit shrewd and sensible Jews to become intimate with them that they may borrow from them, rabbis being held in particularly high esteem and favor by the princes and lords of Poland. So it came about that the aforesaid Prince Radziwill sought out Rabbi Samuel Judah, and revealed his identity, at the same time discovering to him his urgent need of money. The rabbi lent him the sum asked for, and the prince said, 'How can I recompense you, returning good for good?' The rabbi answered, 'First I beg that you deal kindly with the Jews under your power, and then that you do the good you would show me to my son Saul, who lives in Brzesc.' The prince took down the name and place of abode of the rabbi's son, and having arrived at his home, sent for him. He appeared before the prince, who found him so wise and clever that he in every possible way attached the Jew to his own person, gave him many proofs of his favor, sounded his praises in the ears of all the nobles, and raised him to a high position. He was so great a favorite with all the lords that on the day when a king was to be elected, and the peers could not agree, rather than have the day pass without the appointment of a ruler, they unanimously resolved to invest Saul with royal power, calling him Saul Wahl to indicate that he had been *chosen* king.—All this my father told me, and such new matter as I gathered from another source, I will not fail to set down in another chapter."—

"This furthermore I heard from my pious father, when, in 1734, he lay sick in Fürth, where there are many physicians. I went from Marktbreit to Fürth, and stayed with him for three weeks. When I was alone with him, he dictated his will to me, and then said in a low voice: 'This I will tell you that you may know what happened to our ancestor Saul Wahl: After the nobles had elected a king for Poland, and our ancestor had become great in the eyes of the Jews, he unfortunately grew haughty. He had a beautiful daughter, Händele, famed throughout Poland for her wit as well as her beauty. Many sought her in marriage, and among her suitors was a young Talmudist, the son of one of the most celebrated rabbis. (My father did not mention the name, either because he did not know, or because he did not wish to say it, or mayhap he had forgotten it.) The great rabbi himself came to Brzesc with his learned son to urge the suit. They both lodged with the chief elder of the congregation.

But the pride of our ancestor was overweening In his heart he considered himself the greatest, and his daughter the best, in the land, and he said that his daughter must marry one more exalted than this suitor. Thus he showed his scorn for a sage revered in Israel and for his son, and these two were sore offended at the discourtesy. The Jewish community had long been murmuring against our ancestor Saul Wahl, and it was resolved to make amends for his unkindness. One of the most respected men in the town gave his daughter to the young Talmudist for wife, and from that day our ancestor had enemies among his people, who constantly sought to do him harm. It happened at that time that the wife of the king whom the nobles had chosen died, and several Jews of Brzesc, in favor with the powerful of the land, in order to administer punishment to Saul Wahl, went about among the nobles praising his daughter for her exceeding beauty and cleverness, and calling her the worthiest to wear the queenly crown. One of the princes being kindly disposed to Saul Wahl betrayed their evil plot, and it was frustrated.'"[1]

Rabbi Pinchas' ingenuous narrative, charming in its simple directness, closes wistfully: "He who has not seen that whole generation, Saul Wahl amid his sons, sons-in-law, and grandsons, has failed to see the union of the Law with mundane glory, of wealth with honor and princely rectitude. May the Lord God bless us by permitting us to rejoice thus in our children and children's children!"

[1] Cmp. Edelmann, *Gedulath Shaul*, Introduction.

Other rabbis of that time have left us versions of the Saul Wahl legend. They report that he founded a *Beth ha-Midrash* (college for Jewish studies) and a little synagogue, leaving them, together with numerous bequests, to the community in which he had lived, with the condition that the presidency of the college be made hereditary in his family. Some add that they had seen in Brzesc a gold chain belonging to him, his coat of arms emblazoned with the lion of Judah, and a stone tablet on which an account of his meritorious deeds was graven. Chain, escutcheon, and stone have disappeared, and been forgotten, the legend alone survives.

. . .

Now, what has history to say?

Unquestionably, an historical kernel lies hidden in the legend. Neither the Polish chronicles of those days nor Jewish works mention a Jewish king of Poland; but from certain occurrences, hints can be gleaned sufficient to enable us to establish the underlying truth. When Stephen Báthori died, Poland was hard pressed. On all sides arose pretenders to the throne. The most powerful aspirant was Archduke Maximilian of Austria, who depended on his gold and Poland's well-known sympathy for Austria to gain him the throne. Next came the Duke of Ferrara backed by a great army and the favor of the Czar, and then, headed by the crown-prince of Sweden, a crowd of less powerful claimants, so motley that a Polish nobleman justly exclaimed: " If you think any one will do to wear Poland's crown upon his pate, I'll set up my coachman as king!" Great Poland espoused the cause of Sweden, Little Poland supported Austria, and the Lithuanians furthered the wishes of the Czar. In reality, however, the election of the king was the occasion for bringing to a crisis the conflict between the two dominant families of Zamoiski and Zborowski.

The election was to take place on August 18, 1587. The electors, armed to the teeth, appeared on the place designated for the election, a fortified camp on the Vistula, on the other side of which stood the deputies of the claimants. Night was approaching, and the possibility of reconciling the parties seemed as remote as ever. Christopher Radziwill, the "castellan" of the realm, endeavoring to make peace between the factions, stealthily crept from camp to camp, but evening deepened into night, and still the famous election cry, "*Zgoda!*" (Agreed!), was not heard.

According to the legend, this is the night of Saul Wahl's brief royalty. It is said that he was an agent employed by Prince Radziwill, and when the electors could not be induced to come to an agreement, it occurred to the prince to propose Saul as a compromise-king. With shouts of "Long live King Saul!" the proposal was greeted by both factions, and this is the nucleus of the legend, which with remarkable tenacity has perpetuated itself down to our generation. For the historical truth of the episode we have three witnesses. The chief is Prince Nicholas Christopher of Radziwill, duke of Olyka and Nieswiesz, the son of the founder of this still flourishing line of princes. His father had left the Catholic church, and joined the Protestants, but he himself returned to Catholicism, and won fame by his pilgrimage to Jerusalem, described in both Polish and Latin in the work *Peregrinatio Hierosolymitana*. Besides, he offered 5000 ducats for the purchase of extant copies of the Protestant " Radziwill Bible," published by his father, intending to have them destroyed. On his return journey from the Holy Land he was attacked at Pescara by robbers, and at Ancona on a Palm Sunday, according to his own account, he found himself destitute of means. He applied to the papal governor, but his story met with incredulity. Then he appealed to a Jewish merchant, offering him, as a pawn, a gold box made of a piece of the holy cross obtained in Palestine, encircled with diamonds, and bearing on its top the *Agnus dei*. The Jew advanced one hundred crowns, which sufficed exactly to pay his lodging and attendants. Needy as before, he again turned to the Jew, who gave him another hundred crowns, this time without exacting a pledge, a glance at his papal passport having convinced him of the prince's identity.[1]

This is Radziwill's account in his itinerary. As far as it goes, it bears striking similarity to the narrative of Rabbi Pinchas of Anspach, and leads to the certain conclusion that the legend rests upon an

[1] Cmp. H. Goldbaum, *Entlegene Culturen*, p. 299 *ff.*

historical substratum. A critic has justly remarked that the most vivid fancy could not, one hundred and thirty-one years after their occurrence, invent, in Anspach, the tale of a Polish magnate's adventures in Italy. Again, it is highly improbable that Saul Wahl's great-grandson read Prince Radziwill's Latin book, detailing his experiences to his contemporaries.

There are other witnesses to plead for the essential truth of our legend. The rabbis mentioned before have given accounts of Saul's position, of his power, and the splendor of his life. Negative signs, it is true, exist, arguing against the historical value of the legend. Polish history has not a word to say about the ephemeral king. In fact, there was no day fixed for the session of the electoral diet. Moreover, critics might adduce against the probability of its correctness the humble station of the Jews, and the low esteem in which the Radziwills were then held by the Polish nobility. But it is questionable whether these arguments are sufficiently convincing to strip the Saul Wahl legend of all semblance of truth. Polish historians are hardly fair in ignoring the story. Though it turn out to have been a wild prank, it has some historical justification. Such practical jokes are not unusual in Polish history. Readers of that history will recall the *Respublika Babinska*, that society of practical jokers which drew up royal charters, and issued patents of nobility. A Polish nobleman had founded the society in the sixteenth century, its membership being open only to those distinguished as wits. It perpetrated the oddest political jokes, appointing spendthrifts as overseers of estates, and the most quarrelsome as justices of the peace. With such proclivities, Polish factions, at loggerheads with each other, can easily be imagined uniting to crown a Jew, the most harmless available substitute for a real king.

Our last and strongest witness—one compelling the respectful attention of the severest court and the most incisive attorney general—is the Russian professor Berschadzky, the author of an invaluable work on the history of the Jews in Lithuania. He vouches, not indeed for the authenticity of the events related by Rabbi Pinchas, but for the reality of Saul Wahl himself. From out of the Russian archives he has been resurrected by Professor Berschadzky, the first to establish that Saul was a man of flesh and blood.[1] He reproduces documents of incontestable authority, which report that Stephen Báthori, in the year 1578, the third of his reign, awarded the salt monopoly for the whole of Poland to Saul Juditsch, that is, Saul the Jew. Later, upon the payment of a high security, the same Saul the Jew became farmer of the imposts. In 1580, his name, together with the names of the heads of the Jewish community of Brzesc, figures in a lawsuit instituted to establish the claim of the Jews upon the fourth part of all municipal revenues. He rests the claim on a statute of Grandduke Withold, and the verdict was favorable to his side. This was the

[1] *Woschod*, 1889, No. 10 *ff*.

time of the election of Báthori's successor, Sigismund III., and after his accession to the throne, Saul Juditsch again appears on the scene. On February 11, 1588, the king issued the following notice: "Some of our councillors have recommended to our attention the punctilious business management of Saul Juditsch, of the town of Brzesc, who, on many occasions during the reigns of our predecessors, served the crown by his wide experience in matters pertaining to duties, taxes, and divers revenues, and advanced the financial prosperity of the realm by his conscientious efforts." Saul was now entrusted, for a period of ten years, with the collection of taxes on bridges, flour, and brandies, paying 150,000 gold florins for the privilege. A year later he was honored with the title *sluga królewski*, "royal official," a high rank in the Poland of the day, as can be learned from the royal decree conferring it: "We, King of Poland, having convinced ourself of the rare zeal and distinguished ability of Saul Juditsch, do herewith grant him a place among our royal officials, and that he may be assured of our favor for him we exempt him and his lands for the rest of his life from subordination to the jurisdiction of any 'castellan,' or any municipal court, or of any court in our land, of whatever kind or rank it may be; so that if he be summoned before the court of any judge or district, in any matter whatsoever, be it great or small, criminal or civil, he is not obliged to appear and defend himself. His goods may not be distrained, his estates not used as security, and he himself can neither be arrested, nor kept a prisoner. His refusal to appear before a judge or to give bail shall in no wise be punishable; he is amenable to no law covering such cases. If a charge be brought against him, his accusers, be they our subjects or aliens, of any rank or calling whatsoever, must appeal to ourself, the king, and Saul Juditsch shall be in honor bound to appear before us and defend himself."

This royal patent was communicated to all the princes, lords, *voivodes*, marshals, "castellans," starosts, and lower officials, in town and country, and to the governors and courts of Poland. Saul Juditsch's name continues to appear in the state documents. In 1593, he pleads for the Jews of Brzesc, who desire to have their own jurisdiction. In consequence of his intercession, Sigismund III. forbids the *voivodes* (mayors) and their proxies to interfere in the quarrels of the Jews, of whatever kind they may be. The last mention of Saul Juditsch's name occurs in the records of 1596, when, in conjunction with his Christian townsmen, he pleads for the renewal of an old franchise, granted by Grandduke Withold, exempting imported goods from duty.

Saul Wahl probably lived to the age of eighty, dying in the year 1622. The research of the historian has established his existence beyond a peradventure. He has proved that there was an individual by the name of Saul Wahl, and that is a noteworthy fact in the history of Poland and in that of the Jews in the middle ages.

After history, criticism has a word to say. A legend, as a rule, rests on analogy, on remarkable deeds, on notable events, on extraordinary historical phenomena. In the case of the legend under consideration, all these originating causes are combined. Since the time of Sigismund I., the position of the Jews in Lithuania and Poland had been favorable. It is regarded as their golden period in Poland. In general, Polish Jews had always been more favorably situated than their brethren in faith in other countries. At the very beginning of Polish history, a legend, similar to that attached to Saul Wahl's name, sprang up. After the death of Popiel, an assembly met at Kruszwica to fill the vacant throne. No agreement could be reached, and the resolution was adopted to hail as king the first person to enter the town the next morning. The guard stationed at the gate accordingly brought before the assembly the poor Jew Abraham, with the surname Powdermaker (*Prochownik*), which he had received from his business, the importing of powder. He was welcomed with loud rejoicing, and appointed king. But he refused the crown, and pressed to accept it, finally asked for a night's delay to consider the proposal. Two days and two nights passed, still the Jew did not come forth from his room. The Poles were very much excited, and a peasant, Piast by name, raising his voice, cried out: " No, no, this will not do! The land cannot be without a head, and as Abraham does not come out, I will bring him out." Swinging his axe, he rushed into the house, and led the trembling Jew before the crowd. With ready wit, Abraham said, " Poles, here you see the peasant Piast, he is the one to be your king. He is sensible, for he recognized that a land may not be without a king. Besides, he is courageous; he disregarded my command not to enter my house. Crown him, and you will have reason to be grateful to God and His servant Abraham!" So Piast was proclaimed king, and he became the ancestor of a great dynasty.

It is difficult to discover how much of truth is contained in this legend of the tenth century. That it in some remote way rests upon historical facts is attested by the existence of Polish coins bearing the inscriptions: "Abraham *Dux*" and "*Zevach* Abraham" ("Abraham the Prince" and "Abraham's Sacrifice"). Casimir the Great, whose *liaison* with the Jewess Esterka has been shown by modern historians to be a pure fabrication, confirmed the charter of liberties (*privilegium libertatis*) held by the Jews of Poland from early times, and under Sigismund I. they prospered, materially and intellectually, as never before. Learning flourished among them, especially the study of the Talmud being promoted by three great men, Solomon Shachna, Solomon Luria, and Moses Isserles.

Henry of Anjou, the first king elected by the Diet (1573), owed his election to Solomon Ashkenazi, a Jewish physician and diplomat, who ventured to remind the king of his services: "To me more than to any one else does your Majesty owe your election.

Whatever was done here at the Porte, I did, although, I believe, M. d'Acqs takes all credit unto himself." This same diplomat, together with the Jewish prince Joseph Nasi of Naxos, was chiefly instrumental in bringing about the election of Stephen Báthori. Simon Günsburg, the head of the Jewish community of Posen, had a voice in the king's council, and Bona Sforza, the Italian princess on the Polish throne, was in the habit of consulting with clever Jews. The papal legate Commendoni speaks in a vexed tone, yet admiringly, of the brilliant position of Polish Jews, of their extensive cattle-breeding and agricultural interests, of their superiority to Christians as artisans, of their commercial enterprise, leading them as far as Dantzic in the north and Constantinople in the south, and of their possession of that sovereign means which overcomes ruler, starost, and legate alike.[1]

These are the circumstances to be borne in mind in examining the authenticity of the legend about the king of a night. As early as the beginning of his century, recent historians inform us, three Jews, Abraham, Michael, and Isaac Josefowicz, rose to high positions in Lithuania. Abraham was made chief rabbi of Lithuania, his residence being fixed at Ostrog; Isaac became starost of the cities of Smolensk and Minsk (1506), and four years later, he was invested with the governorship of Lithuania. He always kept up his connection with his brothers, protected his co-religionists, and appointed Michael

[1] Graetz, *Geschichte der Juden*, IX., p. 480.

chief elder of the Lithuanian Jews. On taking
the oath of allegiance to Albert of Prussia, he was
raised to the rank of a nobleman. A Jew of the
sixteenth century a nobleman! Surely, this fact is
sufficiently startling to serve as the background of
a legend. We have every circumstance necessary:
An analogous legend in the early history of Poland,
the favored condition of the Jews, the well-attested
reality of Saul Juditsch, and an extraordinary event,
the ennobling of a Jew. Saul Wahl probably did
not reign—not even for a single night—but he certainly was attached to the person of the king, and
later, ignorant of grades of officials, the Jews were
prone to magnify his position. Indeed, the abject
misery of their condition in the seventeenth century
seems better calculated to explain the legend than
their prosperity in the fifteenth and the sixteenth
century. Bogdan Chmielnicki's campaign against
the rebellious Cossacks wrought havoc among the
Jews. From the southern part of the Ukraine to
Lemberg, the road was strewn with the corpses of
a hundred thousand Jews. The sad memory of a
happy past is the fertile soil in which legends thrive.
It is altogether likely that at this time of degradation the memory of Saul Wahl, redeemer and hero,
was first celebrated, and the report of his coat of
arms emblazoned with a lion clutching a scroll of
the Law, and crowning an eagle, of his golden
chain, of his privileges, and all his memorials, spread
from house to house.

Parallel cases of legend-construction readily suggest themselves. In our own time, in the glare of nineteenth century civilization, legends originate in the same way. Here is a case in point: In 1875, the Anthropological Society of Western Prussia instituted a series of investigations, in the course of which the complexion and the color of the hair and eyes of the children at the public schools were to be noted, in order to determine the prevalence of certain racial traits. The most extravagant rumors circulated in the districts of Dantzic, Thorn, Kulm, all the way to Posen. Parents, seized by unreasoning terror, sent their children, in great numbers, to Russia. One rumor said that the king of Prussia had lost one thousand blonde children to the sultan over a game of cards; another, that the Russian government had sold sixty thousand pretty girls to an Arab prince, and to save them from the sad fate conjectured to be in store for them, all the pretty girls at Dubna were straightway married off.—Similarly, primitive man, to satisfy his intellectual cravings, explained the phenomena of the heavens, the earth, and the waters by legends and myths, the germs of polytheistic nature religions. In our case, the tissue of facts is different, the process the same.

But legends express the idealism of the masses; they are the highest manifestations of spiritual life. The thinker's flights beyond the confines of reality, the inventor's gift to join old materials in new combinations, the artist's creative impulse, the poet's inspiration, the seer's prophetic vision—every emanation from man's ideal nature clothes itself with sinews, flesh, and skin, and lives in a people's legends, the repositories of its art, poetry, science, and ethics.

Legends moreover are characteristic of a people's culture. As a child delights in iridescent soap-bubbles, so a nation revels in reminiscences. Though poetry lend words, painting her tints, architecture a rule, sculpture a chisel, music her tones, the legend itself is dead, and only a thorough understanding of national traits enables one to recognize its ethical bearings. From this point of view, the legend of the Polish king of a night is an important historical argument, testifying to the satisfactory condition of the Jews of Poland in the fifteenth and the sixteenth century. The simile that compares nations, on the eve of a great revolution, to a seething crater, is true despite its triteness, and if to any nation, is applicable to the Poland of before and after that momentous session of the Diet. Egotism, greed, ambition, vindictiveness, and envy added fuel to fire, and hastened destruction. Jealousy had planted discord between two families, dividing the state into hostile, embittered factions. Morality was undermined, law trodden under foot, duty neglected, justice violated, the promptings of good sense disregarded. So it came about that the land was flooded by ruin as by a mighty stream, which, a tiny spring at first, gathers strength and volume from its tributaries, and overflowing its bounds, rushes over blooming meadows, fields, and pastures, drawing into its destructive depths the peasant's every joy and hope. That is the soil from which a legend like ours sprouts and grows.

This legend distinctly conveys an ethical lesson. The persecutions of the Jews, their ceaseless wanderings from town to town, from country to country, from continent to continent, have lasted two thousand years, and how many dropped by the wayside! Yet they never parted with the triple crown placed upon their heads by an ancient sage: the crown of royalty, the crown of the Law, and the crown of a good name. Learning and fair fame were indisputably theirs: therefore, the first, the royal crown, never seemed more resplendent than when worn in exile. The glory of a Jewish king of the exile seemed to herald the realization of the Messianic ideal. So it happens that many a family in Poland, England, and Germany, still cherishes the memory of Rabbi Saul the king, and that "Malkohs" everywhere still boast of royal ancestry. Rabbis, learned in the Law, were his descendants, and men of secular fame, Gabriel Riesser among them, proudly mention their connection, however distant, with Saul Wahl. The memory of his deeds perpetuates itself in respectable Jewish homes, where grandams, on quiet Sabbath afternoons, tell of them, as they show in confirmation the seal on coins to an awe-struck progeny.

Three crowns Israel bore upon his head. If the crown of royalty is legendary, then the more emphatically have the other two an historical and ethical value. The crown of royalty has slipped from us, but the crown of a good name and especially the crown of the Law are ours to keep and bequeath to our children and our children's children unto the latest generation.

JEWISH SOCIETY IN THE TIME OF MENDELSSOHN

On an October day in 1743, in the third year of the reign of Frederick the Great, a delicate lad of about fourteen begged admittance at the Rosenthal gate of Berlin, the only gate by which non-resident Jews were allowed to enter the capital. To the clerk's question about his business in the city, he briefly replied: "Study" (*Lernen*). The boy was Moses Mendelssohn, and he entered the city poor and friendless, knowing in all Berlin but one person, his former teacher Rabbi David Fränkel. About twenty years later, the Royal Academy of Sciences awarded him the first prize for his essay on the question: "Are metaphysical truths susceptible of mathematical demonstration?" After another period of twenty years, Mendelssohn was dead, and his memory was celebrated as that of a "sage like Socrates, the greatest philosophers of the day exclaiming, 'There is but one Mendelssohn!'"—

The Jewish Renaissance of a little more than a century ago presents the whole historic course of Judaism. Never had the condition of the Jews been more abject than at the time of Mendelssohn's appearance on the scene. It must be remembered that for Jews the middle ages lasted three hundred years after all other nations had begun to enjoy the blessings of the modern era. Veritable slaves, degenerate in language and habits, purchasing the right to live by a tax (*Leibzoll*), in many cities still wearing a yellow badge, timid, embittered, pale, eloquently silent, the Jews herded in their Ghetto with its single Jew-gate—they, the descendants of the Maccabees, the brethren in faith of proud Spanish grandees, of Andalusian poets and philosophers. The congregations were poor; immigrant Poles filled the offices of rabbis and teachers, and occupied themselves solely with the discussion of recondite problems. The evil nonsense of the Kabbalists was actively propagated by the Sabbatians, and on the other hand the mystical *Chassidim* were beginning to perform their witches' dance. The language commonly used was the *Judendeutsch* (the Jewish German jargon) which, stripped of its former literary dignity, was not much better than thieves' slang. Of such pitiful elements the life of the Jews was made up during the first half of the eighteenth century.

Suddenly there burst upon them the great, overwhelming Renaissance! It seemed as though Ezekiel's vision were about to be fulfilled:[1] "The hand of the Lord was upon me, and carried me out in the spirit of the Lord, and set me down in the midst of the valley which was full of bones... there were very many in the open valley; and, lo, they

[1] Ezekiel xxxvii. 1-11.

were very dry. And he said unto me, Son of man, can these bones live? And I answered, O Lord God, thou knowest. Again he said unto me, Prophesy upon these bones, and say unto them, O ye dry bones, hear the word of the Lord. Thus saith the Lord God unto these bones; Behold, I will cause breath to enter into you, and ye shall live... and ye shall know that I am the Lord. So I prophesied as I was commanded: and as I prophesied, there was a noise, and behold a shaking, and the bones came together, bone to his bone . . . the sinews and the flesh came up upon them, and the skin covered them above: but there was no breath in them. Then said he unto me, Prophesy unto the wind, prophesy, son of man, and say to the wind, Thus saith the Lord God; Come from the four winds, O breath, and breathe upon these slain, that they may live. So I prophesied as he commanded me, and the breath came into them, and they lived, and stood up upon their feet, an exceeding great army. Then he said unto me, Son of man, these bones are the whole house of Israel."

Is this not a description of Israel's history in modern days? Old Judaism, seeing the marvels of the Renaissance, might well exclaim: "Who hath begotten me these?" and many a pious mind must have reverted to the ancient words of consolation: "I remember unto thee the kindness of thy youth, the love of thy espousals, thy going after me in the wilderness, through a land that is not sown."

In the face of so radical a transformation, Herder,

poet and thinker, reached the natural conclusion that "such occurrences, such a history with all its concomitant and dependent circumstances, in brief, such a nation cannot be a lying invention. Its development is the greatest poem of all times, and still unfinished, will probably continue until every possibility hidden in the soul life of humanity shall have obtained expression."[1]

An unparalleled revival had begun; and in Germany, in which it made itself felt as an effect of the French Revolution, it is coupled first and foremost with the name of Moses Mendelssohn.

Society as conceived in these modern days is based upon men's relations to their families, their disciples, and their friends. They are the three elements that determine a man's usefulness as a social factor. Our first interest, then, is to know Mendelssohn in his family.[2] Many years were destined to elapse, after his coming to Berlin, before he was to win a position of dignity. When, a single ducat in his pocket, he first reached Berlin, the reader remembers, he was a pale-faced, fragile boy. A contemporary of his relates: "In 1746 I came to Berlin, a penniless little chap of fourteen, and in the Jewish school I met Moses Mendelssohn. He grew fond of me, taught me reading and writing, and often shared his scanty meals with me. I tried to show my gratitude by doing him any small service

[1] J. G. Herder.
[2] M. Kayserling: *Moses Mendelssohn*, and L. Geiger, *Geschichte der Juden in Berlin*, II.

in my power. Once he told me to fetch him a German book from some place or other. Returning with the book in hand, I was met by one of the trustees of the Jewish poor fund. He accosted me, not very gently, with, 'What have you there? I venture to say a German book!' Snatching it from me, and dragging me to the magistrate's, he gave orders to expel me from the city. Mendelssohn, learning my fate, did everything possible to bring about my return; but his efforts were of no avail." It is interesting to know that it was the grandfather of Herr von Bleichröder who had to submit to so relentless a fate.

German language and German writing Mendelssohn acquired by his unaided efforts. With the desultory assistance of a Dr. Kisch, a Jewish physician, he learnt Latin from a book picked up at a second-hand book stall. General culture was at that time an unknown quantity in the possibilities of Berlin Jewish life. The schoolmasters, who were not permitted to stay in the city more than three years, were for the most part Poles. One Pole, Israel Moses, a fine thinker and mathematician, banished from his native town, Samosz, on account of his devotion to secular studies, lived with Aaron Gumpertz, the only one of the famous family of court-Jews who had elected a better lot. From the latter, Mendelssohn imbibed a taste for the sciences, and to him he owed some direction in his studies; while in mathematics he was instructed by Israel Samosz, at the time when the latter, busily engaged with his great commentary on Yehuda Halevi's *Al-Chazari*, was living at the house of the Itzig family, on the *Burgstrasse*, on the very spot where the talented architect Hitzig, the grandson of Mendelssohn's contemporary, built the magnificent Exchange. To enable himself to buy books, Mendelssohn had to deny himself food. As soon as he had hoarded a few *groschen*, he stealthily slunk to a dealer in second-hand books. In this way he managed to possess himself of a Latin grammar and a wretched lexicon. Difficulties did not exist for him; they vanished before his industry and perseverance. In a short time he knew far more than Gumpertz himself, who has become famous through his entreaty to Magister Gottsched at Leipsic, whilom absolute monarch in German literature: "I would most respectfully supplicate that it may please your worshipful Highness to permit me to repair to Leipsic to pasture on the meadows of learning under your Excellency's protecting wing."

After seven years of struggle and privation, Moses Mendelssohn became tutor at the house of Isaac Bernhard, a silk manufacturer, and now began better times. In spite of faithful performance of duties, he found leisure to acquire a considerable stock of learning. He began to frequent social gatherings, his friend Dr. Gumpertz introducing him to people of culture, among others to some philosophers, members of the Berlin Academy. What smoothed the way for him more than his sterling character and his fine intellect was his good chess-playing. The Jews have always been celebrated as chess-players, and since the twelfth century a literature in Hebrew prose and verse has grown up about the game. Mendelssohn in this respect, too, was the heir of the peculiar gifts of his race.

In a little room two flights up in a house next to the Nicolai churchyard lived one of the acquaintances made by Mendelssohn through Dr. Gumpertz, a young newspaper writer—Gotthold Ephraim Lessing. Lessing was at once strongly attracted by the young man's keen, untrammelled mind. He foresaw that Mendelssohn would "become an honor to his nation, provided his fellow-believers permit him to reach his intellectual maturity. His honesty and his philosophic bent make me see in him a second Spinoza, equal to the first in all but his errors."[1] Through Lessing, Mendelssohn formed the acquaintance of Nicolai, and as they were close neighbors, their friendship developed into intimacy. Nicolai induced him to take up the study of Greek, and old Rector Damm taught him.

At this time (1755), the first coffee-house for the use of an association of about one hundred members, chiefly philosophers, mathematicians, physicians, and booksellers, was opened in Berlin. Mendelssohn, too, was admitted, making his true entrance into society, and forming many attachments. One evening it was proposed at the club that each

[1] Lessing, *Gesammelte Schriften*, Vol. XII., p. 247.

of the members describe his own defects in verse; whereupon Mendelssohn, who stuttered and was slightly hunchbacked, wrote:

> "Great you call Demosthenes,
>   Stutt'ring orator of Greece ;
>   Hunchbacked Æsop you deem wise;—
>   In your circle, I surmise,
>   I am doubly wise and great.
>   What in each was separate
>   You in me united find,—
>   Hump and heavy tongue combined."

Meanwhile his worldly affairs prospered; he had become bookkeeper in Bernhard's business. His biographer Kayserling tells us that at this period he was in a fair way to develop into "a true *bel esprit*"; he took lessons on the piano, went to the theatre and to concerts, and wrote poems. During the winter he was at his desk at the office from eight in the morning until nine in the evening. In the summer of 1756, his work was lightened; after two in the afternoon he was his own master. The following year finds him comfortably established in a house of his own with a garden, in which he could be found every evening at six o'clock, Lessing and Nicolai often joining him. Besides, he had laid by a little sum, which enabled him to help his friends, especially Lessing, out of financial embarrassments. Business cares did, indeed, bear heavily upon him, and his complaints are truly touching: "Like a beast of burden laden down, I crawl through life, self-love unfortunately whispering into my ear that nature had perhaps mapped out a poet's career for me. But what can we do, my friends? Let us pity one another, and be content. So long as love for science is not stifled within us, we may hope on." Surely, his love for learning never diminished. On the contrary, his zeal for philosophic studies grew, and with it his reputation in the learned world of Berlin. The Jewish thinker finally attracted the notice of Frederick the Great, whose poems he had had the temerity to criticise adversely in the "Letters on Literature" (*Litteraturbriefe*). He says in that famous criticism:[1] "What a loss it has been for our mother-tongue that this prince has given more time and effort to the French language. We should otherwise possess a treasure which would arouse the envy of our neighbors." A certain Herr von Justi, who had also incurred the unfavorable notice of the *Litteraturbriefe*, used this review to revenge himself on Mendelssohn. He wrote to the Prussian state-councillor: "A miserable publication appears in Berlin, letters on recent literature, in which a Jew, criticising court-preacher Cramer, uses irreverent language in reference to Christianity, and in a bold review of *Poésies diverses*, fails to pay the proper respect to his Majesty's sacred person." Soon an interdict was issued against the *Litteraturbriefe*, and Mendelssohn was summoned to appear before the attorney general Von Uhden. Nicolai has given us an account of the interview between the high and mighty officer of the state and the poor Jewish philosopher:

[1] Mendelssohn, *Gesammelte Schriften*, Vol. IV^2, 68 *ff.*

Attorney General: "Look here! How can you venture to write against Christians?"

Mendelssohn: "When I bowl with Christians, I throw down all the pins whenever I can."

Attorney General: "Do you dare mock at me? Do you know to whom you are speaking?"

Mendelssohn: "Oh yes. I am in the presence of privy councillor and attorney general Von Uhden, a just man."

Attorney General: "I ask again: What right have you to write against a Christian, a court-preacher at that?"

Mendelssohn: "And I must repeat, truly without mockery, that when I play at nine-pins with a Christian, even though he be a court-preacher, I throw down all the pins, if I can. Bowling is a recreation for my body, writing for my mind. Writers do as well as they can."

In this strain the conversation continued for some time. Another version of the affair is that Mendelssohn was ordered to appear before the king at Sanssouci on a certain Saturday. When he presented himself at the gate of the palace, the officer in charge asked him how he happened to have been honored with an invitation to come to court. Mendelssohn said: "Oh, I am a juggler!" In point of fact, Frederick read the objectionable review some time later, Venino translating it into French for him. It was probably in consequence of this vexatious occurrence that Mendelssohn made application for the privilege to be considered a *Schutzjude*, that is, a Jew with rights of residence. The Marquis d'Argens who lived with the king at Potsdam in the capacity of his Majesty's philosopher-companion, earnestly supported his petition: "*Un philosophe mauvais catholique supplie un philosophe mauvais protestant de donner le privilège à un philosophe mauvais juif. Il y a trop de philosophie dans tout ceci que la raison ne soit pas du côté de la demande.*" The privilege was accorded to Mendelssohn on November 26, 1763.

Being a *Schutzjude*, he could entertain the idea of marriage. Everybody is familiar with the pretty anecdote charmingly told by Berthold Auerbach. Mendelssohn's was a love-match. In April 1760, he undertook a trip to Hamburg, and there became affianced to a "blue-eyed maiden," Fromet Gugenheim. The story goes that the girl shrank back startled at Mendelssohn's proposal of marriage. She asked him: "Do you believe that matches are made in heaven?" "Most assuredly," answered Mendelssohn; "indeed, a singular thing happened in my own case. You know that, according to a Talmud legend, at the birth of a child, the announcement is made in heaven: So and so shall marry so and so. When I was born, my future wife's name was called out, and I was told that she would unfortunately be terribly humpbacked. 'Dear Lord,' said I, 'a deformed girl easily gets embittered and hardened. A girl ought to be beautiful. Dear Lord! Give me the hump, and let the girl be pretty, graceful, pleasing to the eye.'"

His engagement lasted a whole year. He was naturally desirous to improve his worldly position; but never did it occur to him to do so at the expense of his immaculate character. Veitel Ephraim and his associates, employed by Frederick the Great to debase the coin of Prussia, made him brilliant offers in the hope of gaining him as their partner. He could not be tempted, and entered into a binding engagement with Bernhard. His married life was happy, he was sincerely in love with his wife, and she became his faithful, devoted companion.

Six children were the offspring of their union: Abraham, Joseph, Nathan, Dorothea, Henriette, and Recha. In Moses Mendelssohn's house, the one in which these children grew up, the barriers between the learned world and Berlin general society first fell. It was the rallying place of all seeking enlightenment, of all doing battle in the cause of enlightenment. The rearing of his children was a source of great anxiety to Mendelssohn, whose means were limited. One day, shortly before his death, Mendelssohn, walking up and down before his house in Spandauer street, absorbed in meditation, was met by an acquaintance, who asked him: "My dear Mr. Mendelssohn, what is the matter with you? You look so troubled." "And so I am," he replied; "I am thinking what my children's fate will be, when I am gone."

Moses Mendelssohn was wholly a son of his age, which perhaps explains the charm of his personality.

His faults as well as his fine traits must be accounted for by the peculiarities of his generation. From this point of view, we can understand his desire to have his daughters make a wealthy match. On the other hand, he could not have known, and if he had known, he could not have understood, that his daughters, touched by the breath of a later time, had advanced far beyond his position. The Jews of that day, particularly Jewish women, were seized by a mighty longing for knowledge and culture. They studied French, read Voltaire, and drew inspiration from the works of the English freethinkers. One of those women says: "We all would have been pleased to be heroines of romance; there was not one of us who did not rave over some hero or heroine of fiction." At the head of this band of enthusiasts stood Dorothea Mendelssohn, brilliant, captivating, and gifted with a vivid imagination. She was the leader, the animating spirit of her companions. To the reading-club organized by her efforts all the restless minds belonged. In the private theatricals at the houses of rich Jews, she filled the principal rôles; and the mornings after her social triumphs found her a most attentive listener to her father, who was in the habit of holding lectures for her and her brother Joseph, afterward published under the name *Morgenstunden*. And this was the girl whom her father wished to see married at sixteen. When a rich Vienna banker was proposed as a suitable match, he said, "Ah! a man like Eskeles would greatly please my pride!" Dorothea did marry Simon Veit, a banker, a worthy man, who in no way could satisfy the demands of her impetuous nature. Yet her father believed her to be a happy wife. In her thirtieth year she made the acquaintance, at the house of her friend Henriette Herz, of a young man, five years her junior, who was destined to change the course of her whole life. This was Friedrich von Schlegel, the chief of the romantic movement. Dorothea Veit, not beautiful, fascinated him by her brilliant wit. Under Schleiermacher's encouragement, the relation between the two quickly assumed a serious aspect. But it was not until long after her father's death that Dorothea abandoned her husband and children, and became Schlegel's life-companion, first his mistress, later his wife. As Gutzkow justly says, his novel "Lucinde" describes the relation in which Schlegel "permitted himself to be discovered. Love for Schlegel it was that consumed her, and led her to share with him a thousand follies—Catholicism, Brahmin theosophy, absolutism, and the Christian asceticism of which she was a devotee at the time of her death." Neither distress, nor misery, nor care, nor sorrow could alienate her affections. Finally, she became a bigoted Catholic, and in Vienna, their last residence, the daughter of Moses Mendelssohn was seen, a lighted taper in her hand, one of a Catholic procession wending its way to St. Stephen's Cathedral.

The other daughter had a similar career. Henriette Mendelssohn filled a position as governess first in Vienna, then in Paris. In the latter city, her home was the meeting-place of the most brilliant men and women. She, too, denied her father and her faith. Recha, the youngest daughter, was the unhappy wife of a merchant of Strelitz. Later on she supported herself by keeping a boarding-school at Altona. Nathan, the youngest son, was a mechanician; Abraham, the second, the father of the famous composer, Felix Mendelssohn-Bartholdy, established with the oldest, Joseph, a still flourishing banking-business. Abraham's children and grandchildren all became converts to Christianity, but Moses and Fromet died before their defection from the old faith. Fromet lived to see the development of the passion for music which became hereditary in the family. It is said that when, at the time of the popularity of Schulz's "Athalia," one of the choruses, with the refrain *tout l'univers*, was much sung by her children, the old lady cried out irritably, "*Wie mies ist mir vor tout l'univers*" (" How sick I am of 'all the world!'").[1]

To say apologetically that the circumstances of the times produced such feeling and action may be a partial defense of these women, but it is not the truth. Henriette Mendelssohn's will is a characteristic document. The introduction runs thus: "In these the last words I address to my dear relatives, I express my gratitude for all their help and affection, and also that they in no wise hindered me in the practice of my religion. I have only myself to blame if the Lord God did not deem me worthy to

[1] Hensel, *Die Familie Mendelssohn*, Vol. I., p. 86.

be the instrument for the conversion of all my brothers and sisters to the Catholic Church, the only one endowed with saving grace. May the Lord Jesus Christ grant my prayer, and bless them all with the light of His countenance. Amen!" Such were the sentiments of Moses Mendelssohn's daughters!

The sons inclined towards Protestantism. Abraham is reported to have said that at first he was known as the son of his father, and later as the father of his son. His wife was Leah Salomon, the sister of Salomon Bartholdy, afterwards councillor of legation. His surname was really only Salomon; Bartholdy he had assumed from the former owner of a garden in Köpenikerstrasse on the Spree which he had bought. To him chiefly the formal acceptance of Christianity by Abraham's family was due. When Abraham hesitated about having his children baptized, Bartholdy wrote: "You say that you owe it to your father's memory (not to abandon Judaism). Do you think that you are committing a wrong in giving your children a religion which you and they consider the better? In fact, you would be paying a tribute to your father's efforts in behalf of true enlightenment, and he would have acted for your children as you have acted for them, perhaps for himself as I am acting for myself." This certainly is the climax of frivolity! So it happened that one of Mendelssohn's grandsons, Philip Veit, became a renowned Catholic church painter, and another, Felix Mendelssohn-Bartholdy, one of the most celebrated of Protestant composers.

After his family, we are interested in the philosopher's disciples. They are men of a type not better, but different. What in his children sprang from impulsiveness and conviction, was due to levity and imitativeness in his followers. Mendelssohn's co-workers and successors formed the school of *Biurists*, that is, expounders. In his commentary on the Pentateuch he was helped by Solomon Dubno, Herz Homberg, and Hartwig Wessely. Solomon Dubno, the tutor of Mendelssohn's children, was a learned Pole, devoted heart and soul to the work on the Pentateuch. His literary vanity having been wounded, he secretly left Mendelssohn's house, and could not be induced to renew his interest in the undertaking. Herz Homberg, an Austrian, took his place as tutor. When the children were grown, he went to Vienna, and there was made imperial councillor, charged with the superintendence of the Jewish schools of Galicia. It is a mistake to suppose that he used efforts to further the study of the Talmud among Jews. From letters recently published, written by and about him, it becomes evident that he was a common informer. Mendelssohn, of course, was not aware of his true character. The noblest of all was Naphtali Hartwig Wessely, a poet, a pure man, a sincere lover of mankind.

The other prominent members of Mendelssohn's circle were: Isaac Euchel, the "restorer of Hebrew prose," as he has been called, whose chief purpose was the reform of the Jewish order of service and Jewish pedagogic methods; Solomon Maimon, a wild fellow, who in his autobiography tells his own misdeeds, by many of which Mendelssohn was caused annoyance; Lazarus ben David, a modern Diogenes, the apostle of Kantism; and, above all, David Friedländer, an enthusiastic herald of the new era, a zealous champion of modern culture, a pure, serious character with high ethical ideals, whose aims, inspired though they were by most exalted intentions, far overstepped the bounds set to him as a Jew and the disciple of Mendelssohn. Kant's philosophy found many ardent adherents among the Jews at that time. Beside the old there was growing up a new generation which, having no obstructions placed in its path after Mendelssohn's death, aggressively asserted its principles.

The first Jew after Mendelssohn to occupy a position of prominence in the social world of Berlin was his pupil Marcus Herz, with the title professor and aulic councillor, "praised as a physician, esteemed as a philosopher, and extolled as a prodigy in the natural sciences. His lectures on physics, delivered in his own house, were attended by members of the highest aristocracy, even by royal personages."

In circles like his, the equalization of the Jews with the other citizens was animatedly discussed, by partisans and opponents. In the theatre-going public, a respectable minority, having once seen "Nathan the Wise" enacted, protested against the appearance upon the stage of the trade-Jew, speaking the singsong, drawling German vulgarly supposed to be peculiar to all Jews (*Mauscheln*). As early as 1771,

Marcus Herz had entered a vigorous protest against *mauscheln,* and at the first performance of "The Merchant of Venice" on August 16, 1788, the famous actor Fleck declaimed a prologue, composed by Ramler, in which he disavowed any intention to "sow hatred against the Jews, the brethren in faith of wise Mendelssohn," and asserted the sole purpose of the drama to be the combating of folly and vice wherever they appear.

Marcus Herz's wife was Henriette Herz, and in 1790, when Alexander and Wilhelm Humboldt first came to her house, the real history of the Berlin *salon* begins. The Humboldts' acquaintance with the Herz family dates from the visit of state councillor Kunth, the tutor of the Humboldt brothers, to Marcus Herz to advise with him about setting up a lightning-rod, an extraordinary novelty at the time, on the castle at Tegel. Shortly afterward, Kunth introduced his two pupils to Herz and his wife. So the Berlin *salon* owed its origin to a lightning-rod; indeed, it may itself be called an electrical conductor for all the spiritual forces, recently brought into play, and still struggling to manifest their undeveloped strength. Up to that time there had been nothing like society in the city of intelligence. Of course there was no dearth of scholars and clever, brilliant people, but insuperable obstacles seemed to prevent their social contact with one another. Outside of Moses Mendelssohn's house, until the end of the eighties the only *rendezvous* of wits, scholars, and literary men, the preference was for magnificent banquets and noisy carousals, each rank entertaining its own members. In the middle class, the burghers, the social instinct had not awakened at all. Alexander Humboldt significantly dated his first letter to Henriette Herz from *Schloss Langeweile*. In the course of time the desire for spiritual sympathy led to the formation of reading-clubs and *conversazioni*. These were the elements that finally produced Berlin society.

The prototype of the German *salon* naturally was the *salon* of the rococo period. Strangely enough, Berlin Jews, disciples, friends, and descendants of Moses Mendelssohn, were the transplanters of the foreign product to German soil. Untrammelled as they were in this respect by traditions, they hearkened eagerly to the new dispensation issuing from Weimar, and they were in no way hampered in the choice of their hero-guides to Olympus. Berlin irony, French sparkle, and Jewish wit moulded the social forms which thereafter were to be characteristic of society at the capital, and called forth pretty much all that was charming in the society and pleasing in the light literature of the Berlin of the day.

To judge Henriette Herz justly we must beware alike of the extravagance of her biographer and the malice of her friend Varnhagen von Ense; the former extols her cleverness to the skies, the other degrades her to the level of the commonplace. The two seem equally unreliable. She was neither extremely witty nor extremely cultured. She had a singularly clear mind, and possessed the rare faculty of spreading about her an atmosphere of ease and cheer—good substitutes for wit and intellectuality. Upon her beauty and amiability rested the popularity of her *salon*, which succeeded in uniting all the social factors of that period.

The nucleus of her social gatherings consisted of the representatives of the old literary traditions, Nicolai, Ramler, Engel, and Moritz, and they curiously enough attracted the theologians Spalding, Teller, Zöllner, and later Schleiermacher, whose intimacy with his hostess is a matter of history. Music was represented by Reichardt and Wesseli; art, by Schadow; and the nobility by Bernstorff, Dotina, Brinkmann, Friedrich von Gentz, and the Humboldts. Her drawing-room was the hearth of the romantic movement, and as may be imagined, her example was followed for better and for worse by her friends and sisters in faith, so that by the end of the century, Berlin could boast a number of *salons*, meeting-places of the nobility, literary men, and cultured Jews, for the friendly exchange of spiritual and intellectual experiences. Henriette Herz's *salon* became important not only for society in Berlin, but also for German literature, three great literary movements being sheltered in it: the classical, the romantic, and, through Ludwig Börne, that of "Young Germany." Judaism alone was left unrepresented. In fact, she and all her cultured Jewish friends hastened to free themselves of their troublesome Jewish affiliations, or, at least, concealed them as best they could. Years afterwards, Börne spent his ridicule upon the Jewesses of the Berlin *salons*, with their enormous racial noses and their great gold crosses at their throats, pressing into Trinity church to hear Schleiermacher preach. But justice compels us to say that these women did not know Judaism, or knew it only in its slave's garb. Had they had a conception of its high ethical standard, of the wealth of its poetic and philosophic thoughts, being women of rare mental gifts and broad liberality, they certainly would not have abandoned Judaism. But the Judaism of their Berlin, as represented by its religious teachers and the leaders of the Jewish community, most of them, according to Mendelssohn's own account, immigrant Poles, could not appeal to women of keen, intellectual sympathies, and tastes conforming to the ideals of the new era.

As for Mendelssohn's friends who flocked to his hospitable home—their names are household words in the history of German literature. Nicolai and Lessing must be mentioned before all others, but no one came to Berlin without seeking Moses Mendelssohn—Goethe, Herder, Wieland, Hennings, Abt, Campe, Moritz, Jerusalem. Joachim Campe has left an account of his visit at Mendelssohn's house, which is probably a just picture of its attractions.[1] He says: "On a Friday afternoon, my wife and myself, together with some of the distinguished representatives of Berlin scholarship, visited Mendelssohn. We were chatting over our coffee, when Mendelssohn, about an hour before sundown, rose

[1] Cmp. I. Heinemann, *Moses Mendelssohn*, p. 21.

from his seat with the words: 'Ladies and gentlemen, I must leave you to receive the Sabbath. I shall be with you again presently; meantime my wife will enjoy your company doubly.' All eyes followed our amiable philosopher-host with reverent admiration as he withdrew to an adjoining room to recite the customary prayers. At the end of half an hour he returned, his face radiant, and seating himself, he said to his wife: 'Now I am again at my post, and shall try for once to do the honors in your place. Our friends will certainly excuse you, while you fulfil your religious duties.' Mendelssohn's wife excused herself, joined her family, consecrated the Sabbath by lighting the Sabbath lamp, and returned to us. We stayed on for some hours." Is it possible to conceive of a more touching picture?

When Duchess Dorothea of Kurland, and her sister Elise von der Recke were living at Friedrichsfelde near Berlin in 1785, they invited Mendelssohn, whom they were eager to know, to visit them. When dinner was announced, Mendelssohn was not to be found. The companion of the two ladies writes in her journal:[1] "He had quietly slipped away to the inn at which he had ordered a frugal meal. From a motive entirely worthy I am sure, this philosopher never permits himself to be invited to a meal at a Christian's house. Not to be deprived of Mendelssohn's society too long, the duchess rose from the table as soon as possible." Mendelssohn returned, stayed a long time, and, on bidding adieu

[1] Cmp. Buker and Caro, *Vor hundert Jahren*, p. 123.

to the duchess, he said: "To-day, I have had a chat with mind."

This was Berlin society at Mendelssohn's time, and its toleration and humanity are the more to be valued as the majority of Jews by no means emulated Mendelssohn's enlightened example. All their energies were absorbed in the effort of compliance with the charter of Frederick the Great, which imposed many vexatious restrictions. On marrying, they were still compelled to buy the inferior porcelain made by the royal manufactory. The whole of the Jewish community continued to be held responsible for a theft committed by one of its members. Jews were not yet permitted to become manufacturers. Bankrupt Jews, without investigation of each case, were considered cheats. Their use of land and waterways was hampered by many petty obstructions. In every field an insurmountable barrier rose between them and their Christian fellow-citizens. Mendelssohn's great task was the moral and spiritual regeneration of his brethren in faith. In all disputes his word was final. He hoped to bring about reforms by influencing his people's inner life. Schools were founded, and every means used to further culture and education, but he met with much determined opposition among his fellow-believers. Of Ephraim, the debaser of the coin, we have spoken; also of the king's manner towards Jews. Here is another instance of his brusqueness: Abraham Posner begged for permission to shave his beard. Frederick wrote on the margin of his petition: "*Der Jude Posner soll mich und seinen Bart ungeschoren lassen.*"

Lawsuits of Jews against French and German traders made a great stir in those days. It was only after much annoyance that a naturalization patent was obtained by the family of Daniel Itzig, the father-in-law of David Friedländer, founder of the Jews' Free School in Berlin. In other cases, no amount of effort could secure the patent, the king saying: " Whatever concerns your trade is well and good. But I cannot permit you to settle tribes of Jews in Berlin, and turn it into a young Jerusalem."—

This is a picture of Jewish society in Berlin one hundred years ago. It united the most diverse currents and tendencies, emanating from romanticism, classicism, reform, orthodoxy, love of trade, and efforts for spiritual regeneration. In all this queer tangle, Moses Mendelssohn alone stands untainted, his form enveloped in pure, white light.

LEOPOLD ZUNZ[1]

We are assembled for the solemn duty of paying a tribute to the memory of him whose name graces our lodge. A twofold interest attaches us to Leopold Zunz, appealing, as he does, to our local pride, and, beyond and above that, to our Jewish feelings. Leopold Zunz was part of the Berlin of the past, every trace of which is vanishing with startling rapidity. Men, houses, streets are disappearing, and soon naught but a memory will remain of old Berlin, not, to be sure, a City Beautiful, yet filled for him that knew it with charming associations. A precious remnant of this dear old Berlin was buried forever, when, on one misty day of the spring of 1886, we consigned to their last resting place the mortal remains of Leopold Zunz. Memorial addresses are apt to abound in such expressions as "immortal," "imperishable," and in flowery tributes. This one shall not indulge in them, although to no one could they more fittingly be applied than to Leopold Zunz, a pioneer in the labyrinth of science, and the architect of many a stately palace adorning the path but lately discovered by himself. Surely, such an one deserves the cordial recognition and enduring gratitude of posterity.

[1] Address delivered at the installation of the Leopold Zunz Lodge at Berlin.

Despite the fact that Zunz was born at Detmold (August 10, 1794), he was an integral part of old Berlin—a Berlin citizen, not by birth, but by vocation, so to speak. His being was intertwined with its life by a thousand tendrils of intellectual sympathy. The city, in turn, or, to be topographically precise, the district between *Mauerstrasse* and *Rosenstrasse* knew and loved him as one of its public characters. Time was when his witticisms leapt from mouth to mouth in the circuit between the Varnhagen *salon* and the synagogue in the *Heidereutergasse*, everywhere finding appreciative listeners. An observer stationed *Unter den Linden* daily for more than thirty years might have seen a peculiar couple stride briskly towards the *Thiergarten* in the early afternoon. The loungers at Spargnapani's *café* regularly interrupted their endless newspaper reading to crane their necks and say to one another, "There go Dr. Zunz and his wife."

In his obituary notice of the poet Mosenthal, Franz Dingelstedt roguishly says: "He was of poor, albeit Jewish parentage." The same applies to Zunz, only the saying would be truer, if not so witty, in this form: "He was of Jewish, hence of poor, parentage." Among German Jews throughout the middle ages and up to the first half of this century, poverty was the rule, a comfortable competency a rare exception, wealth an unheard of condition. But Jewish poverty was relieved of sordidness by a precious gift of the old rabbis, who said: "Have a tender care of the children of the poor;

from them goeth forth the Law"; an admonition and a prediction destined to be illustrated in the case of Zunz. Very early he lost his mother, and the year 1805 finds him bereft of both parents, under the shelter and in the loving care of an institution founded by a pious Jew in Wolfenbüttel. Here he was taught the best within the reach of German Jews of the day, the *alpha* and *omega* of whose knowledge and teaching were comprised in the Talmud. The Wolfenbüttel school may be called progressive, inasmuch as a teacher, watchmaker by trade and novel-writer by vocation, was engaged to give instruction four times a week in the three R's. We may be sure that those four lessons were not given with unvarying regularity.

In his scholastic home, Leopold Zunz met Isaac Marcus Jost, a waif like himself, later the first Jewish historian, to whom we owe interesting details of Zunz's early life. In his memoirs[1] he tells the following: "Zunz had been entered as a pupil before I arrived. Even in those early days there were evidences of the acumen of the future critic. He was dominated by the spirit of contradiction. On the sly we studied grammar, his cleverness helping me over many a stumbling-block. He was very witty, and wrote a lengthy Hebrew satire on our tyrants, from which we derived not a little amusement as each part was finished. Unfortunately, the misdemeanor was detected, and the *corpus delicti* consigned to the flames, but the sobriquet *chotsuf* (impudent fellow) clung to the writer."

[1] In *Sippurim*, I., 165 ff.

It is only just to admit that in this *Beth ha-Midrash* Zunz laid the foundation of the profound, comprehensive scholarship on Talmudic subjects, the groundwork of his future achievements as a critic. The circumstance that both these embryo historians had to draw their first information about history from the Jewish German paraphrase of " Yosippon," an historical compilation, is counterbalanced by careful instruction in Rabbinical literature, whose labyrinthine ways soon became paths of light to them.

A new day broke, and in its sunlight the condition of affairs changed. In 1808 the *Beth ha-Midrash* was suddenly transformed into the " Samson-school," still in useful operation. It became a primary school, conducted on approved pedagogic principles, and Zunz and Jost were among the first registered under the new, as they had been under the old, administration. Though the one was thirteen, and the other fourteen years old, they had to begin with the very rudiments of reading and writing. Campe's juvenile books were the first they read. A year later finds them engaged in secretly studying Greek, Latin, and mathematics during the long winter evenings, by the light of bits of candles made by themselves of drippings from the great wax tapers in the synagogue. After another six months, Zunz was admitted to the first class of the Wolfenbüttel, and Jost to that of the Brunswick, *gymnasium*. It characterizes the men to say that Zunz was the first, and Jost the third, Jew in Germany to enter a *gymnasium*. Now progress was rapid. The classes of the *gymnasium* were passed through with astounding ease, and in 1811, with a minimum of luggage, but a very considerable mental equipment, Zunz arrived in Berlin, never to leave it except for short periods. He entered upon a course in philology at the newly founded university, and after three years of study, he was in the unenviable position to be able to tell himself that he had attained to—nothing.

For, to what could a cultured Jew attain in those days, unless he became a lawyer or a physician? The Hardenberg edict had opened academical careers to Jews, but when Zunz finished his studies, that provision was completely forgotten. So he became a preacher. A rich Jew, Jacob Herz Beer, the father of two highly gifted sons, Giacomo and Michael Beer, had established a private synagogue in his house, and here officiated Edward Kley, C. Günsburg, J. L. Auerbach, and, from 1820 to 1822, Leopold Zunz. It is not known why he resigned his position, but to infer that he had been forced to embrace the vocation of a preacher by the stress of circumstances is unjust. At that juncture he probably would have chosen it, if he had been offered the rectorship of the Berlin university; for, he was animated by somewhat of the spirit that urged the prophets of old to proclaim and fulfil their mission in the midst of storms and in despite of threatening dangers.

Zunz's sermons delivered from 1820 to 1822 in

the first German reform temple are truly instinct with the prophetic spirit. The breath of a mighty enthusiasm rises from the yellowed pages. Every word testifies that they were indited by a writer of puissant individuality, disengaged from the shackles of conventional homiletics, and boldly striking out on untrodden paths. In the Jewish Berlin of the day, a rationalistic, half-cultured generation, swaying irresolutely between Mendelssohn and Schleiermacher, these new notes awoke sympathetic echoes. But scarcely had the music of his voice become familiar, when it was hushed. In 1823, a royal cabinet order prohibited the holding of the Jewish service in German, as well as every other innovation in the ritual, and so German sermons ceased in the synagogue. Zunz, who had spoken like Moses, now held his peace like Aaron, in modesty and humility, yielding to the inevitable without rancor or repining, always loyal to the exalted ideal which inspired him under the most depressing circumstances. He dedicated his sermons, delivered at a time of religious enthusiasm, to "youth at the crossroads," whom he had in mind throughout, in the hope that they might "be found worthy to lead back to the Lord hearts, which, through deception or by reason of stubbornness, have fallen away from Him."

The rescue of the young was his ideal. At the very beginning of his career he recognized that the old were beyond redemption, and that, if response and confidence were to be won from the young, the expounding of the new Judaism was work, not for the pulpit, but for the professor's chair. "Devotional exercises and balmy lotions for the soul" could not heal their wounds. It was imperative to bring their latent strength into play. Knowing this to be his pedagogic principle, we shall not go far wrong, if we suppose that in the organization of the "Society for Jewish Culture and Science" the initial step was taken by Leopold Zunz. In 1819 when the mobs of Würzburg, Hamburg, and Frankfort-on-the-Main revived the "Hep, hep!" cry, three young men, Edward Gans, Moses Moser, and Leopold Zunz conceived the idea of a society with the purpose of bringing Jews into harmony with their age and environment, not by forcing upon them views of alien growth, but by a rational training of their inherited faculties. Whatever might serve to promote intelligence and culture was to be nurtured: schools, seminaries, academies, were to be erected, literary aspirations fostered, and all public-spirited enterprises aided; on the other hand, the rising generation was to be induced to devote itself to arts, trades, agriculture, and the applied sciences; finally, the strong inclination to commerce on the part of Jews was to be curbed, and the tone and conditions of Jewish society radically changed—lofty goals for the attainment of which most limited means were at the disposal of the projectors. The first fruits of the society were the "Scientific Institute," and the "Journal for the Science of Judaism," published in the spring of 1822, under the editorship of Zunz. Only three numbers appeared, and they met with so small a sale that the cost of printing was not realized. Means were inadequate, the plans magnificent, the times above all not ripe for such ideals. The "Scientific Institute" crumbled away, too, and in 1823, the society was breathing its last. Zunz poured out the bitterness of his disappointment in a letter written in the summer of 1824 to his Hamburg friend Immanuel Wohlwill:

"I am so disheartened that I can nevermore believe in Jewish reform. A stone must be thrown at this phantasm to make it vanish. Good Jews are either Asiatics, or Christians (unconscious thereof), besides a small minority consisting of myself and a few others, the possibility of mentioning whom saves me from the imputation of conceit, though, truth to say, the bitterness of irony cares precious little for the forms of good society. Jews, and the Judaism which we wish to reconstruct, are a prey to disunion, and the booty of vandals, fools, money-changers, idiots, and *parnassim*.[1] Many a change of season will pass over this generation, and leave it unchanged: internally ruptured; rushing into the arms of Christianity, the religion of expediency; without stamina and without principle; one section thrust aside by Europe, and vegetating in filth with longing eyes directed towards the Messiah's ass or other member of the long-eared fraternity; the other occupied with fingering state securities and the pages of a cyclopædia, and constantly oscillating between wealth and bankruptcy, oppression and

[1] Administrators of the secular affairs of Jewish congregations. [Tr.]

tolerance. Their own science is dead among Jews, and the intellectual concerns of European nations do not appeal to them, because, faithless to themselves, they are strangers to abstract truth and slaves of self-interest. This abject wretchedness is stamped upon their penny-a-liners, their preachers, councillors, constitutions, *parnassim*, titles, meetings, institutions, subscriptions, their literature, their book-trade, their representatives, their happiness, and their misfortune. No heart, no feeling! All a medley of prayers, banknotes, and *rachmones*,[1] with a few strains of enlightenment and *chilluk!*[2]—

Now, my friend, after so revolting a sketch of Judaism, you will hardly ask why the society and the journal have vanished into thin air, and are missed as little as the temple, the school, and the rights of citizenship. The society might have survived despite its splitting up into sections. That was merely a mistake in management. The truth is that it never had existence. Five or six enthusiasts met together, and like Moses ventured to believe that their spirit would communicate itself to others. That was self-deception. *The only imperishable possession rescued from this deluge is the science of Judaism. It lives even though not a finger has been raised in its service since hundreds of years. I confess that, barring submission to the judgment of God, I find solace only in the cultivation of the science of Judaism.*

As for myself, those rough experiences of mine shall assuredly not persuade me into a course of

[1] Compassion, charity. [Tr.]   [2] Talmudical dialectics. [Tr.]

action inconsistent with my highest aspirations. I did what I held my duty. I ceased to preach, not in order to fall away from my own words, but because I realized that I was preaching in the wilderness. *Sapienti sat.* . . After all that I have said, you will readily understand that I cannot favor an unduly ostentatious mode of dissolution. Such a course would be prompted by the vanity of the puffed-out frog in the fable, and affect the Jews . . as little as all that has gone before. There is nothing for the members to do but to remain unshaken, and radiate their influence in their limited circles, leaving all else to God."

The man who wrote these words, it is hard to realize, had not yet passed his thirtieth year, but his aim in life was perfectly defined. He knew the path leading to his goal, and—most important circumstance—never deviated from it until he attained it. His activity throughout life shows no inconsistency with his plans. It is his strength of character, rarest of attributes in a time of universal defection from the Jewish standard, that calls for admiration, accorded by none so readily as by his companions in arms. Casting up his own spiritual accounts, Heinrich Heine in the latter part of his life wrote of his friend Zunz:[1] "In the instability of a transition period he was characterized by incorruptible constancy, remaining true, despite his acumen, his scepticism, and his scholarship, to self-imposed promises, to the exalted hobby of his soul. A man

[1] Cmp. Strodtmann: *H. Heine*, Vol. I., p. 316.

of thought and action, he created and worked when others hesitated, and sank discouraged," or, what Heine prudently omitted to say, deserted the flag, and stealthily slunk out of the life of the oppressed.

In Zunz, strength of character was associated with a mature, richly stored mind. He was a man of talent, of character, and of science, and this rare union of traits is his distinction. At a time when the majority of his co-religionists could not grasp the plain, elementary meaning of the phrase, "the science of Judaism," he made it the loadstar of his life.

Sad though it be, I fear that it is true that there are those of this generation who, after the lapse of years, are prompted to repeat the question put by Zunz's contemporaries, "What is the science of Judaism?" Zunz gave a comprehensive answer in a short essay, "On Rabbinical Literature," published by Mauer in 1818:[1] "When the shadows of barbarism were gradually lifting from the mist-shrouded earth, and light universally diffused could not fail to strike the Jews scattered everywhere, a remnant of old Hebrew learning attached itself to new, foreign elements of culture, and in the course of centuries enlightened minds elaborated the heterogeneous ingredients into the literature called rabbinical." To this rabbinical, or, to use the more fitting name proposed by himself, this neo-Hebraic, Jewish literature and science, Zunz devoted his love, his work, his life. Since centuries this field of

[1] Zunz, *Gesammelte Schriften*, Vol. I., p. 3 *ff.*

knowledge had been a trackless, uncultivated waste. He who would pass across, had need to be a pathfinder, robust and energetic, able to concentrate his mind upon a single aim, undisturbed by distracting influences. Such was Leopold Zunz, who sketched in bold, but admirably precise outlines the extent of Jewish science, marking the boundaries of its several departments, estimating its resources, and laying out the work and aims of the future. The words of the prophet must have appealed to him with peculiar force: " I remember unto thee the kindness of thy youth, the love of thy espousals, thy going after me in the wilderness, through a land that is not sown."

Again, when there was question of cultivating the desert soil, and seeking for life under the rubbish, Zunz was the first to present himself as a laborer. The only fruit of the Society for Jewish Culture and Science, during the three years of its existence, was the " Journal for the Science of Judaism," and its publication was due exclusively to Zunz's perseverance. Though only three numbers appeared, a positive addition to our literature was made through them in Zunz's biographical essay on Rashi, the old master expounder of the Bible and the Talmud. By its arrangement of material, by its criticism and grouping of facts, and not a little by its brilliant style, this essay became the model for all future work on kindred subjects. When the society dissolved, and Zunz was left to enjoy undesired leisure, he continued to work on the lines laid down therein.

Besides, Zunz was a political journalist, for many years political editor of "Spener's Journal," and a contributor to the *Gesellschafter*, the *Iris*, *Die Freimütigen*, and other publications of a literary character. From 1825 to 1829, he was a director of the newly founded Jewish congregational school; for one year he occupied the position of preacher at Prague; and from 1839 to 1849, the year of its final closing, he acted as trustee of the Jewish teachers' seminary in Berlin. Thereafter he had no official position.

As a politician he was a pronounced democrat. Reading his political addresses to-day, after a lapse of half a century, we find in them the clearness and sagacity that distinguish the scientific productions of the investigator. Here is an extract from his words of consolation addressed to the families of the heroes of the March revolution of 1848:[1]

"They who walked our streets unnoticed, who meditated in their quiet studies, toiled in their workshops, cast up accounts in offices, sold wares in the shops, were suddenly transformed into valiant fighters, and we discovered them at the moment when like meteors they vanished. When they grew lustrous, they disappeared from our sight, and when they became our deliverers, we lost the opportunity of thanking them. Death has made them great and precious to us. Departing they poured unmeasured wealth upon us all, who were so poor. Our heads, parched like a summer sky, produced no fruitful

[1] *Ibid.*, p. 301.

rain of magnanimous thoughts. The hearts in our bosoms, turned into stone, were bereft of human sympathies. Vanity and illusions were our idols; lies and deception poisoned our lives; lust and avarice dictated our actions; a hell of immorality and misery, corroding every institution, heated the atmosphere to suffocation, until black clouds gathered, a storm of the nations raged about us, and purifying streaks of lightning darted down upon the barricades and into the streets. Through the storm-wind, I saw chariots of fire and horses of fire bearing to heaven the men of God who fell fighting for right and liberty. I hear the voice of God, O ye that weep, knighting your dear ones. The freedom of the press is their patent of nobility, our hearts, their monuments. Every one of us, every German, is a mourner, and you, survivors, are no longer abandoned."

In an election address of February 1849,[1] Zunz says: "The first step towards liberty is to miss liberty, the second, to seek it, the third, to find it. Of course, many years may pass between the seeking and the finding." And further on: "As an elector, I should give my vote for representatives only to men of principle and immaculate reputation, who neither hesitate nor yield; who cannot be made to say cold is warm, and warm is cold; who disdain legal subtleties, diplomatic intrigues, lies of whatever kind, even when they redound to the advantage of the party. Such are worthy of the confi-

[1] *Ibid.*, p. 310.

dence of the people, because conscience is their monitor. They may err, for to err is human, but they will never deceive."

Twelve years later, on a similar occasion, he uttered the following prophetic words:[1] " A genuinely free form of government makes a people free and upright, and its representatives are bound to be champions of liberty and progress. If Prussia, unfurling the banner of liberty and progress, will undertake to provide us with such a constitution, our self-confidence, energy, and trustfulness will return. Progress will be the fundamental principle of our lives, and out of our united efforts to advance it will grow a firm, indissoluble union. Now, then, Germans! Be resolved, all of you, to attain the same goal, and your will shall be a storm-wind scattering like chaff whatever is old and rotten. In your struggle for a free country, you will have as allies the army of mighty minds that have suffered for right and liberty in the past. Now you are split up into tribes and clans, held together only by the bond of language and a classic literature. You will grow into a great nation, if but all brother-tribes will join us. Then Germany, strongly secure in the heart of Europe, will be able to put an end to the quailing before attacks from the East or the West, and cry a halt to war. The empire, some one has said, means peace. Verily, with Prussia at its head, the German empire means peace."

Such utterances are characteristic of Zunz, the

[1] *Ibid.*, p. 316.

politician. His best energies and efforts, however, were devoted to his researches. Science, he believed, would bring about amelioration of political conditions; science, he hoped, would preserve Judaism from the storms and calamities of his generation, for the fulfilment of its historical mission. Possessed by this idea, he wrote *Die Gottesdienstlichen Vorträge der Juden* (" Jewish Homiletics," 1832), the basis of the future science of Judaism, the first clearing in the primeval forest of rabbinical writings, through which the pioneer led his followers with steady step and hand, as though walking on well trodden ground. Heinrich Heine, who appreciated Zunz at his full worth, justly reckoned this book " among the noteworthy productions of the higher criticism," and another reviewer with equal justice ranks it on a level with the great works of Böckh, Diez, Grimm, and others of that period, the golden age of philological research in Germany.

Like almost all that Zunz wrote, *Die Gottesdienstlichen Vorträge der Juden* was the result of a polemic need. By nature Zunz was a controversialist. Like a sentinel upon the battlements, he kept a sharp lookout upon the land. Let the Jews be threatened with injustice by ruler, statesman, or scholar, and straightway he attacked the enemy with the weapons of satire and science. One can fancy that the cabinet order prohibiting German sermons in the synagogue, and so stifling the ambition of his youth, awakened the resolve to trace the development of the sermon among Jews, and show that thousands of years ago the wellspring of religious instruction bubbled up in Judah's halls of prayer, and has never since failed, its wealth of waters overflowing into the popular Midrash, the repository of little known, unappreciated treasures of knowledge and experience, accumulated in the course of many centuries.

In the preface to this book, Zunz, the democrat, says that for his brethren in faith he demands of the European powers, "not rights and liberties, but right and liberty. Deep shame should mantle the cheek of him who, by means of a patent of nobility conferred by favoritism, is willing to rise above his *co-religionists*, while the law of the land brands him by assigning him a place among the lowest of his *co-citizens*. Only in the rights common to all citizens can we find satisfaction; only in unquestioned equality, the end of our pain. Liberty unshackling the hand to fetter the tongue; tolerance delighting not in our progress, but in our decay; citizenship promising protection without honor, imposing burdens without holding out prospects of advancement; they all, in my opinion, are lacking in love and justice, and such baneful elements in the body politic must needs engender pestiferous diseases, affecting the whole and its every part."

Zunz sees a connection between the civil disabilities of the Jews and their neglect of Jewish science and literature. Untrammelled, instructive speech he accounts the surest weapon. Hence the homilies of the Jews appear to him to be worthy, and to stand in need, of historical investigation, and the results of his research into their origin, development, and uses, from the time of Ezra to the present day, are laid down in this epoch-making work.

The law forbidding the bearing of German names by Jews provoked Zunz's famous and influential little book, "The Names of the Jews," like most of his later writings polemic in origin, in which respect they remind one of Lessing's works.

In the ardor of youth Zunz had borne the banner of reform; in middle age he became convinced that the young generation of iconoclasts had rushed far beyond the ideal goal of the reform movement cherished in his visions. As he had upheld the age and sacred uses of the German sermon against the assaults of the orthodox; so for the benefit and instruction of radical reformers, he expounded the value and importance of the Hebrew liturgy in profound works, which appeared during a period of ten years, crystallizing the results of a half-century's severe application. They rounded off the symmetry of his spiritual activity. For, when Midrashic inspiration ceased to flow, the *piut*—synagogue poetry—established itself, and the transformation from the one into the other was the active principle of neo-Hebraic literature for more than a thousand years. Zunz's vivifying sympathies knit the old and the new into a wondrously firm historical thread. Nowhere have the harmony and continuity of Jewish literary development found such adequate expression as in his *Synagogale Poesie des Mittelal-*

ters ("Synagogue Poetry of the Middle Ages," 1855), *Ritus des synagogalen Gottesdienstes* ("The Ritual of the Synagogue," 1859), and *Litteraturgeschichte der synagogalen Poesie* ("History of Synagogue Poetry," 1864), the capstone of his literary endeavors.

In his opinion, the only safeguard against error lies in the pursuit of science, not, indeed, dryasdust science, but science in close touch with the exuberance of life regulated by high-minded principles, and transfigured by ideal hopes. Sermons and prayers in harmonious relation, he believed,[1] will "enable some future generation to enjoy the fruits of a progressive, rational policy, and it is meet that science and poetry should be permeated with ideas serving the furtherance of such policy. Education is charged with the task of moulding enlightened minds to think the thoughts that prepare for rightdoing, and warm, enthusiastic hearts to execute commendable deeds. For, after all is said and done, the well-being of the community can only grow out of the intelligence and the moral life of each member. Every individual that strives to apprehend the harmony of human and divine elements attains to membership in the divine covenant. The divine is the aim of all our thoughts, actions, sentiments, and hopes. It invests our lives with dignity, and supplies a moral basis for our relations to one another. Well, then, let us hope for redemption—for the universal recognition of a form of government under

[1] *Ibid.*, p. 133.

which the rights of man are respected. Then free citizens will welcome Jews as brethren, and Israel's prayers will be offered up by mankind."

These are samples of the thoughts underlying Zunz's great works, as well as his numerous smaller, though not less important, productions: biographical and critical essays, legal opinions, sketches in the history of literature, reviews, scientific inquiries, polemical and literary fragments, collected in his work *Zur Geschichte und Litteratur* ("Contributions to History and Literature," 1873), and in three volumes of collected writings. Since the publication of his "History of Synagogue Poetry," Zunz wrote only on rare occasions. His last work but one was *Deutsche Briefe* (1872) on German language and German intellect, and his last, an incisive and liberal contribution to Bible criticism (*Studie zur Bibelkritik*, 1874), published in the *Zeitschrift der deutschen morgenländischen Gesellschaft* in Leipsic. From that time on, when the death of his beloved wife, Adelheid Zunz, a most faithful helpmate, friend, counsellor, and support, occurred, he was silent.

Zunz had passed his seventieth year when his "History of Synagogue Poetry" appeared. He could permit himself to indulge in well-earned rest, and from the vantage-ground of age inspect the bustling activity of a new generation of friends and disciples on the once neglected field of Jewish science.

Often as the cause of religion and civil liberty

received a check at one place or another, during those long years when he stood aside from the turmoil of life, a mere looker-on, he did not despair; he continued to hope undaunted. Under his picture he wrote sententiously: " Thought is strong enough to vanquish arrogance and injustice without recourse to arrogance and injustice."

Zunz's life and work are of incalculable importance to the present age and to future generations. With eagle vision he surveyed the whole domain of Jewish learning, and traced the lines of its development. Constructive as well as critical, he raised widely scattered fragments to the rank of a literature which may well claim a place beside the literatures of the nations. Endowed with rare strength of character, he remained unflinchingly loyal to his ancestral faith, " the exalted hobby of his soul "— a model for three generations. Jewish literature owes to him a scientific style. He wrote epigrammatic, incisive, perspicuous German, stimulating and suggestive, such as Lessing used. The reform movement he supported as a legitimate development of Judaism on historical lines. On the other hand, he fostered loyalty to Judaism by lucidly presenting to young Israel the value of his faith, his intellectual heritage, and his treasures of poetry. Zunz, then, is the originator of a momentous phase in our development, producing among its adherents as among outsiders a complete revolution in the appreciation of Judaism, its religious and intellectual aspects. Together with self-knowledge he taught his brethren self-respect. He was, in short, a clear thinker and acute critic; a German, deeply attached to his beloved country, and fully convinced of the supremacy of German mind; at the same time, an ardent believer in Judaism, imbued with some of the spirit of the prophets, somewhat of the strength of Jewish heroes and martyrs, who sacrificed life for their conviction, and with dying lips made the ancient confession: "Hear, O Israel, the Lord, our God, the Lord is one!"

His name is an abiding possession for our nation; it will not perish from our memory. "Good night, my prince! O that angel choirs might lull thy slumbers!"

HEINRICH HEINE AND JUDAISM

I

No modern poet has aroused so much discussion as Heinrich Heine. His works are known everywhere, and quotations from them—gorgeous butterflies, stinging gnats, buzzing bees—whizz and whirr through the air of our century. They are the *vade mecum* of modern life in all its moods and variations.

This high regard is a recent development. Within the last thirty years a complete change has taken place in public opinion. Soon after the poet's death, he was entirely neglected. The *Augsburger Allgemeine Zeitung*, whose columns had for decades been enriched with his contributions, took three months to get up a little obituary notice. Then followed a period of acrimonious detraction; at last, cordial appreciation has come.

The conviction has been growing that in Heine the German nation must revere its greatest lyric poet since Goethe, and as time removes him from us, the baser elements of his character recede into the background, his personality is lost sight of, and his poetry becomes the paramount consideration.

What is the attitude of Judaism? Does it acknowledge Heine as its son? Is it disposed to accept *cum beneficio inventarii* the inheritance he has bequeathed to it? To answer these questions we must review Heine's life, his relations to Judaism, his opinions on Jewish subjects, and the qualities which prove him heir to the peculiarities of the Jewish race.

Heine's family was Jewish. On the paternal side it can be traced to Meyer Samson Popert and Fromet Heckscher of Altona; on the maternal side further back, to Isaac van Geldern, who emigrated in about 1700 from Holland to the duchy of Jülich-Berg. He and his son Lazarus van Geldern were people of importance at Düsseldorf, and his other sons, Simon and Gottschalk, were known and respected beyond the confines of their city. Simon van Geldern was the author of "The Israelites on Mount Horeb," a didactic poem in English, and on his trip to the East he kept a Hebrew journal, which can still be seen. His younger brother Gottschalk was a distinguished physician, and occupied a position of high dignity in the Jewish congregations in the duchies of Jülich and Berg. It is said that he provided for the welfare of his brethren in faith " as a father provides for his children." His only daughter Betty (Peierche) van Geldern, urged by her family and in obedience to the promptings of her own heart, married Samson Heine, and became the mother of the poet. Heine himself has written much about his family,[1] particularly about his mother's

[1] Cmp. *Memoiren* in his Collected Works, Vol. VI., p. 375 *ff.*

brother. Of his paternal grandfather, he knew only what his father had told him, that he was "a little Jew with a great beard." On the whole, his education was strictly religious, but it was tainted with the deplorable inconsistency so frequently found in Jewish homes. Themselves heedless of religious ceremonies, parents exact from their children punctilious observance of minute regulations. Samson Heine was one of the Jews often met with in the beginning of this century who, lacking true culture, caught up some of the encyclopædist phrases with which the atmosphere of the period was heavy. Heine describes his father's extraordinary buoyancy: "Always azure serenity and fanfares of good humor." The reproach is characteristic which he addressed to his son, when the latter was charged with atheism: "Dear son! Your mother is having you instructed in philosophy by Rector Schallmeier —that is her affair. As for me, I have no love for philosophy; it is nothing but superstition. I am a merchant, and need all my faculties for my business. You may philosophize as much as you please, only, I beg of you, don't tell any one what you think. It would harm my business, were people to discover that my son does not believe in God. Particularly the Jews would stop buying velvets from me, and they are honest folk, and pay promptly. And they are right in clinging to religion. Being your father, therefore older than you, I am more experienced, and you may take my word for it, atheism is a great sin."

Two instances related by Joseph Neunzig, one of his playmates, show how rigorously Harry was compelled to observe religious forms in his paternal home. On a Saturday the children were out walking, when suddenly a fire broke out. The fire extinguishers came clattering up to the burning house, but as the flames were spreading rapidly, all bystanders were ordered to range themselves in line with the firemen. Harry refused point-blank to help: "I may not do it, and I will not, because it is *Shabbes* to-day." But another time, when it jumped with his wishes, the eight year old boy managed to circumvent the Law. He was playing with some of his schoolmates in front of a neighbor's house. Two luscious bunches of grapes hung over the arbor almost down to the ground. The children noticed them, and with longing in their eyes passed on. Only Harry stood still before the grapes. Suddenly springing on the arbor, he bit one grape after another from the bunch. "Red-head Harry!" the children exclaimed horrified, "what are you doing?" "Nothing wrong," said the little rogue. "We are forbidden to pluck them with our hands, but the law does not say anything about biting and eating." His education was not equable and not methodical. Extremely indulgent towards themselves, the parents were extremely severe in their treatment of their children. So arose the contradictions in the poet's character. He is one of those to whom childhood's religion is a bitter-sweet remembrance unto the end of days. Jewish sympathies were his inalienable heritage, and from this point of view his life must be considered.

The poet's mother was of a different stamp from his father. Like most of the Jews in the Rhenish provinces, his father hailed Napoleon, the first legislator to establish equality between Jews and Christians, as a savior. His mother, on the other hand, was a good German patriot and a woman of culture, who exercised no inconsiderable influence upon the heart and mind of her son. Heine calls her a disciple of Rousseau, and his brother Maximilian tells us that Goethe was her favorite among authors.

The boy was first taught by Rintelsohn at a Jewish school, but his knowledge of Hebrew seems to have been very limited. It is an interesting fact that his first poem, "Belshazzar," which he tells us he wrote at the age of sixteen, was inspired by his childhood's faith and is based upon Jewish history. Towards the end of his life he said to a friend:[1] "Do you know what inspired me? A few words in the Hebrew hymn, *Wayhee bechatsi halaïla*, sung, as you know, on the first two evenings of the Passover. This hymn commemorates all momentous events in the history of the Jews that occurred at midnight; among them the death of the Babylonian tyrant, snatched away at night for desecrating the holy Temple vessels. The quoted words are the refrain of the hymn, which forms part of the Haggada, the curious medley of legends and songs, recited by pious Jews at the *Seder*." Ay, the Passover cele-

[1] Ludwig Kalisch, *Pariser Skizzen*, p. 331.

bration, the *Seder*, remained in the poet's memory till the day of his death. He describes it still later in one of his finest works:[1] "Sweetly sad, joyous, earnest, sportive, and elfishly mysterious is that evening service, and the traditional chant with which the Haggada is recited by the head of the family, the listeners sometimes joining in as a chorus, is thrillingly tender, soothing as a mother's lullaby, yet impetuous and inspiring, so that Jews who long have drifted from the faith of their fathers, and have been pursuing the joys and dignities of the stranger, even they are stirred in their inmost parts when the old, familiar Passover sounds chance to fall upon their ears."

My esteemed friend Rabbi Dr. Frank of Cologne has in his possession a Haggada, admirably illustrated, an heirloom at one time of the Van Geldern family, and it is not improbable that it was out of this artistic book that Heinrich Heine asked the *Mah nishtannah*, the traditional question of the *Seder*.

Heine left home very young, and everybody knows that he was apprenticed to a merchant at Frankfort, and that his uncle Solomon's kindness enabled him to devote himself to jurisprudence. But this, of important bearing on our subject, is not a matter of common knowledge: *Always and everywhere, especially when he had least intercourse with Jews, Jewish elements appear most prominently in Heine's life.*

[1] Collected Works, Vol. IV., p. 227.

A merry, light-hearted student, he arrived in Berlin in 1821. A curious spectacle is presented by the Jewish Berlin of the day, dominated by the *salons*, and the women whose tact and scintillating wit made them the very centre of general society. The traditions of Rahel Levin, Henriette Herz, and other clever women, still held sway. But the state frustrated every attempt to introduce reforms into Judaism. Two great parties opposed each other more implacably than ever, the one clutching the old, the other yearning for the new. Out of the breach, salvation was in time to sprout. In the first quarter of our century, more than three-fourths of the Jewish population of Berlin embraced the ruling faith. This was the new, seditious element with which young Heine was thrown. His interesting personality attracted general notice. All circles welcomed him. The *salons* did their utmost to make him one of their votaries. Romantic student clubs at Lutter's and Wegener's wine-rooms left nothing untried to lure him to their nocturnal carousals. Even Hegel, the philosopher, evinced marked interest in him. To whose allurements does he yield? Like his great ancestor, he goes to "his brethren languishing in captivity." Some of his young friends, Edward Gans, Leopold Zunz, and Moses Moser, had formed a "Society for Jewish Culture and Science," with Berlin as its centre, and Heinrich Heine became one of its most active members. He taught poor Jewish boys from Posen several hours a week in the school established by the society, and all questions that came up interested him. Joseph Lehmann took pleasure in repeatedly telling how seriously Heine applied himself to a review which he had undertaken to write on the compilation of a German prayer-book for Jewish women.

To the Berlin period belongs his *Almansor*, a dramatic poem which has suffered the most contradictory criticism. In my opinion, it has usually been misunderstood. *Almansor* is intelligible only if regarded from a Jewish point of view, and then it is seen to be the hymn of vengeance sung by Judaism oppressed. Substitute the names of a converted Berlin banker and his wife for "Aly" and "Suleima," Berlin under Frederick William III. for "Saragossa," the Berlin Thiergarten for the "Forest," and the satire stands revealed. The following passage is characteristic of the whole poem:[1]

> "Go not to Aly's castle! Flee
> That noxious house where new faith breeds.
> With honeyed accents there thy heart
> Is wrenched from out thy bosom's depths,
> A snake bestowed on thee instead.
> Hot drops of lead on thy poor head
> Are poured, and nevermore thy brain
> From madding pain shall rid itself.
> Another name thou must assume,
> That if thy angel warning calls,
> And calls thee by thy olden name,
> He call in vain."

Such were Heine's views at that time, and with them he went to Göttingen. There, though Jewish

[1] *Ibid.*, Vol. III., p. 13.

society was entirely lacking, and correspondence with his Berlin friends desultory, his Jewish interests grew stronger than ever. There, inspired by the genius of Jewish history, he composed his *Rabbi von Bacharach*, the work which, by his own confession, he nursed with unspeakable love, and which, he fondly hoped, would "become an immortal book, a perpetual lamp in the dome of God." Again Jewish conversions, a burning question of the day, were made prominent. Heine's solution is beyond a cavil enlightened. The words are truly remarkable with which Sarah, the beautiful Jewess, declines the services of the gallant knight:[1] "Noble sir! Would you be my knight, then you must meet nations in a combat in which small praise and less honor are to be won. And would you be rash enough to wear my colors, then you must sew yellow wheels upon your mantle, or bind a blue-striped scarf about your breast. For these are my colors, the colors of my house, named Israel, the unhappy house mocked at on the highways and the byways by the children of fortune."

Another illustration of Heine's views at that time of his life, and with those views he one day went to the neighboring town of Heiligenstadt—to be baptized.

Who can sound the depths of a poet's soul? Who can divine what Heine's thoughts, what his hopes were, when he took this step? His letters and confessions of that period must be read to gain an idea

[1] *Ibid.*, Vol. IV., p. 257 *ff.*

of his inner world. On one occasion he wrote to Moser, to whom he laid bare his most intimate thoughts:[1] "Mentioning Japan reminds me to recommend to you Golovnin's 'Journey to Japan.' Perhaps I may send you a poem to-day from the *Rabbi*, in the writing of which I unfortunately have been interrupted again. I beg that you speak to nobody about this poem, or about what I tell you of my private affairs. A young Spaniard, at heart a Jew, is beguiled to baptism by the arrogance bred of luxury. He sends the translation of an Arabic poem to young Yehuda Abarbanel, with whom he is corresponding. Perhaps he shrinks from directly confessing to his friend an action hardly to be called admirable. . . . Pray do not think about this."

And the poem? It is this:

TO EDOM

"Each with each has borne in patience
  Longer than a thousand year—
Thou dost tolerate my breathing,
  I thy ravings calmly hear.

Sometimes only, in the darkness,
  Thou didst have sensations odd,
And thy paws, caressing, gentle,
  Crimson turned with my rich blood.

Now our friendship firmer groweth,
  Daily keeps on growing straight.
I myself incline to madness,
  Soon, in faith, I'll be thy mate."

[1] *Ibid.*, Vol. VIII., p. 390 *ff.*

A few weeks later he writes to Moser in a still more bitter strain: " I know not what to say. Cohen assures me that Gans is preaching Christianity, and trying to convert the children of Israel. If this is conviction, he is a fool; if hypocrisy, a knave. I shall not give up loving him, but I confess that I should have been better pleased to hear that Gans had been stealing silver spoons. That you, dear Moser, share Gans's opinions, I cannot believe, though Cohen assures me of it, and says that you told him so yourself. I should be sorry, if my own baptism were to strike you more favorably. I give you my word of honor—if our laws allowed stealing silver spoons, I should not have been baptized." Again he writes mournfully: " As, according to Solon, no man may be called happy, so none should be called honest, before his death. I am glad that David Friedländer and Bendavid are old, and will soon die. Then we shall be certain of them, and the reproach of having had not a single immaculate representative cannot be attached to our time. Pardon my ill humor. It is directed mainly against myself."

" Upon how true a basis the myth of the wandering Jew rests!" he says in another letter. " In the lonely wooded valley, the mother tells her children the grewsome tale. Terror-stricken the little ones cower close to the hearth. It is night . . . the postilion blows his horn . . . Jew traders are journeying to the fair at Leipsic. We, the heroes of the legend, are not aware of our part in it. The white beard, whose tips time has rejuvenated, no barber can remove." In those days he wrote the following poem, published posthumously:[1]

TO AN APOSTATE

"Out upon youth's holy flame!
　　Oh! how quickly it burns low!
Now, thy heated blood grown tame,
　　Thou agreest to love thy foe!

And thou meekly grovell'st low
　　At the cross which thou didst spurn;
Which not many weeks ago,
　　Thou didst wish to crush and burn.

Fie! that comes from books untold—
　　There are Schlegel, Haller, Burke—
Yesterday a hero bold,
　　Thou to-day dost scoundrel's work."

The usual explanation of Heine's formal adoption of Christianity is that he wished to obtain a government position in Prussia, and make himself independent of his rich uncle. As no other offers itself, we are forced to accept it as correct. He was fated to recognize speedily that he had gained nothing by baptism. A few weeks after settling in Hamburg he wrote: "I repent me of having been baptized. I cannot see that I have bettered my position. On the contrary, I have had nothing but disappointment and bad luck." Despite his baptism, his enemies called him "the Jew," and at heart he never did become a Christian.

[1] *Ibid.*, Vol. I., p. 196.

At Hamburg, in those days, Heine was repeatedly drawn into the conflict between reform and orthodoxy, between the Temple and the synagogue. His uncle Solomon Heine was a warm supporter of the Temple, but Heine, with characteristic inconsistency, admired the old rigorous rabbinical system more than the modern reform movement, which often called forth his ridicule. Yet, at bottom, his interest in the latter was strong, as it continued to be also in the Berlin educational society, and its "Journal for the Science of Judaism," of which, however, only three numbers were issued. He once wrote from Hamburg to his friend Moser: "Last Saturday I was at the Temple, and had the pleasure with my own ears to hear Dr. Salomon rail against baptized Jews, and insinuate that they are tempted to become faithless to the religion of their fathers only by the hope of preferment. I assure you, the sermon was good, and some day I intend to call upon the man. Cohen is doing the generous thing by me. I take my *Shabbes* dinner with him; he heaps fiery *Kugel* upon my head, and contritely I eat the sacred national dish, which has done more for the preservation of Judaism than all three numbers of the Journal. To be sure, it has had a better sale. If I had time, I would write a pretty little Jewish letter to Mrs. Zunz. I am getting to be a thoroughbred Christian; I am sponging on the rich Jews."

They who find nothing but jest in this letter, do not understand Heine. A bitter strain of disgust, of unsparing self-denunciation, runs through it—the feelings that dictate the jests and accusations of his *Reisebilder*. This was the period of Heine's best creations: for as such his "Book of Songs," *Buch der Lieder*, and his *Reisebilder* must be considered. With a sudden bound he leapt into greatness and popularity.

The reader may ask me to point out in these works the features to be taken as the expression of the genius of the Jewish race. To understand our poet, we must keep in mind that *Heinrich Heine was a Jew born in the days of romanticism in a town on the Rhine*. His intellect and his sensuousness, of Jewish origin, were wedded with Rhenish fancy and blitheness, and over these qualities the pale moonshine of romanticism shed its glamour.

The most noteworthy characteristic of his writings, prose and verse, is his extraordinary subjectivity, pushing the poet's *ego* into the foreground. With light, graceful touch, he demonstrates the possibility of unrestrained self-expression in an artistic guise. The boldness and energy with which "he gave voice to his hidden self" were so novel, so surprising, that his melodies at once awoke an echo. This subjectivity is his Jewish birthright. It is Israel's ingrained combativeness, for more than a thousand years the genius of its literature, which throughout reveals a predilection for abrupt contrasts, and is studded with unmistakable expressions of strong individuality. By virtue of his subjectivity, which never permits him to surrender himself unconditionally, the Jew establishes a connection between his *ego* and whatever subject he treats of. "He does not sink his own identity, and lose himself in the depths of the cosmos, nor roam hither and thither in the limitless space of the world of thought. He dives down to search for pearls at the bottom of the sea, or rises aloft to gain a bird's-eye view of the whole. The world encloses him as the works of a clock are held in a case. His *ego* is the hammer, and there is no sound unless, swinging rhythmically, itself touches the sides, now softly, now boldly." Not content to yield to an authority which would suppress his freedom of action, he traverses the world, and compels it to promote the development of his energetic nature. To these peculiarities of his race Heine fell heir—to the generous traits growing out of marked individuality, its grooves deepened by a thousand years of martyrdom, as well as to the petty faults following in the wake of excessive self-consciousness, which have furnished adversaries of the Jews with texts and weapons.

This subjectivity, traceable in his language and in his ancient literature, it is that unfits the Jew for objective, philosophic investigation. It is, moreover, responsible for that energetic self-assertiveness for which the Aramæan language has coined the word *chutspa*, only partially rendered by arrogance. Possibly it is the root of another quality which Heine owes to his Jewish extraction—his wit. Heine's scintillations are composed of a number of elements—of English humor, French sparkle, German irony, and Jewish wit, all of which, saving the last, have been analyzed by the critics. Proneness to censure, to criticism, and discussion, is the concomitant of keen intellect given to scrutiny and analysis. From the buoyancy of the Jewish disposition, and out of the force of Jewish subjectivity, arose Jewish wit, whose first manifestations can be traced in the Talmud and the Midrash. Its appeals are directed to both fancy and heart. It delights in antithesis, and, as was said above, is intimately connected with Jewish subjectivity. Its distinguishing characteristic is the desire to have its superiority acknowledged without wounding the feelings of the sensitive, and an explanation of its peculiarity can be found in the sad fate of the Jews. The heroes of Shakespere's tragedies are full of irony. Frenzy at its maddest pitch breaks out into merry witticisms and scornful laughter. So it was with the Jews. The waves of oppression, forever dashing over them, strung their nerves to the point of reaction. The world was closed to them in hostility. There was nothing for them to do but laugh—laugh with forced merriment from behind prison bars, and out of the depths of their heartrending resignation. Complaints it was possible to suppress, but no one could forbid their laughter, ghastly though it was. M. G. Saphir, one of the best exponents of Jewish wit, justly said: "The Jews seized the weapon of wit, since they were interdicted the use of every other sort of weapon." Whatever humdrum life during the middle ages offered them, had to submit to the scalpel of their wit.

As a rule, Jewish wit springs from a lively appreciation of what is ingenious. A serious beginning suddenly and unexpectedly takes a merry, jocose turn, producing in Heine's elegiac passages the discordant endings so shocking to sensitive natures. But it is an injustice to the poet to attribute these rapid transitions to an artist's vain fancy. His satire is directed against the ideals of his generation, not against the ideal. Harsh, discordant notes do not express the poet's real disposition. They are exaggerated, romantic feeling, for which he himself, led by an instinctively pure conception of the good and the beautiful, which is opposed alike to sickly sentimentality and jarring dissonance, sought the outlet of irony.

Heine's humor, as I intimated above, springs from his recognition of the tragedy of life. It is an expression of the irreconcilable difference between the real and the ideal, of the perception that the world, despite its grandeur and its beauty, is a world of folly and contradictions; that whatever exists and is formed, bears within itself the germ of death and corruption; that the Lord of all creation himself is but the shuttlecock of irresistible, absolute force, compelling the unconditional surrender of subject and object.

Humor, then, grows out of the contemplation of the tragedy of life. But it does not stop there. If the world is so pitiful, so fragile, it is not worth a tear, not worth hatred, or contempt. The only sensible course is to accept it as it is, as a nothing, an absolute contradiction, calling forth ridicule. At this point, a sense of tragedy is transformed into demoniac glee. No more is this a permanent state. The humorist is too impulsive to accept it as final. Moreover, he feels that with the world he has annihilated himself. In the phantom realm into which he has turned the world, his laughter reverberates with ghostlike hollowness. Recognizing that the world meant more to him than he was willing to admit, and that apart from it he has no being, he again yields to it, and embraces it with increased passion and ardor. But scarcely has the return been effected, scarcely has he begun to realize the beauties and perfections of the world, when sadness, suffering, pain, and torture, obtrude themselves, and the old overwhelming sense of life's tragedy takes possession of him. This train of thought, plainly discernible in Heine's poems, he also owes to his descent. A mind given to such speculations naturally seeks poetic solace in *Weltschmerz*, which, as everybody knows, is still another heirloom of his race.

These are the most important characteristics, some admirable, some reprehensible, which Heine has derived from his race, and they are the very ones that raised opponents against him, one of the most interesting and prominent among them being the German philosopher Arthur Schopenhauer. His two opinions on Heine, expressed at almost the same time, are typical of the antagonism aroused by the poet. In his book, "The World as Will and

Idea,"[1] he writes: "Heine is a true humorist in his *Romanzero*. Back of all his quips and gibes lies deep seriousness, *ashamed* to speak out frankly." At the same time he says in his journal, published posthumously: "Although a buffoon, Heine has genius, and the distinguishing mark of genius, ingenuousness. On close examination, however, his ingenuousness turns out to have its root in Jewish shamelessness; for he, too, belongs to the nation of which Riemer says that it knows neither shame nor grief."

The contradiction between the two judgments is too obvious to need explanation; it is an interesting illustration of the common experience that critics go astray when dealing with Heine.

II

When, as Heine puts it, "a great hand solicitously beckoned," he left his German fatherland in his prime, and went to Paris. In its sociable atmosphere, he felt more comfortable, more free, than in his own home, where the Jew, the author, the liberal, had encountered only prejudices. The removal to Paris was an inauspicious change for the poet, and that he remained there until his end was still less calculated to redound to his good fortune. He gave much to France, and Paris did little during

[1] Vol. II., p. 110. Cmp. Frauenstädt, *A. Schopenhauer*, p. 467 *ff*.

his life to pay off the debt. The charm exercised upon every stranger by Babylon on the Seine, wrought havoc in his character and his work, and gives us the sole criterion for the rest of his days. Yet, despite his devotion to Paris, home-sickness, yearning for Germany, was henceforth the dominant note of his works. At that time Heine considered Judaism "a long lost cause." Of the God of Judaism, the philosophical demonstrations of Hegel and his disciples had robbed him; his knowledge of doctrinal Judaism was a minimum; and his keen race-feeling, his historical instinct, was forced into the background by other sympathies and antipathies. He was at that time harping upon the long cherished idea that men can be divided into *Hellenists* and *Nazarenes*. Himself, for instance, he looked upon as a well-fed Hellenist, while Börne was a Nazarene, an ascetic. It is interesting, and bears upon our subject, that most of the verdicts, views, and witticisms which Heine fathers upon Börne in the famous imaginary conversation in the Frankfort *Judengasse*, might have been uttered by Heine himself. In fact, many of them are repeated, partly in the same or in similar words, in the jottings found after his death.

This conversation is represented as having taken place during the Feast of *Chanukka*. Heine who, as said above, took pleasure at that time in impersonating a Hellenist, gets Börne to explain to him that this feast was instituted to commemorate the victory of the valiant Maccabees over the king of

Syria. After expatiating on the heroism of the Maccabees, and the cowardice of modern Jews, Börne says:[1]

"Baptism is the order of the day among the wealthy Jews. The evangel vainly announced to the poor of Judæa now flourishes among the rich. Its acceptance is self-deception, if not a lie, and as hypocritical Christianity contrasts sharply with the old Adam, who will crop out, these people lay themselves open to unsparing ridicule.—In the streets of Berlin I saw former daughters of Israel wear crosses about their necks longer than their noses, reaching to their very waists. They carried evangelical prayer books, and were discussing the magnificent sermon just heard at Trinity church. One asked the other where she had gone to communion, and all the while their breath smelt. Still more disgusting was the sight of dirty, bearded, malodorous Polish Jews, hailing from Polish sewers, saved for heaven by the Berlin Society for the Conversion of Jews, and in turn preaching Christianity in their slovenly jargon. Such Polish vermin should certainly be baptized with cologne instead of ordinary water."

This is to be taken as an expression of Heine's own feelings, which come out plainly, when, "persistently loyal to Jewish customs," he eats, "with good appetite, yes, with enthusiasm, with devotion, with conviction," *Shalet*, the famous Jewish dish, about which he says: "This dish is delicious, and it

[1] Collected Works, Vol. VII., p. 255 *ff*.

is a subject for painful regret that the Church, indebted to Judaism for so much that is good, has failed to introduce *Shalet*. This should be her object in the future. If ever she falls on evil times, if ever her most sacred symbols lose their virtue, then the Church will resort to *Shalet*, and the faithless peoples will crowd into her arms with renewed appetite. At all events the Jews will then join the Church from conviction, for it is clear that it is only *Shalet* that keeps them in the old covenant. Börne assures me that renegades who have accepted the new dispensation feel a sort of home-sickness for the synagogue when they but smell *Shalet*, so that *Shalet* may be called the Jewish *ranz des vaches*."

Heine forgot that in another place he had uttered this witticism in his own name. He long continued to take peculiar pleasure in his dogmatic division of humanity into two classes, the lean and the fat, or rather, the class that continually gets thinner, and the class which, beginning with modest dimensions, gradually attains to corpulency. Only too soon the poet was made to understand the radical falseness of his definition. A cold February morning of 1848 brought him a realizing sense of his fatal mistake. Sick and weary, the poet was taking his last walk on the boulevards, while the mob of the revolution surged in the streets of Paris. Half blind, half paralyzed, leaning heavily on his cane, he sought to extricate himself from the clamorous crowd, and finally found refuge in the Louvre, almost empty during the days of excitement. With difficulty he dragged himself to the hall of the gods and goddesses of antiquity, and suddenly came face to face with the ideal of beauty, the smiling, witching Venus of Milo, whose charms have defied time and mutilation. Surprised, moved, almost terrified, he reeled to a chair, tears, hot and bitter, coursing down his cheeks. A smile was hovering on the beautiful lips of the goddess, parted as if by living breath, and at her feet a luckless victim was writhing. A single moment revealed a world of misery. Driven by a consciousness of his fate, Heine wrote in his "Confessions": "In May of last year I was forced to take to my bed, and since then I have not risen. I confess frankly that meanwhile a great change has taken place in me. I no longer am a fat Hellenist, the freest man since Goethe, a jolly, somewhat corpulent Hellenist, with a contemptuous smile for lean Jews—I am only a poor Jew, sick unto death, a picture of gaunt misery, an unhappy being."

This startling change was coincident with the first symptoms of his disease, and kept pace with it. The pent-up forces of faith pressed to his bedside; religious conversations, readings from the Bible, reminiscences of his youth, of his Jewish friends, filled his time almost entirely. Alfred Meissner has culled many interesting data from his conversations with the poet. For instance, on one occasion Heine breaks out with:[1]

"Queer people this! Downtrodden for thousands of years, weeping always, suffering always,

[1] Alfred Meissner, *Heinrich Heine*, p. 138 *ff.*

abandoned always by its God, yet clinging to Him tenaciously, loyally, as no other under the sun. Oh, if martyrdom, patience, and faith in despite of trial, can confer a patent of nobility, then this people is noble beyond many another.—It would have been absurd and petty, if, as people accuse me, I had been ashamed of being a Jew. Yet it were equally ludicrous for me to call myself a Jew.—As I instinctively hold up to unending scorn whatever is evil, timeworn, absurd, false, and ludicrous, so my nature leads me to appreciate the sublime, to admire what is great, and to extol every living force." Heine had spoken so much with deep earnestness. Jestingly he added: "Dear friend, if little Weill should visit us, you shall have another evidence of my reverence for hoary Mosaism. Weill formerly was precentor at the synagogue. He has a ringing tenor, and chants Judah's desert songs according to the old traditions, ranging from the simple monotone to the exuberance of Old Testament cadences. My wife, who has not the slightest suspicion that I am a Jew, is not a little astonished by this peculiar musical wail, this trilling and cadencing. When Weill sang for the first time, Minka, the poodle, crawled into hiding under the sofa, and Cocotte, the polly, made an attempt to throttle himself between the bars of his cage. 'M. Weill, M. Weill!' Mathilde cried terror-stricken, 'pray do not carry the joke too far.' But Weill continued, and the dear girl turned to me, and asked imploringly: 'Henri, pray tell me what sort of songs these are.' 'They are our German folk songs,' said I, and I have obstinately stuck to that explanation."

Meissner reports an amusing conversation with Madame Mathilde about the friends of the family, whom the former by their peculiarities recognized as Jews. "What!" cried Mathilde, "Jews? They are Jews?" "Of course, Alexander Weill is a Jew, he told me so himself;—why he was going to be a rabbi." "But the rest, all the rest? For instance, there is Abeles, the name sounds so thoroughly German." "Rather say it sounds Greek," answered Meissner. "Yet I venture to insist that our friend Abeles has as little German as Greek blood in his veins." "Very well! But Jeiteles—Kalisch—Bamberg—Are they, too . . . O no, you are mistaken, not one is a Jew," cried Mathilde. "You will never make me believe that. Presently you will make out Cohn to be a Jew. But Cohn is related to Heine, and Heine is a Protestant." So Meissner found out that Heine had never told his wife anything about his descent. He gravely answered: "You are right. With regard to Cohn I was of course mistaken. Cohn is certainly not a Jew."

These are mere jests. In point of fact, his friends' reports on the religious attitude of the Heine of that period are of the utmost interest. He once said to Ludwig Kalisch, who had told him that the world was all agog over his conversion:[1] "I do not make a secret of my Jewish allegiance, to which I have not returned, because I never abjured it. I was not

[1] Ludwig Kalisch, *Pariser Skizzen*, p. 334.

baptized from aversion to Judaism, and my professions of atheism were never serious. My former friends, the Hegelians, have turned out scamps. Human misery is too great for men to do without faith."

The completest picture of the transformation, truer than any given in letters, reports, or reminiscences, is in his last two productions, the *Romanzero* and the "Confessions." There can be no more explicit description of the poet's conversion than is contained in these "confessions." During his sickness he sought a palliative for his pains—in the Bible. With a melancholy smile his mind reverted to the memories of his youth, to the heroism which is the underlying principle of Judaism. The Psalmist's consolations, the elevating principles laid down in the Pentateuch, exerted a powerful attraction upon him, and filled his soul with exalted thoughts, shaped into words in the "Confessions":[1] "Formerly I felt little affection for Moses, probably because the Hellenic spirit was dominant within me, and I could not pardon the Jewish lawgiver for his intolerance of images, and every sort of plastic representation. I failed to see that despite his hostile attitude to art, Moses was himself a great artist, gifted with the true artist's spirit. Only in him, as in his Egyptian neighbors, the artistic instinct was exercised solely upon the colossal and the indestructible. But unlike the Egyptians he did not shape his works of art out of brick or granite. His pyra-

[1] Collected Works, Vol. VII., 473 *ff.*

mids were built of men, his obelisks hewn out of human material. A feeble race of shepherds he transformed into a people bidding defiance to the centuries—a great, eternal, holy people, God's people, an exemplar to all other peoples, the prototype of mankind: he created Israel. With greater justice than the Roman poet could this artist, the son of Amram and Jochebed the midwife, boast of having erected a monument more enduring than brass.

As for the artist, so I lacked reverence for his work, the Jews, doubtless on account of my Greek predilections, antagonistic to Judaic asceticism. My love for Hellas has since declined. Now I understand that the Greeks were only beautiful youths, while the Jews have always been men, powerful, inflexible men, not only in early times, to-day, too, in spite of eighteen hundred years of persecution and misery. I have learnt to appreciate them, and were pride of birth not absurd in a champion of the revolution and its democratic principles, the writer of these leaflets would boast that his ancestors belonged to the noble house of Israel, that he is a descendant of those martyrs to whom the world owes God and morality, and who have fought and bled on every battlefield of thought."

In view of such avowals, Heine's return to Judaism is an indubitable fact, and when one of his friends anxiously inquired about his relation to God, he could well answer with a smile: *Dieu me pardonnera; c'est son metier*. In those days Heine made his will, his true, genuine will, to have been the first to publish which the present writer will always consider the distinction of his life. The introduction reads: "I die in the belief in one God, Creator of heaven and earth, whose mercy I supplicate in behalf of my immortal soul. I regret that in my writings I sometimes spoke of sacred things with levity, due not so much to my own inclination, as to the spirit of my age. If unwittingly I have offended against good usage and morality, which constitute the true essence of all monotheistic religions, may God and men forgive me."

With this confession on his lips Heine passed away, dying in the thick of the fight, his very bier haunted by the spirits of antagonism and contradiction. . . .

> "Greek joy in life, belief in God of Jew,
>   And twining in and out like arabesques,
>   Ivy tendrils gently clasp the two."

In Heine's character, certainly, there were sharp contrasts. Now we behold him a Jew, now a Christian, now a Hellenist, now a romanticist; to-day laughing, to-morrow weeping, to-day the prophet of the modern era, to-morrow the champion of tradition. Who knows the man? Yet who that steps within the charmed circle of his life can resist the temptation to grapple with the enigma?

One of the best known of his poems is the plaint:

> "Mass for me will not be chanted,
>   *Kadosh* not be said,
>   Naught be sung, and naught recited,
>   Round my dying bed."

The poet's prophecy has not come true. As this tribute has in spirit been laid upon his grave, so always thousands will devote kindly thought to him, recalling in gentleness how he struggled and suffered, wrestled and aspired; how, at the dawn of the new day, enthusiastically proclaimed by him, his spirit fled aloft to regions where doubts are set at rest, hopes fulfilled, and visions made reality.

THE MUSIC OF THE SYNAGOGUE[1]

Ladies and Gentlemen:—Let the emotions aroused by the notes of the great masters, now dying away upon the air, continue to reverberate in your souls. More forcibly and more eloquently than my weak words, they express the thoughts and the feelings appropriate to this solemn occasion.

A festival like ours has rarely been celebrated in Israel. For nearly two thousand years the muse of Jewish melody was silent; during the whole of that period, a new chord was but seldom won from the unused lyre. The Talmud[2] has a quaint tale on the subject: Higros the Levite living at the time of the decadence of Israel's nationality, was the last skilled musician, and he refused to teach his art. When he sang his exquisite melodies, touching his mouth with his thumb, and striking the strings with his fingers, it is said that his priestly mates, transported by the magic power of his art, fell prostrate, and wept. Under the Oriental trappings of this tale is concealed regretful anguish over the decay of old Hebrew song. The altar at Jerusalem was demolished, and the songs of Zion, erst sung by the Levitical choirs under the leadership of the Korachides,

[1] Address at the celebration of Herr Lewandowski's fiftieth anniversary as director of music.
[2] *Yoma*, 38^a.

were heard no longer. The silence was unbroken, until, in our day, a band of gifted men disengaged the old harps from the willows, and once more lured the ancient melodies from their quavering strings.

Towering head and shoulders above most of the group of restorers is he in whose honor we are assembled, to whom we bring greeting and congratulation. To you, then, Herr Lewandowski, I address myself to offer you the deep-felt gratitude and the cordial wishes of your friends, of the Berlin community, and, I may add, of the whole of Israel. You were appointed for large tasks—large tasks have you successfully performed. At a time when Judaism was at a low ebb, only scarcely discernible indications promising a brighter future, Providence sent you to occupy a guide's position in the most important, the largest, and the most intelligent Jewish community of Germany. For fifty years your zeal, your diligence, your faithfulness, your devotion, your affectionate reverence for our past, and your exalted gifts, have graced the office. Were testimony unto your gifts and character needed, it would be given by this day's celebration, proving, as it does, that your brethren have understood the underlying thought of your activities, have grasped their bearing upon Jewish development, and have appreciated their influence.

You have remodelled the divine service of the Jewish synagogue, superadding elements of devotion and sacredness. Under your touch old lays have clothed themselves with a modern garb—a new rhythm vibrates through our historic melodies, keener strength in the familiar words, heightened dignity in the cherished songs. Two generations and all parts of the world have hearkened to your harmonies, responding to them with tears of joy or sorrow, with feelings stirred from the recesses of the heart. To your music have listened entranced the boy and the girl on the day of declaring their allegiance to the covenant of the fathers; the youth and the maiden in life's most solemn hour; men and women in all the sacred moments of the year, on days of mourning and of festivity.

A quarter of a century ago, when you celebrated the end of twenty-five years of useful work, a better man stood here, and spoke to you. Leopold Zunz on that occasion said to you: "Old thoughts have been transformed by you into modern emotions, and long stored words seasoned with your melodies have made delicious food."

This is your share in the revival of Jewish poesy, and what you have resuscitated, and remodelled, and re-created, will endure, echoing and re-echoing through all the lands. In you Higros the Levite has been restored to us. But your melodies will never sink into oblivious silence. They have been carried by an honorable body of disciples to distant lands, beyond the ocean, to communities in the remote countries of civilization. Thus they have become the perpetual inheritance of the congregation of Jacob, the people that has ever loved and wooed music, only direst distress succeeding in flinging the pall of silence over song and melody.

Holy Writ places the origin of music in the primitive days of man, tersely pointing out, at the same time, music's conciliatory charms: it is the descendant of Cain, the fratricide, a son of Lemech, the slayer of a man to his own wounding, who is said to be the "father of all such as play on the harp and guitar" (*Kinnor* and *Ugab*). Another of Lemech's sons was the first artificer in every article of copper and iron, the inventor of weapons of war, as the former was the inventor of stringed instruments. Both used brass, the one to sing, the other to fight. So music sprang from sorrow and combat. Song and roundelay, timbrels and harp, accompanied our forefathers on their wanderings, and preceded the armed men into battle. So, too, the returning victor was greeted, and in the Temple on Moriah's crest, joyful songs of gratitude extolled the grace of the Lord. From the harp issued the psalm dedicated to the glory of God—love of art gave rise to the psalter, a song-book for the nations, and its author David may be called the founder of the national and Temple music of the ancient Hebrews. With his song, he banished the evil spirit from Saul's soul; with his skill on the psaltery, he defeated his enemies, and he led the jubilant chorus in the Holy City singing to the honor and glory of the Most High.

Compare the Hebrew and the Hellenic music of ancient times: Orpheus with his music charms wild beasts; David's subdues demons. By means of Amphion's lyre, living walls raise themselves; Israel's cornets make level the ramparts of Jericho.

Arion's melodies lure dolphins from the sea; Hebrew music infuses into the prophet's disciples the spirit of the Lord. These are the wondrous effects of music in Israel and in Hellas, the foremost representatives of ancient civilization. Had the one united with the other, what celestial harmonies might have resulted! But later, in the time of Macedonian imperialism, when Alexandria and Jerusalem met, the one stood for enervated paganism, the other for a Judaism of compromise, and a union of such tones produces no harmonious chords.

But little is known of the ancient Hebrew music of the Temple, of the singers, the songs, the melodies, and the instruments. The Hebrews had songs and instrumental music on all festive, solemn occasions, particularly during the divine service. At their national celebrations, in their homes, at their diversions, even on their journeys and their pilgrimages to the sanctuary, their hymns were at once religious, patriotic, and social.[1] They had the viol and the cithara, flutes, cymbals, and castanets, and, if our authorities interpret correctly, an organ (*magrepha*), whose volume of sound surpassed description. When, on the Day of Atonement, its strains pealed through the chambers of the Temple, they were heard in the whole of Jerusalem, and all the people bowed in humble adoration before the Lord of hosts. The old music ceased with the overthrow of the Jewish state. The Levites hung their

[1] Cmp. Fétis, *Histoire générale de la Musique*, Vol. I., p. 563 *ff.*

harps on the willows of Babylon's streams, and every entreaty for the "words of song" was met by the reproachful inquiry: "How should we sing the song of the Lord on the soil of the stranger?" Higros the Levite was the last of Israelitish tone-artists.

Israel set out on his fateful wanderings, his unparalleled pilgrimage, through the lands and the centuries, along an endless, thorny path, drenched with blood, watered with tears, across nations and thrones, lonely, terrible, sublime with the stern sublimity of tragic scenes. They are not the sights and experiences to inspire joyous songs—melody is muffled by terror. Only lamentation finds voice, an endless, oppressive, anxious wail, sounding adown, through two thousand years, like a long-drawn sigh, reverberating in far-reaching echoes: "How long, O Lord, how long!" and "When shall a redeemer arise for this people?" These elegiac refrains Israel never wearies of repeating on all his journeyings. Occasionally a fitful gleam of sunlight glides into the crowded Jewish quarters, and at once a more joyous note is heard, rising triumphant above the doleful plaint, a note which asserts itself exultingly on the celebration in memory of the Maccabean heroes, on the days of *Purim*, at wedding banquets, at the love-feasts of the pious brotherhood. This fusion of melancholy and of rejoicing is the keynote of mediæval Jewish music growing out of the grotesque contrasts of Jewish history. Yet, despite its romantic woe, it is informed with the spirit of a remote past, making it the legitimate offspring of ancient Hebrew music, whose characteristics, to be sure, we arrive at only by guesswork. Of that mediæval music of ours, the poet's words are true: "It rejoices so pathetically, it laments so joyfully."

Whoever has heard, will never forget Israel's melodies, breaking forth into rejoicing, then cast down with sadness; flinging out their notes to the skies, then sinking into an abyss of grief; now elated, now oppressed; now holding out hope, now moaning forth sorrow and pain. They convey the whole of Judah's history—his glorious past, his mournful present, his exalted future promised by God. As their tones flood our soul, a succession of visions passes before our mental view: the Temple in all its unexampled splendor, the exultant chorus of Levites, the priests discharging their holy office, the venerable forms of the patriarchs, the lawgiver-guide of the people, prophets with uplifted finger of warning, worthy rabbis, pale-faced martyrs of the middle ages; but the melodies conjuring before our minds all these shadowy figures have but one burden: "How should we sing the song of the Lord on the soil of the stranger?"

That is the ever-recurring *motif* of the Jewish music of the middle ages. But the blending of widely different emotions is not favorable to the creation of melody. Secular occurrences set their seal upon religious music, of which some have so high a conception as to call it one of the seven liberal arts, or even to extol it beyond poetry. Jacob

Levi of Mayence (Maharil), living at the beginning of the fifteenth century, is considered the founder of German synagogue music, but his productions remained barren of poetic and devotional results. He drew his best subjects from alien sources. At the time of the Italian Renaissance, music had so firmly established itself in the appreciation of the people that a preacher, Judah Muscato, devoted the first of his celebrated sermons to music, assigning to it a high mission among the arts. He interpreted the legend of David's Æolian harp as a beautiful allegory. Basing his explanation on a verse in the Psalms, he showed that it symbolizes a spiritual experience of the royal bard. Another writer, Abraham ben David Portaleone, found the times still riper; he could venture to write a theory of music, as taught him by his teachers, Samuel Arkevolti and Menahem Lonsano, both of whom had strongly opposed the use of certain secular melodies then current in Italy, Germany, France, and Turkey for religious songs. Among Jewish musicians in the latter centuries of the middle ages, the most prominent was Solomon Rossi. He, too, failed to exercise influence on the shaping of Jewish music, which more and more delighted in grotesqueness and aberrations from good taste. The origin of synagogue melodies was attributed to remoter and remoter periods; the most soulful hymns were adapted to frivolous airs. Later still, at a time when German music had risen to its zenith, when Bach, Handel, Haydn, Mozart, and Beethoven flourished, the Jewish strolling musician *Klesmer*, a mendicant in the world of song as in the world of finance, was wandering through the provinces with his two mates.

Suddenly a new era dawned for Israel, too. The sun of humanity sent a few of its rays into the squalid Ghetto. Its walls fell before the trumpet blast of deliverance. On all sides sounded the cry for liberty. The brotherhood of man, embracing all, did not exclude storm-baptized Israel. The old synagogue had to keep pace with modern demands, and was arrayed in a new garb. Among those who designed and fashioned the new garment, he is prominent in whose honor we have met to-day.

From our short journey through the centuries of music, we have returned to him who has succeeded in the great work of restoring to its honorable place the music of the synagogue, sorely missed, ardently longed for, and bringing back to us old songs in a new guise. An old song and a new melody! The old song of abiding love, loyalty, and resignation to the will of God! His motto was the beautiful verse: "My strength and my song is the Lord"; and his unchanging refrain, the jubilant exclamation: "Blessed be thou, fair Musica!" A wise man once said: "Hold in high honor our Lady of Music!" The wise man was Martin Luther—another instance this of the conciliatory power of music, standing high above the barriers raised by religious differences. It is worthy of mention, on this occasion, that at the four hundredth anniversary celebration in honor of Martin Luther, in the Sebaldus church at Nuremberg, the most Protestant of the cities of Germany, called by Luther himself "the eye of God," a psalm of David was sung to music composed by our guest of the day.

"Hold in high honor our Lady of Music!" We will be admonished by the behest, and give honor to the artist by whose fostering care the music of the synagogue enjoys a new lease of life; who, with pious zeal, has collected our dear old melodies, and has sung them to us with all the ardor and power with which God in His kindness endowed him.

> "The sculptor must simulate life, of the poet I demand intelligence;
> The soul can be expressed only by Polyhymnia!"

An orphan, song wandered hither and thither through the world, met, after many days, by the musician, who compassionately adopted it, and clothed it with his melodies. On the pinions of music, it now soars whithersoever it listeth, bringing joy and blessing wherever it alights. "The old song, the new melody!" Hark! through the silence of the night in this solemn moment, one of those old songs, clad by our *maestro* in a new melody, falls upon our ears: "I remember unto thee the kindness of thy youth, the love of thy espousals, thy going after me in the wilderness, through a land that is not sown!"

Hearken! Can we not distinguish in its notes, as they fill our ears, the presage of a music of the future, of love and good-will? We seem to hear the rustle of the young leaves of a new spring, the resurrection foretold thousands of years agone by our poets and prophets. We see slowly dawning that great day on which mankind, awakened from the fitful sleep of error and delusion, will unite in the profession of the creed of brotherly love, and Israel's song will be mankind's song, myriads of voices in unison sending aloft to the skies the psalm of praise: Hallelujah, Hallelujah!

INDEX

Aaron, medical writer, 79
Abbahu, Haggadist, 21
Abbayu, rabbi, quoted, 232-233
Abina, rabbi, 19
Abitur, poet, 24
Aboab, Isaac, writer, 45, 130
Aboab, Samuel, Bible scholar, 45
Abrabanel, Isaac, scholar and statesman, 42, 99
Abrabanel, Judah, 42, 95
Abraham in Africa, 255
Abraham Bedersi, poet, 171
Abraham ben Chiya, scientist, 83, 93
Abraham ben David Portaleone, musician, 376
Abraham de Balmes, physician, 95
Abraham deï Mansi, Talmudist, 116
Abraham ibn Daud, philosopher, 35
Abraham ibn Ezra, exegete, 36
mathematician, 83
Abraham ibn Sahl, poet, 34, 88
Abraham Judæus. See Abraham ibn Ezra
Abraham of Sarteano, poet, 224
Abraham Portaleone, archæologist, 45, 97
Abraham Powdermaker, legend of, 285-286
Abt and Mendelssohn, 314
Abyssinia, the Ten Tribes in, 262-263
Ackermann, Rachel, novelist, 119

Acosta, Uriel, alluded to, 100
Acta Esther et Achashverosh, drama, 244
Actors, Jewish, 232, 246, 247-248
Adia, poet, 24
Adiabene, Jews settle in, 251
Æsop's fables translated into Hebrew, 34
"A few words to the Jews by one of themselves," by Charlotte Montefiore, 133
Afghanistan, the Ten Tribes in, 259
Africa, interest in, 249-250
  in the Old Testament, 255
  the Talmud on, 254
  the Ten Tribes in, 262
Agau spoken by the Falashas, 265
Aguilar, Grace, author, 134-137
  testimonial to, 136-137
"Ahasverus," farce, 244
Ahaz, king, alluded to, 250
Akiba ben Joseph, rabbi, 19, 58
  quoted, 253, 256
Albert of Prussia, alluded to, 288
Albertus Magnus and Maimonides, 156, 164
  philosopher, 82
  proscribes the Talmud, 85
Albo, Joseph, philosopher, 42
Al-Chazari, by Yehuda Halevi, 31
  commentary on, 298

INDEX

Alemanno, Jochanan, Kabbalist, 95
Alessandro Farnese, alluded to, 98
Alexander III, pope, and Jewish diplomats, 99
Alexander the Great, 229, 254
Alexandria, centre of Jewish life, 17
 philosophy in, 75
Alfonsine Tables compiled, 92
Alfonso V of Portugal and Isaac Abrabanel, 99
Alfonso X, of Castile, patron of Jewish scholars, 92, 93
Alfonso XI, of Castile, 170, 260
Alityros, actor, 232
Alkabez, Solomon, poet, 43
Alliance Israélite Universelle, and the Falashas, 264
"Almagest" by Ptolemy translated, 79
 read by Maimonides, 159
Almansor by Heine, 347
Almohades and Maimonides, 148
Altweiberdeutsch. See *Judendeutsch*
Amatus Lusitanus, physician, 42, 97
Amharic spoken by the Falashas, 265
Amoraïm, Speakers, 58
Amos, prophet, alluded to, 251
Amsterdam, Marrano centre, 128-129
Anahuac and the Ten Tribes, 259
Anatoli. See Jacob ben Abba-Mari ben Anatoli
Anatomy in the Talmud, 77
Anna, Rashi's granddaughter, 118
Anti-Maimunists, 39-40
Antiochus Epiphanes, alluded to, 193

Antonio di Montoro, troubadour, 97, 180-181
Antonio dos Reys, on Isabella Correa, 129
Antonio Enriquez di Gomez. See Enriquez, Antonio.
Antonio Jose de Silva, dramatist, 100, 236-237
Aquinas, Thomas, philosopher, 82
 and Maimonides, 156, 164
 under Gabirol's influence, 94
 works of, translated, 86
Arabia, Jews settle in, 250-251
 the Ten Tribes in, 256-257
Arabs influence Jews, 80
 relation of, to Jews, 22
Argens, d', and Mendelssohn, 303
Aristeas, Neoplatonist, 17
Aristobulus, Aristotelian, 17
Aristotle, alluded to, 250
 and Maimonides, 156
 interpreted by Jews, 85
 quoted, 249
Arkevolti, Samuel, grammarian, 376
Armenia, the Ten Tribes in, 259
Arnstein, Benedict David, dramatist, 245
Art among Jews, 102
"Art of Carving and Serving at Princely Boards, The" translated, 91
Arthurian legends in Hebrew, 87
Ascarelli, Deborah, poetess, 44, 124
Asher ben Yehuda, hero of a romance, 34, 213
Ashi, compiler of the Babylonian Talmud, 19
Ashkenasi, Hannah, authoress, 120
Asireh ha-Tikwah, by Joseph Pensa, 237-238

INDEX

Asiya, Kabbalistic term, 41
Astruc, Bible critic, 13
Auerbach, Berthold, novelist, 49, 50
  quoted, 303
Auerbach, J. L., preacher, 322
Augsburger Allgemeine Zeitung and Heine, 340
Avenare. See Abraham ibn Ezra
Avencebrol. See Gabirol, Solomon
Avendeath, Johannes, translator of "The Fount of Life," 26
Averroës and Maimonides, 163-164
Avicebron. See Gabirol, Solomon
Avicenna and Maimonides, 156, 158
Azariah de Rossi, scholar, 45
Azila, Kabbalistic term, 41

Barrios, de, Daniel, critic, 47, 129
Barruchius, Valentin, romance writer, 171
Bartholdy, Salomon, quoted, 308
Bartolocci, Hebrew scholar, 48
Bassista, Sabbataï, bibliographer, 47
Bath Halevi, Talmudist, 117
Bechaï ibn Pakuda, philosopher, 35, 137
Beck, K., poet, 49
Beena, Kabbalistic term, 41
Beer, Jacob Herz, establishes a synagogue, 322
Beer, M., poet, 49
Behaim, Martin, scientist, 96
Belmonte, Bienvenida Cohen, poetess, 130
"Belshazzar" by Heine, 344
Bendavid. See Lazarus ben David

"Beni Israel" and the Ten Tribes, 259
Benjamin of Tudela, traveller, 37, 258
  quoted, 263
Berachya ben Natronaï (Hanakdan), fabulist, 34, 88
Beria, a character in Immanuel Romi's poem, 221-222
Beria, Kabbalistic term, 41
Bernhard, employer of Mendelssohn, 298, 300, 304
Bernhardt, Sarah, actress, 246
Bernstein, Aaron, Ghetto novelist, 50
  quoted, 272
Bernstorff, friend of Henriette Herz, 313
Berschadzky on Saul Wahl, 282
Beruriah, wife of Rabbi Meïr, 110-112
Bible. See Old Testament, The
Bible critics, 12, 13, 14
Bible dictionary, Jewish German, 100
"Birth and Death" from the Haggada, 66
Biurists, the Mendelssohn school, 309
Blackcoal, a character in "The Gift of Judah," 214
Blanche de Bourbon, wife of Pedro I, 169
Bleichroeder quoted, 296-297
Bloch, Pauline, writer, 140
Boccaccio, alluded to, 35
Böckh, alluded to, 333
Bonet di Lattes, astronomer, 95
Bonifacio, Balthasar, accuser of Sara Sullam, 127
"Book of Diversions, The" by Joseph ibn Sabara, 214
"Book of Samuel," by Litte of Ratisbon, 119, 120
"Book of Songs" by Heine, 353

INDEX

Börne, Ludwig, quoted, 313–314, 359–361
Borromeo, cardinal, alluded to, 98
Brinkmann, friend of Henriette Herz, 313
Bruno di Lungoborgo, work of, translated, 86
Bruno, Giordano, philosopher, 82
Buch der Lieder by Heine, 353
Buffon quoted, 89
Büschenthal, L. M., dramatist, 245
Buxtorf, father and son, scholars, 48
   translates "The Guide of the Perplexed," 155

Calderon, alluded to, 239
Calderon, the Jewish, 100
Calendar compiled by the rabbis, 77
Caliphs and Jewish diplomats, 98
Campe, Joachim, on Mendelssohn, 314–315
Cardinal, Peire, troubadour, 171–172
Casimir the Great, Jews under, 286
Cassel, D., scholar, 49
   quoted, 19–20
Castro, de, Orobio, author, 47
Çeba, Ansaldo, and Sara Sullam, 125–128
Celestina, by Rodrigo da Cota, 97, 235
Chananel, alluded to, 257
Chanukka, story of, 359–360
Charlemagne and Jewish diplomats, 98
Charles of Anjou, patron of Hebrew learning, 92
Chasan, Bella, historian, 120
Chasdaï ben Shaprut, statesman, 82

Chasdaï Crescas, philosopher, 42, 93–94
Chassidism, a form of Kabbalistic Judaism, 46
Chesed, Kabbalistic term, 41
Children in the Talmud, 63–64
Chiya, rabbi, 19
Chiya bar Abba, Halachist, 21
Chmielnicki, Bogdan, and the Jews, 288
Chochma, Kabbalistic term, 41
Chotham Tochnith by Abraham Bedersi, 171
"Chronicle of the Cid," the first, by a Jew, 90, 170
Cicero and the drama, 232
Clement VI, pope, and Levi ben Gerson, 91
Cochin, the Ten Tribes in, 259
Cohen, friend of Heine, 350
Cohen, Abraham, Talmudist, 118
Cohen, Joseph, historian, 44
Coins, Polish, 286
Columbus, alluded to, 181
   and Jews, 96
Comedy, nature of, 195–196
Commendoni, legate, on the Polish Jews, 287
"Commentaries on Aristotle" by Averroës, 163
"Commentary on Ecclesiastes" by Obadiah Sforno, 95
Commerce developed by Jews, 101–102
Comte Lyonnais, Palanus, romance, 90, 171
"Confessions" by Heine, quoted, 365–366
Conforte, David, historian, 43
Consejos y Documentos al Rey Dom Pedro by Santob de Carrion, 173–174
Consolaçam as Tribulações de Ysrael by Samuel Usque, 44

Constantine, translator, 81
"Contemplation of the World" by Yedaya Penini, 40
"Contributions to History and Literature" by Zunz, 337
Copernicus and Jewish astronomers, 86
Correa, Isabella, poetess, 129
Cota, da, Rodrigo, dramatist, 97, 235
"Counsel and Instruction to King Dom Pedro" by Santob de Carrion, 173–174
"Court Secrets" by Rachel Ackermann, 119
Cousin, Victor, on Spinoza, 145
Creation, Maimonides' theory of, 160
Creed, the Jewish, by Maimonides, 151–152
Creizenach, Th., poet, 49
Cromwell, Oliver, and Manasseh ben Israel, 99

Dalalat al-Haïrin, "Guide of the Perplexed," 154
Damm, teacher of Mendelssohn, 299
"Dance of Death," attributed to Santob, 174
Daniel, Immanuel Romi's guide in Paradise, 223
Dansa General, attributed to Santob, 174
Dante and Immanuel Romi, 35, 89, 220, 223
Dante, the Hebrew, 124
"Dark Continent, The." See Africa
David, philosopher, 83
David ben Levi, Talmudist, 46
David ben Yehuda, poet, 223
David d'Ascoli, physician, 97
David della Rocca, alluded to, 124

David de Pomis, physician, 45, 97
Davison, Bogumil, actor, 246
Deborah, as poetess, 106–107
De Causis, by David, 83
Decimal fractions first mentioned, 91
"Deeds of King David and Goliath, The," drama, 244
Delitzsch, Franz, quoted, 24
Del Medigo, Elias. See Elias del Medigo and Joseph del Medigo
De Rossi, Hebrew scholar, 48
Deutsch, Caroline, poetess, 139, 142–143
Deutsch, Emanuel, on the Talmud, 68–70
Deutsche Briefe by Zunz, 337
Dialoghi di Amore by Judah Abrabanel, 42, 95
Dichter und Kaufmann by Berthold Auerbach, 49
Die Freimütigen, Zunz contributor to, 330
Die gottesdienstlichen Vorträge der Juden by Zunz, 48, 333–335
Diez, alluded to, 333
Dingelstedt, Franz, quoted, 319
Dioscorides, botanist, 82
Disciplina clericalis, a collection of tales, 89, 171
Divina Commedia, travestied, 35
imitated, 89, 124
Doctor angelicus, Thomas Aquinas, 94
Doctor Perplexorum, "Guide of the Perplexed," 154, 155
Document hypothesis of the Old Testament, 13
Dolce, scholar and martyr, 119
Donnolo, Sabattaï, physician, 82

Dorothea of Kurland and Mendelssohn, 315
Dotina, friend of Henriette Herz, 313
Drama, the, among the ancient Hebrews, 229
  classical Hebrew, 244–245, 248
  first Hebrew, published, 239
  first Jewish, 234
  Jewish German, 246–247
Drama, the German, Jews in, 245
  the Portuguese, Jews in, 236–237, 238
  the Spanish, Jews in, 235–236
Dramatists, Jewish, 230, 235, 236, 237, 238, 239, 244, 245, 248
Drinking songs, 200–201, 204, 205, 209, 212–213
Dubno, Solomon, commentator, 309
Dukes, L., scholar, 49
Dunash ben Labrat, alluded to, 257
"Duties of the Heart" by Bechaï, 137

Eben Bochan, by Kalonymos ben Kalonymos, 216–219
Egidio de Viterbo, cardinal, 44
Eibeschütz, Jonathan, Talmudist, 47
Eldad ha-Dani, traveller, 37, 80, 257–258
Elias del Medigo, scholar, 44, 94
Elias Kapsali, scholar, 98
Elias Levita, grammarian, 44, 95
Elias Mizrachi, scholar, 98
Elias of Genzano, poet, 224
Elias Wilna, Talmudist, 46
Eliezer, rabbi, quoted, 253
Eliezer ha-Levi, Talmudist, 36

Eliezer of Metz, Talmudist, 36
El Muallima, Karaite, 117
Em beyisrael, Deborah, 107
Emden, Jacob, Talmudist, 47
Emin Pasha, alluded to, 250
"Enforced Apostasy," by Maimonides, 152
Engel, friend of Henriette Herz, 313
Enriquez, Antonio, di Gomez, dramatist, 100, 236.
Enriquez, Isabella, poetess, 130
En-Sof, Kabbalistic term, 40, 41
Ephraim, the Israelitish kingdom, 251
Ephraim, Veitel, financier, 304, 316
Erasmus, quoted, 44
Esheth Lapidoth, Deborah, 106
Eskeles, banker, alluded to, 305
Esterka, supposed mistress of Casimir the Great, 286
"Esther," by Solomon Usque, 235
Esthori Hafarchi, topographer, 93
Ethiopia. See Abyssinia
Euchel, Isaac, Hebrew writer, 48, 309
Eupolemos, historian, 17
Euripides, alluded to, 230
Ewald, Bible critic, 14
"Exodus from Egypt, The" by Ezekielos, 230
Ezekiel, prophet, quoted, 252, 294–295
Ezekielos, dramatist, 17, 230
Ezra, alluded to, 253

Fables translated by Jews, 79, 86–87, 88
Fagius, Paul, Hebrew scholar, 44, 95

Falashas, the, and the missionaries, 263, 267
and the Negus Theodore, 267
customs of, 266
described by Halévy, 264
history of, 263
intellectual eagerness of, 266, 268
Messianic expectations of, 267–268
religious customs of, 265–266
Faust of Saragossa, Gabirol, 199
Faust translated into Hebrew, 248
Felix, Rachel, actress, 246
Ferdinand and Isabella of Spain and Isaac Abrabanel, 99
Ferrara, duke of, candidate in Poland, 278
Figo, Azariah, rabbi, 45
Fischels, Rosa, translator of the Psalms, 120
"Flaming Sword, The," by Abraham Bedersi, 171
"Flea Song" by Yehuda Charisi, 212
Fleck, actor, 311
Foa, Rebekah Eugenie, writer, 139
Folquet de Lunel, troubadour, 171–172
Fonseca Pina y Pimentel, de, Sara, poetess, 130
"Foundation of the Universe, The," by Isaac Israeli, 93
"Foundation of the World, The," by Moses Zacuto, 238–239
"Fount of Life, The," by Gabirol, 26
Fox fables translated, 79
Frank, Rabbi Dr., alluded to, 345

Fränkel, David, teacher of Mendelssohn, 293
Frankel, Z, scholar, 49
Frankl, L. A., poet, 49
Frank-Wolff, Ulla, writer, 139
Franzos, K. E., Ghetto novelist, 50
Frederick II, emperor, patron of Hebrew learning, 40, 85, 89, 92
Frederick the Great and Mendelssohn, 301–303
and the Jews, 316–317
Freidank, German author, 185
Friedländer, David, disciple of Mendelssohn, 48, 317, 350
Fröhlich, Regina, writer, 131
Fürst, J., scholar, 49

Gabirol, Solomon, philosopher, 26–27, 82–83, 94
poet, 24, 25–26, 27, 199
Gad, Esther, alluded to, 132
Galen and Gamaliel, 81
works of, edited by Maimonides, 153
Gama, Ga, Vasco, and Jews, 96–97
Gamaliel, rabbi, 18, 77, 81
Gans, David, historian, 47
Gans, Edward, friend of Heine, 324, 346, 350
Gaspar, Jewish pilot, 96
Gayo, Isaac, physician, 86
Geiger, Abraham, scholar, 49
Geldern, van, Betty, mother of Heine, 341, 344
Geldern, van, Gottschalk, Heine's uncle, 341
Geldern, van, Isaac, Heine's grandfather, 341
Geldern, van, Lazarus, Heine's uncle, 341
Geldern, van, Simon, author, 341
Gentz, von, Friedrich, friend of Henriette Herz, 313

388 INDEX

Geometry in the Talmud, 77
German literature cultivated by Jews, 87
Gerson ben Solomon, scientist, 90
Gesellschafter, Zunz contributor to the, 330
Ghedulla, Kabbalistic term, 41
Ghemara, commentary on the Mishna, 60
Ghetto tales, 50
Ghevoora, Kabbalistic term, 41
Gideon, Jewish king in Abyssinia, 263
"Gift from a Misogynist, A," satire, by Yehuda ibn Sabbataï, 34, 214–216
Glaser, Dr. Edward, on the Falashas, 263
Goethe, alluded to, 314
 and Jewish literature, 103–104
 on Yedaya Penini, 40
Goldschmidt, Henriette, writer, 139
Goldschmidt, Johanna, writer, 139
Goldschmied, M., Ghetto novelist, 50
Goldsmid, Anna Maria, writer, 137
Goldsmid, Isaac Lyon, alluded to, 137
Gottloeber, A., dramatist, 248
Götz, Ella, translator, 120
Graetz, Heinrich, historian, 49
 quoted, 185
Graziano, Lazaro, dramatist, 235
Greece and Judæa contrasted, 194
Grimani, Dominico, cardinal, alluded to, 95
Grimm, alluded to, 333
Guarini, dramatist, 239

Gugenheim, Fromet, wife of Mendelssohn, 303
 quoted, 307
"Guide of the Perplexed, The," contents of, 157–163
 controversy over, 164–166
 English translation of, 155 (note)
 purpose of, 155
Gumpertz, Aaron, and Mendelssohn, 297, 299
 quoted, 298
Gundisalvi, Dominicus, translator of "The Fount of Life," 26
Günsburg, C., preacher, 322
Günsburg, Simon, confidant of Stephen Báthori, 287
"Gustavus Vasa" by Grace Aguilar, 134
Gutzkow, quoted, 306

Haggada and Halacha contrasted, 21, 60, 194–195
Haggada, the, characterized, 18, 54–55, 60–61, 64–70
 cosmopolitan, 33
 described by Heine, 20
 ethical sayings from, 61–63
 poetic quotations from, 65–68
Haggada, the, at the Passover service, 344–345
Haï, Gaon, 22
Halacha and Haggada contrasted, 21, 60, 194–195
Halacha, the, characterized, 18, 54–55
 subjective, 33
Halévy, Joseph, and the Falashas, 264
 quoted, 265–266
Halley's comet and Rabbi Joshua, 77
"Haman's Will and Death," drama, 244
Hamel, Glikel, historian, 120

INDEX

Händele, daughter of Saul Wahl, 276
Hariri, Arabic poet, 32, 34 (note)
Haroun al Rashid, embassy to, 99
Hartmann, M., poet, 49
Hartog, Marian, writer, 137
Hartung, actor, 248
Ha-Sallach, Moses ibn Ezra, 205
Hebrew drama, first, published, 237
Hebrew language, plasticity of, 32–33
Hebrew studies among Christians, 44, 47–48, 95, 98
Heckscher, Fromet, ancestress of Heine, 341
Hegel and Heine, 346
Heine, Heinrich, poet, 49
  and Venus of Milo, 362
  appreciation of, 340
  characterized by Schopenhauer, 357–358
  character of, 367
  conversion of, 348–351
  family of, 341–342, 344
  Ghetto novelist, 50
  in Berlin, 346–347
  in Göttingen, 347–348
  in Paris, 358–359
  Jewish traits of, 345–348, 353–357
  on Gabirol, 25–26
  on the Jews, 362–363, 365–366
  on Yehuda Halevi, 27
  on Zunz, 327–328, 333
  quoted, 9, 20, 28, 206
  religious education of, 343
  return of, to Judaism, 366
  wife of, 363–364
  will of, 366–367
Heine, Mathilde, wife of Heinrich Heine, 363–364
Heine, Maximilian, quoted, 344

"Heine of the middle ages," Immanuel Romi, 219
Heine, Samson, father of Heinrich Heine, 341, 342
Heine, Solomon, uncle of Heinrich Heine, 345, 352
Hellenism and Judaism, 75–76
Hellenists, Heine on, 359, 362
Hennings, alluded to, 314
Henry of Anjou, election of, in Poland, 286–287
Herder, poet, and Mendelssohn, 314
  quoted, 296
Hermeneutics by Maimonides, 162–163
Herod and the stage, 230–231
Herrera, Abraham, Kabbalist, 99
Hertzveld, Estelle and Maria, writers, 140
Herz, Henriette, alluded to, 131, 133, 346
  and Dorothea Mendelssohn, 306
  character of, 312–313
  salon of, 311–314
Herz, Marcus, physicist, 310, 311
Herzberg-Fränkel, L., Ghetto novelist, 50
Herzfeld, L., scholar, 49
Hess, M., quoted, 109
"Highest Faith, The" by Abraham ibn Daud, 36
Higros the Levite, musician, 369, 374
Hildebold von Schwanegau, minnesinger, 182
Hillel, rabbi, 18
  quoted, 255
Hillel ben Samuel, translator 86
Himyarites and Jews, 256
Hirsch, scholar, 49
Hirsch, Jenny, writer, 139

"History and Literature of the Israelites" by Constance and Anna Rothschild, 142
"History of Synagogue Poetry" by Zunz, 336
"History of the Jews in England" by Grace Aguilar, 135
"History of the National Poetry of the Hebrews" by Ernest Meier, 14
Hitzig, architect, alluded to, 298
Hitzig, Bible critic, 13, 14
Hod, Kabbalistic term, 41
Holbein, Hans, illustrates a Jewish book, 102
Holdheim, S., scholar, 49
Holland, exiles in, 128–129
Homberg, Herz disciple of Mendelssohn, 48, 309
"Home Influence" by Grace Aguilar, 134
Hosea, king, alluded to, 250
Hosea, prophet, alluded to, 251
"Hours of Devotion" by Fanny Neuda, 140
Humanism and the Jews, 94–95
Humboldts, the, and Henriette Herz, 311, 312, 313
Humor in antiquity, 191–192
  in Jewish German literature, 225–226
  nature of, 195–195, 356–357
Hurwitz, Bella, historian, 120
Hurwitz, Isaiah, Kabbalist, 43

Ibn Alfange, writer, 170
Ibn Chasdaï, Makamat writer, 35
Ibn Sina and Maimonides, 156
Iggereth ha-Sh'mad by Maimonides, 152
Ikkarim by Joseph Albo, 42
Ima Shalom, Talmudist, 113

Immanuel ben Solomon, poet, 35, 89, 90, 219–221, 222–223
  and Dante, 35, 89, 220, 223
  quoted, 220, 221, 222
Immanuel Romi. See Immanuel ben Solomon
India, the Ten Tribes in, 259
Indians and the Ten Tribes, 259
Innocent III, pope, alluded to, 184
Intelligences, Maimonides' doctrine of the, 159
"Interest and Usury" from the Haggada, 67–68
Iris, Zunz contributor to the, 330
Isaac Alfassi, alluded to, 257
Isaac ben Abraham, Talmudist, 36
Isaac ben Moses, Talmudist, 36
Isaac ben Sheshet, philosopher, 42
Isaac ben Yehuda ibn Ghayyat, poet, 201, 202
Isaac ibn Sid, astronomer, 92
Isaac Israeli, mathematician, 93
Isaac Israeli, physician, 81, 82, 257
Isaiah, prophet, quoted, 251, 252
Ishmael, poet, alluded to, 118
Israel, kingdom of, 250–251
"Israel Defended" translated by Grace Aguilar, 134
"Israelites on Mount Horeb, The," by Simon van Geldern, 341
Isserles, Moses, Talmudist, 46, 100, 286
Italy, Jews of, 45–46, 116
Itzig, Daniel, naturalization of, 317

Jabneh, academy at, 57, 227–228
Jacob ben Abba-Mari ben Anatoli, scholar, 39–40, 85
Jacob ben Elias, poet, 224
Jacob ben Machir, astronomer, 86
Jacob ben Meïr, Talmudist, 36
Jacob ben Nissim, alluded to, 257
Jacob ibn Chabib, Talmudist, 43
Jason, writer, 17
Jayme I, of Aragon, patron of Hebrew learning, 92
Jellinek, Adolf, preacher, 49
quoted, 33, 245–246
Jeremiah, prophet, quoted, 251
Jerusalem, friend of Moses Mendelssohn, 314
Jerusalem, Kabbalists in, 43
Jesus, mediator between Judaism and Hellenism, 76
quotes the Old Testament, 13
"Jewish Calderon, The," Antonio Enriquez di Gomez, 236
Jewish drama, the first, 234
"Jewish Faith, The," by Grace Aguilar, 135
Jewish German drama, the, 246–247
Jewish historical writings, lack of, 23–24
Jewish history, spirit of, 269–271
"Jewish Homiletics" by Zunz, 333–335
Jewish literature and Goethe, 103–104
characterized, 11–12
comprehensiveness of, 37
definition of, 328
extent of, 9–10, 22
Hellenic period of, 16–17

Jewish literature (continued), in Persia, 90
love in, 122–123
name of, 10
rabbinical period of, 38
Jewish philosophers, 17, 22, 23, 35, 40, 42
Jewish poetry, and Syrian, 80
future of, 50
subjects of, 24–25
Jewish poets, 49
Jewish race, the, liberality of, 33–34
morality of, 36
preservation of, 108–109
subjectivity of, 33, 353–354
versatility of, 79
Jewish scholars, 49
Jewish Sybil, the, 17–18
"Jewish Voltaire, The," Immanuel Romi, 219
Jewish wit, 354–356
Jews, academies of, 75, 79
and Columbus, 96
and commerce, 101–102
and Frederick the Great, 316–317
and the invention of printing, 38
and the national poetry of Germany, 87
and the Renaissance, 43–44, 74–75, 94–95, 223, 224
and troubadour poetry, 171–173
and Vasco da Gama, 96–97
as diplomats, 98–99
as economists, 103
as interpreters of Aristotle, 85
as linguists, 75
as literary mediators, 97–98
as physicians, 19, 37, 44, 45, 81–82, 86, 95, 97
as scientific mediators, 78
as teachers of Christians, 95, 98

Jews (cont'd), as traders, 74–75
  as translators, 44, 79, 86–87, 88, 89 90, 91–92
  as travellers, 37–38
  as wood engravers, 102
  characterized by Heine, 362–363, 365–366
  defended by Reuchlin, 95
  in Arabia, 256–257
  in Holland, 46
  in Italy, 45–46, 116
  in Poland, 46, 286–288
  in the modern drama, 235–237, 245
  in the sciences, 102
  of Germany, in the middle ages, 186
  of Germany, poverty of, 319
  of the eighteenth century, 294
  relation of, to Arabs, 22
  under Arabic influences, 78, 80
  under Hellenic influences, 76
  under Roman influences, 76, 77
João II, of Portugal, employs Jewish scholars, 96
Jochanan, compiler of the Jerusalem Talmud, 19, 114
Jochanan ben Zakkaï, rabbi, 18, 56–57, 228
John of Seville, mathematician, 91
Josefowicz brothers in Lithuania, 287–288
Joseph ben Jochanan, wife of, 119
Joseph del Medigo, scholar, 45
Joseph Ezobi, poet, 89
Joseph ibn Aknin, disciple of Maimonides, 155
Joseph ibn Nagdela, wife of, 117
Joseph ibn Sabara, satirist, 34, 214
Joseph ibn Verga, historian, 42
Joseph ibn Zaddik, philosopher, 35
Josephus, Flavius, historian 13, 18, 44
  at Rome, 232
  quoted, 230
Joshua, astronomer, 77
Joshua, Samaritan book of, on the Ten Tribes, 252
Joshua ben Chananya, rabbi, 18
Joshua, Jacob, Talmudist, 47
Jost, Isaac Marcus, historian, 49, 321
  on Zunz, 320
"Journal for the Science of Judaism," 324–325, 329, 352
Juan Alfonso de Bæna, poet, 90, 179
Judæa and Greece contrasted, 194
Judæo-Alexandrian period, 16–17
Judah Alfachar and Maimonides, 165
Judah Hakohen, astronomer, 93
Judah ibn Sabbataï, satirist, 34, 214
Judah ibn Tibbon, translator, 39, 84
Judah Tommo, poet, 224
Judaism and Hellenism, 75–76
  served by women, 115–116
Judendeutsch, patois, 47, 294
  literature in, 47, 100–101
  philological value of, 100
  used by women, 119
Judges, quoted, 107
Judith, queen of the Jewish kingdom in Abyssinia, 262, 263

Kabbala, the, attacked and defended, 45, 46
  influence of, 93, 99

INDEX

Kabbala, the (continued), studied by Christians, 44
  supposed author of, 19
  system of, outlined, 40–41
Kabbalists, 43, 95, 99
Kalâm, Islam theology, 81
Kalila we-Dimna, fox fables, translated, 79
Kalir, Eliezer, poet, 25
"Kaliric," classical in Jewish literature, 25
Kalisch, Ludwig, quoted, 364–365
Kalonymos ben Kalonymos as a satirist, 35, 216–219
  as a scholar, 89
Kant and Maimonides, 146, 164
  's philosophy among Jews, 310
Kara, Abigedor, Talmudist, 47
Karaite doctrines in Castile, 117
Karo, Joseph, compiler of the *Shulchan Aruch*, 43
Kasmune (Xemona), poetess, 24, 118
Kaspi, Joseph, philosopher, 42
Kayserling, M., quoted, 300
Kepler and Jewish astronomers, 91, 92
Kether, Kabbalistic term, 41
Kimchi, David, grammarian, 39, 84
"King Solomon's Seal" by Büschenthal, 245
Kisch, teacher of Moses Mendelssohn, 297
Klesmer, musician, 377
Kley, Edward, preacher, 49, 322
Kohen, Sabbataï, Talmudist, 46
Kompert, Leopold, Ghetto novelist, 50
Korbi, character in "The Gift of Judah," 214
Krochmal, scholar, 49
Kuh, M. E., poet, 49

Kulke, Ghetto novelist, 50
Kunth, tutor of the Humboldts, 311

La Doctrina Christiana, attributed to Santob, 174
La Fontaine, and Hebrew fable translations, 34, 88
Landau, Ezekiel, Talmudist, 47
Laura (Petrarch's) in "Praise of Women," 223
Layesharim Tehillah by Luzzatto, 240–241
"Lay of Zion" by Yehuda Halevi, 28–31, 210
Lazarus ben David, philosopher, 310, 350
Lazarus, Emma, poetess, 140
Lazarus, M., scholar, 49
Lecho Dodi, Sabbath song, 43
Legend-making, 288–289
Legends, value of, 289–292
Lehmann, M., Ghetto novelist, 50
Leibnitz and Maimonides, 146
Leibzoll, tax, 294
Lemech, sons of, inventions of, 372
Leo de Modena, rabbi, 45, 128
Leo Hebræus. See Judah Abrabanel
Leon di Bannolas. See Levi ben Gerson
Lessing, alluded to, 246
  and Mendelssohn, 299, 300, 314
  as fabulist, 88
  on Yedaya Penini, 40
Letteris, M. E., dramatist, 248
"Letters to a Christian Friend on the Fundamental Truths of Judaism," by Clementine Rothschild, 141
Levi ben Abraham, philosopher, 40

Levi ben Gerson, philosopher, 42, 90-91
Levi (Henle), Elise, writer, 139
Levi of Mayence, founder of German synagogue music, 376
Levin (Varnhagen), Rahel, alluded to, 131, 346
and Judaism, 132
and the emancipation movement, 132-133
Levita, Elias. See Elias Levita
Lewandowski, musician, work of, 370-371, 377-378
"Light of God" by Chasdaï Crescas, 42
Lindo, Abigail, writer, 137
Lithuania, Jews in, 282, 285
Litte of Ratisbon, historian, 119
Litteraturbriefe by Mendelssohn, 301
Litteraturgeschichte der synagogalen Poesie by Zunz, 336
Lokman's fables translated into Hebrew, 34
Lonsano, Menahem, writer on music, 376
Lope de Vega, alluded to, 239
Love in Hebrew poetry, 122-123, 225
Love in Jewish and German poetry, 186
Lucian, alluded to, 18
"Lucinde" by Friedrich von Schlegel, 306
Luis de Torres accompanies Columbus, 96
Luria, Solomon, Talmudist, 46, 286
Luther, Martin, and Rashi, 84
quoted, 377
under Jewish influences, 98
Luzzatto, Moses Chayyim, dramatist, 45, 239-241

Luzzatto, S. D., scholar, 49, 137

Maffei, dramatist, 240
Maggidim, itinerant preachers, 227
"Magic Flute, The," first performance of, 247-248
"Magic Wreath, The," by Grace Aguilar, 134
Maharil, founder of German synagogue music, 376
Maimon, Solomon, and Mendelssohn, 310
Maimonides, Moses, philosopher, 34, 35, 84
and Aristotle, 156
and Averroës, 163-164
and Ibn Sina, 156
and modern philosophy, 164
and scholasticism, 85, 156, 164
as astronomer, 93
career of, 147-150
in France, 145-146
medical works of, 153-154
on man's attributes, 160-161
on prophecy, 161-162
on resurrection, 164-165
on revelation, 162
on the attributes of God, 157-158
on the Mosaic legislation, 163
philosophic work of, 154 ff.
quoted, 152, 167
religious works of, 150-153
Maimunists, 39-40
Makamat, a form of Arabic poetry, 34 (note)
Malabar, the Ten Tribes in, 259
Malchuth, Kabbalistic term, 41
Manasseh ben Israel, author, 47, 99-100
and Rembrandt, 102
on the Ten Tribes, 259

Manesse, Rüdiger, compiler, 183–184
Mannheimer, N., preacher, 49
Manoello. See Immanuel ben Solomon
Mantino, Jacob, physician, 95
Manuel, of Portugal, alluded to, 97
Margoles, Jacob, Kabbalist, 95
Maria de Padilla, mistress of Pedro I, 169
Marie de France, fabulist, 88
Mar Sutra on the Ten Tribes, 253
Mashal, parable, 227
Massichtoth, Talmudic treatises, 59
Mauscheln, Jewish slang, 310–311
Maximilian, of Austria, candidate for the Polish crown, 278
Mechabberoth by Immanuel Romi, 219–220
Medicine, origin of, 81
Meier, Ernest, Bible critic, 12
 quoted, 14
Meïr, rabbi, fabulist, 19, 111–112
Meïr ben Baruch, Talmudist, 36
Meïr ben Todros ha-Levi, quoted, 164–165
Meissner, Alfred, recollections of, of Heine, 362–364
Mekirath Yoseph by Beermann, 241–244
Melo, David Abenator, translator, 47
Mendel Gibbor, quoted, 272
Mendels, Edel, historian, 120
Mendelssohn, Abraham, son of Moses Mendelssohn, 307, 308
Mendelssohn, Dorothea, daughter of Moses Mendelssohn, 131, 305–306

Mendelssohn, Henriette, daughter of Moses Mendelssohn, 306–308
Mendelssohn, Joseph, son of Moses Mendelssohn, 305, 307
Mendelssohn, Moses, philosopher, 48
 and Lessing, 299, 300, 314
 and Maimonides, 164
 as critic, 301–302
 as reformer, 316
 as translator, 40
 children of, 304
 disciples of, 309
 friends of, 299, 314–315
 in Berlin, 293, 296 ff
 marriage of, 303–304
 quoted, 300, 301
Mendelssohn, Nathan, son of Moses Mendelssohn, 307
Mendelssohn, Recha, daughter of Moses Mendelssohn, 307
Mendelssohn-Bartholdy, Felix, 307, 308
Mendez, David Franco, dramatist, 244
Meneketh Ribka, by Rebekah Tiktiner, 119
Menelek, son of the Queen of Sheba, 262
Merope by Maffei, 240
Mesgid, Falasha synagogue, 265
Mesopotamia, the Ten Tribes in, 259
Messer Leon, poet, 223
Meyer, Marianne, alluded to, 132
Meyer, Rachel, writer, 139
Meyer, Sarah, alluded to, 132
Meyerbeer, alluded to, 245
Midrash, commentary, 20, 53–54
Midrash Rabba, a Talmudic work, 21
Migdal Oz by Luzzatto, 239

Minchath Yehuda Soneh ha-Nashim, by Judah ibn Sabbataï, 214-216
Minnedienst absent from Jewish poetry, 122
Minnesingers, 182
Miriam, as poetess, 106
Miriam, Rashi's granddaughter, 118
Mishlé Sandabar, romance, 88
Mishna, the, commentary on, 60
compilation of, 58
in poetry, 201
Mishneh Torah by Maimonides, 152-153
Missionaries in Abyssinia, 263-267
Mohammedanism, rise of, 77-78
Montefiore, Charlotte, writer, 133
Montefiore, Judith, philanthropist, 133
Montpellier, "Guide of the Perplexed" burnt at, 155
Jews at academy of, 86, 92
Moreh Nebuchim by Maimonides, 146, 154, 161-162
Morgenstern, Lina, writer, 139
Morgenstunden by Mendelssohn, 305
Moritz, friend of Henriette Herz, 313, 314
Morpurgo, Rachel, poetess, 137-138
Mosaic legislation, the, Maimonides on, 163
"Mosaic" style in Hebrew poetry, 201-202
Mosenthal, S. H., Ghetto novelist, 49, 50
Dingelstedt on, 319
Moser, Moses, friend of Heine, 324, 346
letters to, 350, 352

Moses, prophet, characterized by Heine, 365-366
in Africa, 255
Moses de Coucy, Talmudist, 36
Moses ibn Ezra, poet, 24, 32, 202-206, 207
Moses, Israel, teacher of Mendelssohn, 297-298
Moses of Narbonne, philosopher, 42
Moses Rieti, the Hebrew Dante, 35, 124
Moses Sephardi. See Petrus Alphonsus
Mosessohn, Miriam, writer, 138
Munk, Solomon, scholar, 49
and Gabirol, 26, 83
translates *Moreh Nebuchim*, 146, 155
Münster, Sebastian, Hebrew scholar, 44, 95
Muscato, Judah, preacher, 376
Music among Jews, 372-376
Mussafia, Benjamin, author, 47

Nachmanides, exegete, 39
Nagara, Israel, poet, 43
"Names of the Jews, The," by Zunz, 335
Nasi, Joseph, statesman, 99
and the Polish election, 287
"Nathan the Wise" and tolerance, 185, 310-311
Nazarenes, defined by Heine, 359
Nefesh, Kabbalistic term, 41
Neïlah prayer, A, 104
Neo-Hebraic literature. See Jewish literature
Nero, alluded to, 232
Neshama, Kabbalistic term, 41
Nesirim, Falasha monks, 265
Nestorians and the Ten Tribes, 259
Neto, David, philosopher, 47
Neuda, Fanny, writer, 140

INDEX

Neunzig, Joseph, on Heine, 343
"New Song," anonymous poem, 224
Nezach, Kabbalistic term, 41
Nicolai, friend of Mendelssohn, 299, 300, 313, 314
Nicolas de Lyra, exegete, 84
Noah, Mordecai, and the Ten Tribes, 259
Nöldeke, Theodor, Bible critic, 12
Nomologia, by Isaac Aboab, 45
Numbers, book of, quoted, 71
Nunes, Manuela, de Almeida, poetess, 130

Obadiah Bertinoro, Talmudist, 43
Obadiah Sforno, teacher of Reuchlin, 95
Offenbach, J., alluded to, 245
Old Testament, the, Africa in, 255
  document hypothesis of, 13
  humor in, 191, 193
  in poetry, 201
  interpretation of, 54
  literary value of, 14-16, 73-74
  quoted by Jesus, 13
  study of, 12-13, 18
  time of compilation of, 16
  time of composition of, 13-14
  translations of, 16, 47, 48, 80
Oliver y Fullano, de, Nicolas, author, 129
"On Rabbinical Literature" by Zunz, 328
Ophir, Hebrew name for Africa, 255
Ophra in Yehuda Halevi's poems, 207
Oppenheim, David, rabbi at Prague, 244
Ormus, island, explored by Jews, 96

Ottenheimer, Henriette, poetess, 49, 138-139
Otto von Botenlaube, minnesinger, 182
Owl, character in "The Gift of Judah," 214

Padua, University of, and Elias del Medigo, 94
Palestine described, 93
Palquera, Shemtob, philosopher, 40
Pan, Taube, poetess, 120
"Paradise, The" by Moses Rieti, 35
Parallax computed by Isaac Israeli, 93
Parzival, by Wolfram von Eschenbach, 185
  Jewish contributions to, 35, 87
Pastor Fido by Guarini, 129, 240
Paul III, pope, alluded to, 95
Paula deï Mansi, Talmudist, 116-117
Pedro I, of Castile, and Santob de Carrion, 87, 169, 170
Pedro di Carvallho, navigator, 96
Pekah, king, alluded to, 250
Pensa, Joseph, de la Vega, dramatist, 237-238
Pentateuch, the Jewish German translation of, 100
  Mendelssohn's commentary on, 309
Peregrinatio Hierosolymitana by Radziwill, 280
Persia, Jewish literature in, 90
Pesikta, a Talmudic work, 21
Petachya of Ratisbon, traveller, 37, 117
Petrarch, translated into Spanish, 98
Petrus Alphonsus, writer, 89, 171

Peurbach, humanist, 100
Philipson, L., journalist, 49
Philo, philosopher, 17
Philo the Elder, writer, 17
Phokylides (pseudo-), Neoplatonist, 17
Physicians, Jewish, 81, 95, 97, 179
Pickelhering, a character in *Mekirath Yoseph*, 241
Pico della Mirandola alluded to, 94
and Levi ben Gerson, 91
and the Kabbala, 44
Pilpul, Talmudic method, 46
Pinchas, rabbi, chronicler of the Saul Wahl story, 273, 277, 280
Piut, a form of liturgic Hebrew poetry, 24. 198
" Plant Lore " by Dioscorides, 82
Pliny, alluded to, 250
Pnie, Samson, contributes to *Parzival*, 35, 87
Poésies diverses by Frederick the Great, 301
Poland, election of king in, 278-279
Jews in, 286-288
Pollak, Jacob, Talmudist, 46
Popert, Meyer Samson, ancestor of Heine, 341
Popiel, of Poland, alluded to, 285
Poppæa, empress, alluded to, 232
" Praise of Women," anonymous work, 34
" Praise of Women," by David ben Yehuda, 223
" Praise unto the Righteous," by Luzzatto, 240-241
" Prince and the Dervish, The," by Ibn Chasdaï, 35
Printing, influence of, on Jewish literature, 94

" Prisoners of Hope, The," by Joseph Pensa, 237-238
Prophecy defined by Maimonides, 161-162
Proudhon anticipated by Judah ibn Tibbon, 39
Psalm cxxxiii., 71-72
Psalms, the, translated into Jewish German, 120
into Persian, 90
Ptolemy Philadelphus and the Septuagint, 16
Ptolemy's " Almagest " translated, 79

Rab, rabbi, 19
Rabbinical literature. See Jewish literature
Rabbinowicz, Bertha, 138
Rabbi von Bacharach by Heine, 50, 348, 349
Rachel (Bellejeune), Talmudist, 118
Radziwill, Nicholas Christopher, and Saul Wahl, 274-276, 279-280
" Radziwill Bible, The," 280
Rambam, Jewish name for Maimonides, 146
Ramler and Jews, 311, 313
Rappaport, Moritz, poet, 49
Rappaport, S., scholar, 49
Rashi. See Solomon ben Isaac
Rausnitz, Rachel, historian, 121
Ravenna and Jewish financiers, 101-102
" Recapitulation of the Law " by Maimonides, 152-153
Recke, von der, Elise, and Mendelssohn, 215
Red Sea, coasts of, explored by Jews, 96
Reichardt, musician, 313
Reinmar von Brennenberg, minnesinger, 182

INDEX

Reisebilder by Heine, 353
Rembrandt illustrates a Jewish book, 102
Renaissance, the, and the Jews, 43-44, 74-75, 94-95, 223, 224
Renaissance, the Jewish, 101, 227, 293-295
Renan, Ernest, alluded to, 163, 191
Respublika Babinska, a Polish society, 281-282
Respuestas by Antonio di Montoro, 180
Resurrection, Maimonides on, 164-165
Reuchlin, John, and Jewish scholars, 91, 94-95
and the Talmud, 44
quoted, 89
Revelation defined by Maimonides, 162
Richard I, of England, and Maimonides, 149
Riemer quoted, 358
Riesser, Gabriel, journalist, 49, 291
"Righteous Brethren, The" an Arabic order, 79
Rintelsohn, teacher of Heine, 344
Ritter, Heinrich, on Maimonides, 146
"Ritual of the Synagogue, The," by Zunz, 336
Ritus des synagogalen Gottesdienstes by Zunz, 336
Robert of Anjou, patron of Hebrew learning, 92
Robert of Naples, patron of Hebrew learning, 89
Rodenberg, Julius, quoted, 144
Romanelli, Samuel L., dramatist, 244, 248
Romanzero by Heine, 9, 27, 365
Rossi, Solomon, musician, 376

Rothschild, Anna, historian, 142
Charlotte, philanthropist, 141
Clementine, writer, 141-142
Constance, historian, 142
Rothschild family, women of the, 140-142
Ruach, Kabbalistic term, 41
Rückert, poet, alluded to, 139
"Rules for the Shoeing and Care of Horses in Royal Stables," translated, 91
Rüppell, explorer, quoted, 263

Sa'adia, philosopher, 22, 80-81
Sachs, M., scholar, 49
Saisset, E., on Maimonides, 146
"Sale of Joseph, The" by Beermann, 241-244
Salerno, Jews at academy of, 86, 92
Salomon, Annette, writer, 137
Salomon, G., preacher, 49
Salomon, Leah, wife of Abraham Mendelssohn, 308
Salon, the German, established by Jews, 312
Salonica, Spanish exiles in, 43
Sambation, fabled stream, 249, 258
Samson, history of, dramatized, 236
humor in the, 191, 192
"Samson and the Philistines" by Luzzatto, 239
"Samsonschool" at Wolfenbüttel, 321
Samuel, astronomer, 76
Samuel, physician, 19
Samuel ben Ali, Talmudist, 117
Samuel ben Meïr, exegete, 36, 172
Samuel ibn Nagdela, grand vizir, 98
Samuel Judah, father of Saul Wahl, 273, 274

Samuel the Pious, hymnologist, 36
Santillana, de, on Santob de Carrion, 173
Santo. See Santob de Carrion
Santob de Carrion, troubadour, 34, 87, 169–170, 174–175, 188
  characterized, 173
  character of, 178
  quoted, 169, 175–176, 177–178
  relation of, to Judaism, 176–177
Saphir, M. G., quoted, 355
Sarah, a character in *Rabbi von Bacharach*, 348
Sarastro, played by a Jew, 247
Satirists, 213–223
Saul Juditsch. See Saul Wahl
Saul Wahl, in the Russian archives, 282–284
  relics of, 278
  story of, 273–277
  why so named, 276
Savasorda. See Abraham ben Chiya
Schadow, sculptor, 313
Schallmeier, teacher of Heine, 342
Schlegel, von, Friedrich, husband of Dorothea Mendelssohn, 306
Schleiden, M. J., quoted, 28, 74–75
Schleiermacher and the Jews, 313, 314, 323
Schopenhauer, Arthur, anticipated by Gabirol, 27
  on Heine, 357–358
Schutzjude, a privileged Jew, 302–403
Scotists and Gabirol, 26
Scotus, Duns, philosopher, 82
Scotus, Michael, scholar, 40, 85
Scribes, the compilers of the Old Testament, 16

"Seal of Perfection, The," by Abraham Bedersi, 171
Sechel Hapoel, Active Intellect, 159
Seder described by Heine, 345
Sefer Asaf, medical fragment, 81
Sefer ha-Hechal by Moses Rieti, 124
Sefer Sha'ashuim by Joseph ibn Sabara, 214
Sefiroth, Kabbalistic term, 41
Selicha, a character in "The Sale of Joseph," 241
Selicha, a form of Hebrew liturgical poetry, 24, 25, 198
Septuagint, contents of the, 16
Serach, hero of "The Gift of Judah," 214–216
"Seven Wise Masters, The," romance, 88
Seynensis, Henricus, quoted, 52
Shachna, Solomon, Talmudist, alluded to, 286
Shalet, a Jewish dish, 360–361
Shalmaneser, conquers Israel, 250
  obelisk of, 261
Shammaï, rabbi, 18
Shapiro, Miriam, Talmudist, 117
Shebach Nashim by David ben Yehuda, 223
Shem-Tob. See Santob de Carrion
Sherira, Talmudist, 22
"Shields of Heroes," by Jacob ben Elias, 224
"Shulammith," Jewish German drama, 247
Shulchan Aruch, code, 43
Sigismund I, Jews under, 285, 286
Sigismund III, and Saul Wahl, 283–284

INDEX

Simon ben Yochaï, supposed author of the Kabbala, 19
Sirkes, Joel, Talmudist, 46
"Society for Jewish Culture and Science," in Berlin, 324, 346
Soferim, Scribes, 56
Solomon, king, alluded to, 250
  and Africa, 255
Solomon Ashkenazi, diplomat, 96, 286-287
Solomon ben Aderet, Talmudist, 40
Solomon ben Isaac (Rashi), exegete, 36, 84, 137
  essay on, by Zunz, 329
  family of, 118
Solomon ben Sakbel, satirist, 34, 213
Solomon Yitzchaki. See Solomon ben Isaac
"Song of Joy" by Yehuda Halevi, 207
"Song of Songs," a dramatic idyl, 229
  alluded to, 207
  characterized, 192-193
  epitomized, 223
  explained, 172
  in later poetry, 202
  quoted, 186
Sonnenthal, Adolf, actor, 246
Soudan, the, Moses in, 255
"Source of Life, The" by Gabirol, 82-83
"South, the," Talmud name for Africa, 255
Spalding, friend of Henriette Herz, 313
"Spener's Journal," Zunz editor of, 330
Spinoza, Benedict (Baruch), philosopher, 47, 100
  and Maimonides, 145, 146, 164
  influenced by Chasdaï Crescas, 94

Spinoza, Benedict (continued), under Kabbalistic influence, 99
"Spirit of Judaism, The," by Grace Aguilar, 134
Stein, L., poet, 49
Steinheim, scholar, 49
Steinschneider, M., scholar, 37, 49
Steinthal, H., scholar, 49
Stephen Báthori, of Poland, 278, 282, 287
Studie zur Bibelkritik by Zunz, 337
Sullam, Sara Copia, poetess, 44, 124-128
Surrenhuys, scholar, 48
Süsskind von Trimberg, minnesinger, 35, 87, 182, 184
  and Judaism, 187
  character of, 188
  poetry of, 185-186
  quoted, 182-183, 187-188, 188-189
Synagogale Poesie des Mittelalters, by Zunz, 335
"Synagogue Poetry of the Middle Ages" by Zunz, 336
Syria, the Ten Tribes in, 259
Syrian and Jewish poetry, 80
Syrian Christians as scientific mediators, 78

Tachkemoni by Yehuda Charisi, 211
Talmud, the, burnt, 40, 44
  character of, 52-53
  compilers of, 56, 57-58
  composition of, 16
  contents of, 59-60, 68-70, 76-77
  in poetry, 201
  on Africa, 254
  on the Ten Tribes, 253
  origin of, 53-54

Talmud, the (continued), study of, 17–18
  translations of, 60
  woman in, 110–114
  women and children in, 63–64
Talmud, the Babylonian, 54
  compiler of, 17
Talmud, the Jerusalem, compiler of, 17
Talmudists, 22, 36, 40, 43, 46, 47, 117, 286
Talmudists (women), 116, 117, 118
Tamar, a character in Immanuel Romi's poem, 221–222
Tanaïm, Learners, 56, 57
Tanchuma, a Talmudic work, 19
Targum, the, in poetry, 201
Telescope, the, used by Gamaliel, 77
Teller, friend of Henriette Herz, 313
Ten Tribes, the, English views of, 260–262
  Irish legend of, 261
  the prophets on, 251–252
  the Samaritan Hexateuch on, 252
  the supposed homes of, 256–262
  the Talmud on, 253
Tertullian quoted, 233
Theatre, the, and the rabbis, 230–234
Theodore, Negus of Abyssinia, 263, 267
Theorica by Peurbach, 100
Thomists and Gabirol, 24
"Thoughts suggested by Bible Texts" by Louise Rothschild, 141
Tifereth, Kabbalistic term, 41
Tiglath-Pileser conquers Israel, 250

Tiktiner, Rebekah, scholar, 119
"Till Eulenspiegel," the Jewish German, 101
Tolerance in Germany, 185, 189
"Touchstone" by Kalonymos ben Kalonymos, 33, 216–219
"Tower of Victory" by Luzzatto, 239
Tragedy, nature of, 195
Travellers, Jewish, 80
"Tristan and Isolde" compared with the *Mechabberoth*, 220
Troubadour poetry and the Jews, 171–173
Troubadours, 223
"Truth's Campaign," anonymous work, 32
Turkey, Jews in, 98
"Two Tables of the Testimony, The," by Isaiah Hurwitz, 43
Tycho de Brahe and Jewish astronomers, 92

Uhden, von, and Mendelssohn, 302
Uhland, poet, alluded to, 139
Ulla, itinerant preacher, 114
"Upon the Philosophy of Maimonides," prize essay, 145
Usque, Samuel, poet, 44
Usque, Solomon, poet, 98, 235

"Vale of Weeping, The," by Joseph Cohen, 44
Varnhagen, Rahel. See Levin, Rahel
Varnhagen von Ense, German *littérateur*, 312
Vecinho, Joseph, astronomer, 96
Veit, Philip, painter, 308

Veit, Simon, husband of Dorothea Mendelssohn, 306
Venino, alluded to, 302
Venus of Milo and Heine, 362
Vespasian and Jochanan ben Zakkaï, 57
Walther von der Vogelweide, minnesinger, 182, 189
Wandering Jew, the, myth of, 350
"War of Wealth and Wisdom, The," satire, 34
"Water Song" by Gabirol, 200-201
Weil, Jacob, Talmudist, 102
Weill, Alexander, and Heine, 363-364
Weltschmerz in Gabirol's poetry, 199
in Heine's poetry, 357
Wesseli, musician, 313
Wessely, Naphtali Hartwig, commentator, 48, 309
Wieland, poet, alluded to, 314
Wihl, poet, 49
Wine, creation of, 197-198
Withold, grandduke, and the Lithuanian Jews, 282, 284
Wohllerner, Yenta, poetess, 138
Wohlwill, Immanuel, friend of Zunz, letter to, 325
Wolfenbüttel, Jews' free school at, 320-221
Wolff, Hebrew scholar, 48
Wolfram von Eschenbach, minnesinger, 182, 185, 189
Woman, creation of, 197
in Jewish annals, 110
in literature, 106-107
in the Talmud, 64, 110-114
mental characteristics of, 121-122
satirized and defended, 223-224
services of, to Judaism, 115-116

"Woman's Friend" by Yedaya Penini, 216
Women, Jewish, in the emancipation movement, 133, 139
"Women of Israel, The" by Grace Aguilar, 134
"Women's Shield," by Judah Tommo, 224
"World as Will and Idea, The," by Schopenhauer, 357

Xemona. See Kasmune

Yaltha, wife of Rabbi Nachman, 113-114
Yechiel ben Abraham, financier, 99
Yechiel deï Mansi, alluded to, 116
Yedaya Penini, poet, 40, 216
Yehuda ben Astruc, scientist, 92
Yehuda ben Zakkaï quoted, 68
Yehuda Charisi, poet, 32, 34 (note), 210-213
on Gabirol, 27
quoted, 214
traveller, 37
Yehuda Chayyug, alluded to, 257
Yehuda Hakohen, Talmudist, 36
Yehuda Halevi, as philosopher, 31, 34
as poet, 24, 27-28, 206-210
daughter of, 117
Yehuda Romano, translator, 90
Yehuda Sabbataï, satirist, 34, 214
Yehuda the Prince, Mishna compiler, 19, 58
lament over, 65-66
Yemen, Judaism in, 256
Yesod, Kabbalistic term, 41
Yesod Olam by Moses Zacuto, 238-239

Yezira, Kabbalistic term, 41
"Yosippon," an historical compilation, 120, 249, 250, 321
Yucatan and the Ten Tribes, 259

Zacuto, Abraham, astronomer, 42, 96–97
Zacuto, Moses, dramatist, 238–239
Zarzal, Moses, physician, 179
Zeitschrift der deutschen morgenländischen Gesellschaft, Zunz contributor to, 337
Zeltner, J. G., on Rebekah Tiktiner, 119
Zerubbabel, alluded to, 253
Zohar, the, astronomy in, 91
authorship of, 39
Zöllner, friend of Henriette Herz, 313

Zunz, Adelheid, wife of Leopold Zunz, 337, 352
Zunz, Leopold, scholar, 25, 48
and religious reform, 335
as journalist, 330
as pedagogue, 324
as politician, 330–332
as preacher, 322–323
characterized by Heine, 327–328
described by Jost, 320
education of, 320–322
friend of Heine, 346
importance of, for Judaism, 338
in Berlin, 318–319
quoted, 11–12, 119, 323, 325–327, 330, 331, 332, 334, 336, 371
style of, 338
"Zur Geschichte und Litteratur" by Zunz, 337